THE ANTHROPOLOGY OF SELF AND BEHAVIOR

THE

ANTHROPOLOGY

OF **SELF** AND

BEHAVIOR

GERALD M. ERCHAK

Rutgers University Press
New Brunswick, New Jersey, and London

Second paperback printing, 1998

Library of Congress Cataloging-in-Publication Data
Erchak, Gerald Michael.
The anthropology of self and behavior / Gerald M.
Erchak.
    p.   cm.
Includes bibliographical references (p.) and index.
ISBN 0-8135-1761-3 (cloth)—ISBN 0-8135-1762-1 (pbk.)
1. Ethnopsychology. I. Title.
GN502.E72 1992
155.8—dc20   91-19666
                                                CIP

British Cataloging-in-Publication information available

Contents

Preface

I had two purposes in writing this book: to present an integrated theoretical perspective on some of the major topic areas in psychological anthropology, and to introduce the field to advanced students, scholars in related fields such as psychology and sociology, and other interested readers.

My theoretical perspective—basically cultural constructionist with a focus on adaptation—was developed over twenty-five years of study, research, and teaching in psychological anthropology. I have carried out research on socialization and family life among the Kpelle of Liberia, on domestic violence cross-culturally, on the medicalization of the American classroom, and on alcoholism in the United States, much of which has found its way into this volume.

As an introduction to the field of psychological anthropology for use in undergraduate and graduate courses, the book presents a particular slant on a sometimes chaotic and always diverse field.

Since I personally prefer books that take a definite point of view, I have not hesitated to do so. I see no problem with using texts in the classroom with which I disagree; indeed, disagreement with authors by myself or by my students often leads to much better discussion and writing. I have tried to keep the length down so that other books and materials could be easily assigned by an instructor. Within the text I have used well-known and easily available ethnographies as illustrative examples wherever possible.

The book is designed to truly *introduce* the field, rather than to cover it completely and encyclopedically. I interpret "introduce" to mean to tantalize, to provoke, to encourage further study; therefore the material covered is selective. Many will find work they consider significant to be omitted; all of us have different visions, and I invite you to add other material, and delete anything herein that you find objectionable or unnecessary.

My argument in this volume is roughly fourfold: the self, personality, and behavior are *culturally constructed;* the resulting selves, personalities, and sets of behaviors are in general (although not always) *adaptive,* that is, they contribute to survival and to the attainment of satisfying lives. In addition, the perspective is *cultural relativist,* with American culture portrayed as just as unique—as exotic—as the non-Western cultures so favored by anthropologists. Finally, the orientation is *critical* in many ways: critical of some anthropological theory, of psychology and psychiatry, of Western biomedicine, and of aspects of American life and culture.

In the first chapter, I present some basic concepts and an overview of the theoretical framework. Chapter 2 looks at the developmental process of socialization. In Chapter 3 I continue with the examination of socialization, but only as it applies to gender, seen here in dynamic interaction with the self and culture. The expression of the self in sexuality is also discussed as cultural construction. Chapter 4 deals with the notion of collective, shared behavioral and psychological traits and what these have to do with both normative and unusual behavior. In Chapter 5 I continue the treatment of abnormality and behavioral and mental disorder, especially taking issue with biomedical approaches. Finally, Chapter 6 discusses two important newer directions in the anthropology of self and behavior, the study of cognition and emotion, again emphasizing their cultural construction along with universal features. A brief Epilogue reviews the main arguments.

Acknowledgments

A variety of grants and people contributed to this modest effort. The Liberian research was made possible by a Fulbright Research/ Lecture Grant for 1970–71; my thanks to Michael Cole, John Whiting, and Blake Robinson, among others, for facilitating that project. A sabbatical and Skidmore Faculty Development Grants (Mellon Foundation) made much of the other research possible. Finally, writing the book was facilitated by another sabbatical, a reduced teaching load, and financial support, all of which were extended and coordinated by the Dean of Faculty's Office at Skidmore: special thanks go to Eric Weller, Phyllis Roth, and David Burrows of that office. I also thank David Burrows for granting permission to reprint parts of my article "Culture," which is included in a volume edited by him for the freshman class at Skidmore, *Liberal Studies I: The Human Experience.*

I have profited greatly from the helpful suggestions of many who read earlier drafts of chapters or of the whole manuscript, including Jane Erchak, Fran Hoffman, Pat Oles, Rick Rosenfeld, Marlie Wasserman, and anonymous reviewers. I thank them all.

THE ANTHROPOLOGY OF SELF AND BEHAVIOR

1

Adaptation
and the Cultural Construction
of the Person

We in the West, particularly in the United States, tend to think of "self" or "personality" as something unique to the individual. My personality is . . . well, me! Few of us think of the self as something *shared* by others around us. Just as we think of ourselves as separate somehow from the natural environment—not really part of the ecosystem—we think of the self as something that sets us apart from the others rather than something that helps join us all together in a social system. In fact self *both* sets each of us off as a unique individual, like a sort of psychological fingerprint, but also ties us to the other people in our culture. Why can Europeans, culturally quite similar to North Americans, easily identify Americans in Europe? Why do middle-class American schoolchildren wave their hands wildly in the air to get their teacher's attention, while Inuit and certain other Native American children sit quietly when they know the answer, hoping to avoid the teacher's attention? In both examples public behavior expresses features of the public presentation of the self that are *shared* by members of particular cultures. Europeans often identify Americans (a stereotypical minority, to be sure) by loudness, assertiveness, and extreme informality. Middle-class white American children are trained to be competitive, drawing attention to themselves in the process. Many Native American children, on the other hand, are trained to be cooperative and to avoid competition; demanding a teacher's attention in order to give a correct answer is seen as showing off, putting oneself above others.

This Western emphasis on and valuation of the individual is a tremendous contribution to world culture: where would freedom, rights, self-expression, or the development of one's potential be without it? Yet the individual always and necessarily exists in society as a bearer of culture. To explain human behavior, the scientist must explore and analyze both individual and group.

Traditionally, the study of the self and personality has been dominated by the discipline of psychology, at least in the undergraduate curriculum (psychiatry controls the topic in medical school); one could say that psychology "owns" the subject. Personality and self are therefore generally treated as individual phenomena, rarely seen as products of any social forces beyond the (Western) nuclear family. In addition, theories of personality within psychology (and psychiatry) are based on research that nearly always utilizes *only* Western subjects; in the United States, this means Americans. These theories, and the associated research, are then offered to science as explaining *human* behavior; they are in fact relevant only to American behavior, and say little or nothing about Maasai, Navajo, Asmat, or Tibetan behavior. Sociology teaches us that individuals participate in complex social systems and are products of social forces; cultural anthropology teaches us that the behavior of individuals elsewhere in the world is sometimes like our own behavior, sometimes radically different. If the self and personality were solely unique to each person, we would collide chaotically like bumper cars until extinction.

This book examines how individual selves are shaped by the forces of culture and how different cultures produce adults with personalities characterizing their cultures. Cultural relativism in behavior will be discussed throughout: for example, is behavior considered abnormal or deviant in North America also considered unusual or odd elsewhere in the world? In several sections, my focus is on psychological issues in nonliterate, nonindustrial societies, but I generally contrast these with the same or similar issues in Western societies as well as analyze cultural foundations of American behavior in its own right. In fact a primary purpose in writing this book is to make students aware of the sociocultural forces shaping their own behaviors. The arguments I make rest on a theoretical framework emphasizing psychocultural evolution and adaptation, which means that personalities and behavior are shown to be adapted to or consistent with both natural and cultural environmental realities.

In this sense I present this book as at once a complement and alternative to the more traditional psychological treatments. Rather than the more usual Western approach emphasizing how individuals shape society and culture, anthropology takes a reverse approach, showing how society and culture shape individuals and their behavior. While all persons are of course products of biology, they are also cultural constructs: biology and culture interact to produce ever-changing selves. In the pages that follow, the focus is on the cultural side of the equation.

Culture

Anthropologists utilize the concept of culture in a way that is probably different from what you have previously encountered. To them, culture has nothing to do with refinement or sophistication; nor is it something associated with social elites. It is not purely biological. It is not merely ethnic tradition. Culture is shared symbolic knowledge which people draw on as they make their way through life. It provides its bearers pathways to a satisfying life—or at least survival.

Culture is constructed on a tripartite foundation: mental, material, and social. By "mental," I refer to the obvious fact that culture is a product of the brain and thereby constrained by brain structure. The structure of culture may reflect the structure of the brain at some level, as Claude Levi-Strauss (e.g., 1966) has so elegantly suggested in his many volumes. Culture is also an expression of consciousness pure and simple, reflecting mental (intellectual and emotional) needs. For example, human beings seem to crave order and explanation. Aware and fearful of death, they develop "religious" explanations for it. Intolerant of chaos, they pigeonhole phenomena and objects in their universe, classifying and categorizing kin, events, animals, plants, supernatural beings, and the like. It is as if the brain *cannot help it.*

The material foundation refers to our most basic survival needs: food, shelter, reproduction. These are so essential, so fundamental, that they tend to structure other aspects of culture such as kinship and politics. Karl Marx and, most recently, "cultural materialists" such as Marvin Harris (1979) have written persuasively on the material basis of culture. Often neglected in the intellectual debates concerning the primacy of the mental versus the material is the third foundation, the *social* basis of culture: culture cannot exist without society. Survival, reproduction, production, and child-rearing are all profoundly social. A brief discussion of the defining characteristics of culture should further clarify how essential it is to human survival.

Culture is learned; we are not born with it. We are indeed born with the capacity for culture. Culture is a product of human intelligence and like intelligence, it is made possible by our supreme evolutionary product—the complex brain. Like the microprocessors and electronic circuitry in the computer I am using to write this book, the brain with all its neural circuitry and electrochemical impulses is *hardware.* Like the word-processing program I am using, culture is *software.*

Humans need to be exposed to culture from birth if they are to acquire it fully. Cultural behaviors learned early appear to be more powerful and influential than those learned later. In any case human beings come into the world with an evolved biological competence to learn culture from other human beings.

Culture is also shared, although it is important to note that no two people in any society possess identical versions of their culture, but they nonetheless need to interact in relatively appropriate and predictable ways. We do not need identical knowledge or rules to behave in a relatively orderly, predictable fashion appropriate to a given set of circumstances. A high school classroom is a place to socialize as well as a place to learn; to some students it may be strictly a social arena; to others, strictly educational; and to some it may be primarily a place to sleep. Yet there is enough sharing for relatively predictable interaction to take place. Yanomamo teenagers from the Amazon rain forest would not share enough of the cultural premises upon which the idea of a classroom is based to enable them to interact appropriately.

Culture is a symbolic system. A symbol is something that stands for something else. Language is the most obvious example of a symbolic system since words arbitrarily represent things and ideas; much of culture is encoded in language. Language is only part of cultural knowledge, however. Music and art are symbolic yet nonlinguistic. All people in all societies are surrounded by a world of symbols. A body covered with white chalky clay might indicate that the wearer is ill or perhaps spiritually charged in some way. The clothes you are wearing as you read this symbolically convey gender, status, mood, occasion, personality, and perhaps other characteristics as well. An example that conveys both the extraordinary power of culture as well as its symbolic nature is the white middle- and upper-class Euro-American custom of tanning. Here we have a behavior that is objectively harmful; it causes the drying and premature wrinkling of the skin as well as contributing to skin cancer. It is often excruciating to acquire a "healthy" tan, requiring hours, days, and weeks (usually) lying in the hot sun, sweating profusely while being chafed by sand and bitten by insects. And why? Well, to achieve a skin color closer to that of minority groups discriminated against by the lighter-skinned ruling class! A dark tan on a white person conveys a symbolic message: "I have the leisure time, and the money, to take lengthy vacations in sunny places." A few decades ago, members of the same social group cultivated pale complexions; this in effect said: "I do not have to engage in manual labor out of doors." Culture patterns group and individual behavior, and does so symbolically. Through such symbolic ordering of the world, people enhance their survival. The essence of human as opposed to animal consciousness is the ability to contemplate things that are not near us, that perhaps don't even exist, or that have not yet occurred. The intellectual imposition of a symbolic order on experience and environment allows humans to plan, to manipulate, to communicate—all necessary for survival.

Culture is adaptive, a tool for survival. Humans are not particularly fast or especially strong. We have neither long fur nor curved talons. Our primary specialization is our brain, our intelligence, which along with our opposable thumb and forefinger (developed earlier for tree-dwelling) enabled us to develop tools and technology. All of the many cultures of the world, including about 100,000 distinct cultures from the present to the first humans, are different designs for surviving in varying ecological niches, with different neighbors and unique histories; each is a never-to-be-repeated experiment in survival strategy. It should be noted here that no culture needs to be perfectly adapted to its environment, only *adequately* adapted; it simply has to provide the means for a sufficient number of its members to get by and reproduce.

You are no doubt thinking at this point that culture clearly does much more than merely enable people to survive. While culture originally evolved for survival, as an expression of human intelligence it is always changing and in a sense improving, even in the most technologically simple societies. Humans are not content with brutish survival but also want satisfaction, recreation, and creative expression. Culture everywhere provides the means to satisfying lives (as defined by each culture) as part of overall adaptation. What I am suggesting is that people require more than food and shelter to survive: they also need to impose an intellectual order on the universe around them, to impart meaning to their lives, and to experience pleasure and satisfaction, among other things. Culture provides the means to these ends.

Every culture is constantly changing. Most of the cultures in the world today did not even exist in the not-too-distant past. Could one speak of "the English" or "the French" 700 or 800 years ago? No, these cultures did not exist; instead, there were Celts, Angles, Saxons, Normans, Gauls, Franks, and so on. Corn or maize is now considered the "traditional" staple of South Africans (who call it "mealie") and many other African peoples; yet it is indigenous not to Africa but to the Americas. Maize was introduced to Africa during the sixteenth century. The Zulu, the largest African ethnic group in South Africa today, were formed from a minor kin-based chiefdom in the late eighteenth century. And Americans are still not considered an "ethnic" group: we are one-fourth Swedish, one-fourth African, one-half German, and various other combinations.

While stability, a certain order, is important for culture, change is also essential. The simple fact is that the effective environment of any culture changes; therefore the culture must also change to adapt to the changing environment. Changes might come from an individual, perhaps in the form of an innovation or a prophecy that catches on, or they might originate at the group level, with unconscious changes in, say, child-rearing practices; either way, the capacity for change is a defining characteristic of culture.

Cultural evolution is an extension of biological evolution. The capacity for culture is clearly biological; as an aspect of consciousness and intelligence, culture is based in the brain, a highly evolved biological organ. Yet the content of each culture is learned rather than instinctual; the very plasticity of culture is why it works in so many different environments. The flexible mental basis of culture is psychological rather than biological; that is, while psychological processes may theoretically be reduced to biological processes, to do so is uninformative. Psychological phenomena must be understood at the psychological level. Cultural phenomena, involving the behavior of people in groups, must be understood at the cultural level; to reduce them to individual psychologies is again uninformative; to reduce cultural behavior to mere biology is absurd.

Yet human beings are at once biological animals with varying psychologies, shaped both by culture and biology. With the evolution of culture, biological evolution appears to have slowed down a great deal. While biological microevolution still occurs, especially in the adaptation of human groups to disease pathogens, changes in gross morphology are not as necessary. If a species can build a fire and fashion garments, that species does not need fur; furry members of the species will have no breeding advantage over the less furry members. Humans do not need to change their bodies very much to adapt to their environment if they can change the environment or change their behavior. Such changes may originate with the group or with individuals within the group, and may be conscious or unconscious. Therefore it is most accurate to speak of *psychocultural* evolution rather than simply cultural evolution when speaking of the self and behavior; it is based on biological evolution and extends biological evolution, but it is not the same as biological evolution. Psychocultural evolution operates with different, albeit somewhat analogous, principles.

8

Self and Personality

A self is not an actual thing that you can see and touch; it is a posited entity, an abstraction difficult to define. When asked to explain what they understand by the word, people tend to give responses like "It's me; it's who I am." "It's my spirit, my spiritual part." "It's what makes me different from everybody else." They feel comfortable with the term, but can't really define it. The self and closely related concepts such as "personality" either do not exist linguistically in non-Western culture or else are thought of in such a radically different way that it would be almost silly to claim any sort of meaningful comparability.

We in the West emphasize the uniqueness of each personality, each self, each individual; one's self separates a person from society. Each person is different, special, never to exist again. By contrast, many other cultures, particularly those that are nonliterate and nonindustrial, view the person as continuous with society, an extension of community. For example, Dorothy Lee (1986 [orig. 1976]) argues persuasively that in simpler societies with more integrated communities, the self's submersion in the community provides it with a value and strength that is difficult to replicate in modern impersonal urban society.

Concepts such as person, individual, self, and the like are cultural constructs. The Western (especially Anglo-American) philosophical tradition of extreme individualism has shaped our thinking on matters of the self, emphasizing separation, boundaries, and even solitude. The psychiatrist and anthropologist Arthur Kleinman notes that "the self as we come to know and experience it is a 'construction' of modern culture" (1988:51).

For most of the twentieth century the "self" as a theoretical and analytical concept was little discussed in the social science literature: "personality" was the term employed in contexts wherein the "self" would be used today. Although the two concepts are quite different, there is little agreement within or across disciplines regarding either their definitions or their distinctions. There are scores of competing and overlapping definitions of both concepts: any one offered is bound to annoy significant numbers of scholars in the relevant disciplines. But in general "personality" is a more "inner" theoretical concept, inaccessible to direct observation, whereas the "self" is conceptualized as something "presented" to the community at large and thus accessible to ethnographers and other researchers through behavior observation, autobiographical accounts, and so on. Even this generalization, however, would be protested by many. The psychological anthropologist George DeVos employs both concepts: "cultural traditions of thought influence how the self perceives itself. In turn, this self-perception interacts with, rather than is totally determined by, the operation of underlying coping mechanisms that comprise personality structure" (DeVos and Suarez-Orozco 1990:20).

A conventional definition of "personality" is suggested by the psychological anthropologist Victor Barnouw (1985:8): "Personality is a more or less enduring organization of forces within the individual associated with a complex of fairly consistent attitudes, values, and modes of perception which account, in part, for the individual's consistency of behavior." Note the vagueness: "more or less," "fairly," "in part"; such qualifiers are typical in definitions that try to please everyone. Notice also that the "forces" are *within* the individual. Francis Hsu (1985) pointedly asserts that "the concept of personality is an expression of the western ideal of individualism" and does not even correspond to how Westerners live, let alone to how people in non-Western cultures do; we should replace it with the self, culturally defined within a network of changing social relationships.

"Self" is variously defined as "ego," as "person," and as "individual." DeVos has recently defined "selfhood" as "consciousness," and argues that self must be distinguished from ego: the latter is an external analytic concept in social science, whereas the former is a culture-specific experiential concept (DeVos and Suarez-Orozco 1990:20–21). Self is clearly a more all-encompassing concept than personality, including the mind, the emotions, the body, as well as the individual's cognition or perception of all of these, all in the context of social action; it is a product of the interaction between society and the developing psychobiological human organism; and it changes throughout the life course. The origin of the concept of the self in the social sciences is conventionally traced back to the social psychologist George Herbert Mead (1964 [orig. 1934]), who detailed the social construction of the self in a series of provocative essays in the 1930s. For Mead (1964), the most important characteristic of the self along with its social nature is its reflexivity, the fact that it is at once a subject, an initiator of action, and also an object to itself; the self internalizes the attitudes of other people in the society toward himself or herself (he calls this internal representation the "generalized other"). Mead has been most influential in sociology, especially as interpreted by the extraordinary social observer Erving Goffman (e.g., 1959, 1963, 1971) and other "symbolic interactionists." Goffman and his followers treat social behavior as a drama, with the (American) players presenting ever-changing selves to an ever-changing audience or social situation: psychological aspects of the self are left unexamined. Recently, however, Frank Johnson (1985) argued that these psychological aspects of the Western self typically include describing it as analytic, monotheistic, individualistic, materialistic, and rationalistic. Other scholars might of course come up with different lists, although it is probably fair to assume that all would include individualism as a feature.

In psychoanalytic psychology and psychiatry there has been a great increase in interest in the self in recent years, especially notable in the work of Heinz Kohut (1971, 1977) and Otto Kernberg (1975). The psychoanalyst Roy Schafer (1989), representative of this newer self psychology, sees the self as an active agent, motivated and initiating, the subject of experience, the essence and core of a person's life; and also as the object of action and experience, including one's own; the self must be studied, he says, as a set of "narrative strategies" or "story lines."

Although few followed his lead at the time, the psychological anthropologist A. Irving Hallowell argued in 1955 that "self" was preferable to "personality" for purposes of cross-cultural comparison, presaging Hsu's (1985) arguments just noted. In an essay apparently influenced by G. H. Mead, he argued that self-awareness was universal, that the self is culturally constituted, and that positive valuation by others is an important source of motivation for humans everywhere (Hallowell 1955). He viewed the self "as personal continuity in experience, memory, and social identity" (LeVine 1982:295). In recent years this Hallowellian approach has enjoyed a significant revival: for example, he is cited favorably and frequently in a recent review of current developments in psychocultural theory (Shweder and LeVine 1984); and Walter Gold-schmidt's (1990) *The Human Career: The Self in the Symbolic World* is explicitly indebted to Hallowell.

But in the thirty or so years between these recent developments and Hallowell's essay the concept of the self was little used in psychological anthropology. For example, in the most widely used textbook during much of that period, Barnouw's *Culture and Personality* (fourth ed., 1985), there is not a single entry in the index for "self" but there are many for "personality." The recent collection, *The Making of Psychological Anthropology*, dedicated to Hallowell himself, also does not include a single entry for "self" in its index while again including many for "personality" (Spindler 1978). The tide is changing, however: for better or worse, "self" is at this writing replacing "personality" in psychocultural studies. However, with the reader's indulgence and forgiveness, I will have to zigzag between these two in the following pages according to the usage of the study or author under discussion, reflecting this transition in psychological anthropology.

Looking at some of the current work on the cross-cultural study of the self and behavior, one finds plenty of disagreement among anthropologists. Grace Harris (1989) argues that the words "individual", "self", and "person" should be analytically distinguished as biological, psychological, and sociological conceptualizations, respectively, each referring to different facets of human experience. She controversially asserts that all societies have "working cultural constructs" of all three facets (Harris 1989:607). A more representative point of view is put forth by Shweder and Bourne (1984), who assert that cultures everywhere recognize dual features of a self, "egocentric" and "sociocentric." The egocentric self is the Western ideal of an autonomous individual participating in society almost as a matter of free will. The sociocentric self is the stereotypical (in anthropology) non-Western conception of the person submerged in community. The important difference between the two "ideal types" is not a matter of presence or absence but one of degree of cultural elaboration. So in the West we emphasize the individual over the community but still realize that society helps make us who we are; in rural preindustrial societies the community is valued over the self, but of course everyone recognizes individual differences in temperament, behavioral style, and so on.

The self is also a biological phenomenon, existing everywhere. All children learn to distinguish where their bodies end and other beings and actions begin as part of normal psychophysiological development. Sigmund Freud, Jean Piaget, and G. H. Mead all emphasize this major developmental transition. The biologist Gunther Stent (1975) has argued that the self should even be considered to be a Kantian transcendental concept (that is, something that limits and shapes our thought) just like space, time, and causality. Like them, it is a priori and intuitively obvious, defying explicit definition.

The Self in Ethnography

The self, then, is difficult to define: at once inner and outer, active and passive, biological and social, universal and culturally constructed. However, as suggested above, it is more accessible to study than personality is, and in recent years many ethnographers have produced accounts of selves in non-Western cultures. Robert LeVine (1982:295), whose theory of personality and behavior will be highlighted a little later in this chapter, offers some important assumptions that might guide ethnographic research on the self: (1) individual behavior is deliberate, motivated, and marked by "adaptive goal-orientations"; (2) individuals' goals and how they go about achieving them are conscious, and expressed through the language and beliefs that their culture makes available; (3) these culturally encoded means and ends are transmitted from generation to generation and from person to person as pragmatic local wisdom that aids survival and provides satisfaction; (4) self-consciousness and a certain degree of introspection are found everywhere in the world, and so in every culture one actor is always distinguished from another; and (5) cultures vary in how the self is expected to develop throughout life, in what behaviors are supported or negatively regarded, and in the degree and contexts for autonomy versus cooperation. Methodologically, ethnographic depictions of the self in other cultures are usually presented as "ethnopsychologies," psychological concepts and categories "from the native's point of view" (see, for example, Kirkpatrick and White 1985; Geertz 1984). The emphasis is on actual individuals experiencing life (Turner and Bruner 1986).

The Kpelle of Liberia, among whom I lived and studied in the early 1970s, present a self to others that is warm, respectful, and polite, even a bit formal. But underneath this warm public self is often one that is suspicious and mistrustful. The belief in malign motivations in other people, expressed in a preoccupation with and fear of sorcery and witchcraft, is very strong. "We Kpelle do not like each other," I was told. Suspicious and fearful or not, a proper adult, whether man or woman, should be controlled in behavior, readily generous, and very hardworking. A person who excels at traditional rural activities such as farming, hunting, or roof-thatching is called a "hero," whereas one who succeeds at urban, modern activities such as driving or soccer is a "bullshitter" or *kwii* (foreign, strange): cultural change creates and requires new selves.

Knowledge and respect come only with age, beginning with the process of initiation (see Chapter 3). Such knowledge is in general secret, subject to rules of *ifa mo* ("you can't talk about it"), and gives a person power over others who may lack it. Knowledge acquired through other means, such as experience or schooling, does not command respect within rural Kpelle culture; the self must be managed and presented accordingly. The Kpelle self is also partly spiritual, and this spirit-self can travel about in dreams or in trance while the body-self is sleeping or otherwise unconscious. The self can also be possessed by spirits; when this occurs, as in the wearing of masks during rituals, the everyday self is gone and therefore not responsible for the actions of the possessed body. The permeability and complexity of the Kpelle self is also seen in the *nyina*, a sort of animal double that connects men (I am not sure if women possess *nyina*-selves) with the forest, and which may even take over in times of great stress: it is as if there is a village, or cultural, self, and a forest, or natural, self; the latter is often blamed for aggressive or antisocial behavior.

Karen Ito (1985:320) has argued that the Hawaiian self is defined through interrelationships with others, especially with regard to the emotional tone of these ties: "Self is a socially interactive concept tied to correct social behavior (*hana pono*) between

Self and Other. . . . The Self-Other relationship . . . offers a protective netting when open to positive exchanges, and dangerously exposes the Self when entangled by negative exchanges."

The Sambia (a pseudonym) of the Highlands of New Guinea are rugged individualists who recognize and appreciate significant differences among persons, and who emphasize gender in their conceptualizing of the self (Herdt and Stoller 1990:94–95). Personal characteristics are the result of one's "thought" (*koontu*), which Herdt states is quite similar to our concept of self. Behaviors, morals, and personality traits all stem from one's *koontu*. But it is private situations, private experience, and private knowledge that most directly express selfhood. Since most Sambia, like people everywhere, try to express themselves according to norms of propriety and appropriateness, their communications and narratives must be examined over a long period to minimize normative censors and reveal Sambia selves (Herdt and Stoller 1990:97).

The list of ethnographic analyses of selfhood is growing rapidly, including studies of the Pintupi Aborigines of Australia's Western Desert (Myers 1979), Tahitians (Levy 1973), Marquesans (Kirkpatrick 1985), Ifaluk, Micronesia (Lutz 1988), A'ara of Santa Isabel, Solomon Islands (White 1985), the Ilongot of the Philippines (Rosaldo 1980, 1983), Japanese (Lebra 1983; DeVos 1985), Hindu India (Bharati 1985), Chinese (Chu 1985), and many others. This new road, now taken by so many, will eventually lead to very different conceptualizations of human psyche and behavior.

Self, Personality, and Behavior

In this section I will outline the connections between the self and the personality, on the one hand, and behavior, on the other. I use a simplified version of Robert LeVine's (1982) formulation of these connections, which he himself had derived from an earlier one by the psychologist Irvin Child. I must first point out that LeVine employs the term "personality"; if he were writing in the 1990s, perhaps he would reconceptualize his theory in terms of the "self." I will try to discuss the relation of both to behavior, a difficult task at best.

Personality, according to LeVine, refers to a mental organization of relatively consistent dispositions that underlie behavior. It can only be inferred, never directly observed, so it, like the self, must remain an abstraction. We know it is partly inherited and partly learned, but we do not know proportions. We *think* that features of the personality as well as aspects of the self acquired early in life are more fundamental and more difficult to modify than those acquired later, but this notion remains controversial, especially with regard to details. This psychological system intervenes between raw experience and ensuing behavior (LeVine 1982:5), "filtering" experienced events; any behavior is therefore shaped not only by stimuli from the environment but also by personality and self, which construct both stimulus *and* response.

Although neither the inner self nor the personality can be directly seen, behavior, or at least behavior in a social context, can be observed by others. Behavior does not directly mirror the personality or the self; individuals are capable of behaving in ways that mask inner states, at least for a short while. But of course behavior is all that behavioral scientists have to work with. It is certainly a rough indirect measure of personality and self, and the longer the observational period and the more varied the social settings, the more accurate the measure. The more careful the study, the more closely can behavior be viewed as the self externalized. LeVine notes that "observed behavioral consistencies do not *constitute* personality, they are *indicators* of it, or rather of the internal dispositions that influence overt behavior" (1982:7; emphases in original). A man who strikes and screams at members of his family, who curses other drivers in traffic, and who insults colleagues at the office—and who behaves in this fashion over a significant length of time (so that temporary stressors can be ruled out as the cause of his outbursts)—is an angry person. Anger is a part of his inner self.

Self and personality clearly have some biochemical bases; aspects of both are genetically encoded and are inherited. But no one knows what parts are biological and what parts are purely acquired. For example, scientists know that imbalances in certain brain chemicals such as serotonin are associated with emotional states: too much may bring about hyperactivity, even manic excitement; too little seems to promote depression. There are many such examples, making molecular neurology one of the most exciting research frontiers today. However, it is unknown whether such inner "imbalances" are purely endogenous (that is, arising from within the person), or triggered (or even wholly caused) by environmental stressors. For the purposes of this book, it is simply recognized that human selves and personalities are partly biochemically based, but that learning plays a far greater role, at least in the development (or even the destruction) of "normal" selves or personalities.

Selves and personalities may have evolved in human beings because they aided survival (Goldschmidt 1990:67–69). The acquisition of culture is impossible without a symbolic self; in fact the self (as well as personality) and culture probably coevolved (see Goldschmidt 1990 for further discussion of this issue).

Individuals and culture shape each other, but the balance is far from equal. Each individual influences culture: in our own society, each decision we make regarding food, clothing, shelter, school, sexuality, and so on, contributes to cultural "drift" and change. "I'm on the pill now, so I can enjoy sex freely" (1970); "I'm afraid of herpes, chlamydia, and AIDS, so I have sex infrequently, and only with someone I know well" (1990). Cultural "rules" concerning sexuality are shaped in part by the daily decisions of individuals. However, culture shapes and controls individual selves far more powerfully. While societies continue without any given members, no individual can exist without society. The structure of the family as well as customary gender and age roles, all artifacts of culture, are basic to the formation of the self.

Throughout life, culture rewards and punishes all sorts of personality traits as they are exhibited in behavior. People shun the obnoxious—and try not to be obnoxious so that they can maintain friendships. Violent people have difficulty maintaining viable families; in extreme cases cultural rules may deem them unfit to live in society. In Western capitalist society certain forms of aggressiveness and risk-taking are rewarded while orientation toward family and home rather than corporation and work may be punished. Every culture, from the smallest and simplest to the largest and most complex, is a structure of subtle and not-so-subtle rewards and punishments for personality traits and their expression in behavior. Western society is pluralistic and can absorb a wide variety of behaviors, making it difficult for the Western student of culture and society to see these cultural foundations of the self and personality, but they are most definitely there, as we will see later on.

In the study of tribal cultures, the phenomenon is almost obvious. For example, Jean Briggs (1970) has written movingly about the management of anger and temper among northern Canadian Inuit. An angry person is shunned by the Inuit, just as a sinner is shunned by the Old Order Amish. But unlike the Amish sinner, the ostracized Inuit will die if not taken back by the community. Could the cultural foundations of personality and self be more clearly demonstrated?

Genetic variation is the primary source of vitality for any species in nature. It is this variation that enables organisms to adapt to a changing ecology. If the environment alters too much or too fast and if the genetic variation is too limited, the species becomes extinct. The environment selects individuals with the necessary adaptive traits, rewarding them with survival. Survival is defined as the production of offspring, who in turn live through breeding age. Individual organisms lacking these traits do not live to produce viable offspring; the environment has "punished" them.

A fundamental thesis of this book is that the relationship between selves and culture is similar to the relationship between genes and environment. While a culture is certainly not a species, as a *type* of human organization it is similar to a species. A self is not a gene, but as a source of variation within a culture it is similar to a gene. Selves are the source of cultural vitality, allowing individuals within a culture and, in the aggregate, the culture itself to respond to and adapt to an ever-changing environment. It should be noted that "environment" is everything external to the individual, so that one may speak of the "physical," "cultural," or "caretaking" environment. Another important point to keep in mind is that environmental factors do not *determine* behavior; rather, behavior is adapted to environmental realities. Furthermore, adaptation is never a passive response to an environment because individuals and societies transform their environments while adapting to them. As their selves are forming, active, developing human children interact with and grow within the cultural and natural environments. While individuals exist in physical nature, they also exist in, and only in, *cultures* that make up their effective immediate environments. Personalities, selves, ways of thinking, and behavioral patterns, in other words, are built within individual biographies on cultural foundations.

LeVine's Evolutionary Theory of Personality

Robert LeVine is a psychoanalytically trained anthropologist with an interest in how human personalities (and selves in his more recent work) promote adaptation and contribute to cultural evolution. At the outset I must emphasize that LeVine's theory of psychosocial adaptation is neither the only nor the first theory in studies of culture and personality to emphasize adaptation, but it *is* by far the most explicit, articulated, developed, and influential theory to do so. I will discuss some of the others in the next section.

LeVine's theory is highly technical and elaborate. At the risk of oversimplifying, I am "translating" the theory into a version more suitable to those encountering psychocultural studies for the first time. His model is "Darwinian," explicitly invoking biological terminology; he refers to human societies as "populations," and to his evolutionary model as "population psychology." For LeVine, personalities are statistically varying features of societies that can be measured from observations of the behavior(s) of individuals; behavior is viewed as a personality *indicator.*

The culture (or "sociocultural system") is a selective environment that interacts with individual behavior just as the natural environment interacts with the behavior of all organisms. The culture is made up of all sorts of social institutions which make demands on members but also provide opportunities for them. To achieve a satisfying life of successful conformity, an individual is better off with certain personality traits rather than others since people with different personalities behave differently in social roles and are therefore rewarded differently by the culture. This selection of personality traits by the culture and the shaping of their own behavior by individuals is the process of "psychosocial adaptation." Adaptation is in general an unconscious process, although humans, unlike other animals, can become aware of what they are doing and thereby can quite deliberately direct their behavior (LeVine 1982:103–104; see also Boehm 1982).

One problem with these assumptions is that human beings interact with both the natural and cultural environments, making it difficult to establish with certainty precisely which environment is functioning as the selective environment at any given time. This problem is especially salient with regard to small-scale cultures whose members live out of doors—"in" nature as it were—and in attempting to understand behaviors such as those involved in environmental pollution in complex societies such as our own. In the latter example both environments shape the behaviors in the end. In my view LeVine does not come to grips with this problem.

The primary concepts in LeVine's evolutionary model are the personality "genotype," the personality "phenotype," and "deliberate" socialization. While LeVine is in my estimation advancing the frontiers of knowledge, his concepts are sometimes confusing. Let me explain.

In biological usage the genotype is the actual genetic makeup of an organism; the phenotype consists of the observable characteristics of an organism, or the genotype modified by environmental factors. In LeVine's analogy, the personality genotype is the same as what I have defined as simply "personality" earlier in this chapter: it refers to the internal organization of personality dispositions (LeVine 1982:115–116). It is acquired early and is resistant to later elimination yet can be inhibited under certain conditions. The personality genotype is formed in the first five or six years of life, when the child's experiences of the world are filtered through caretakers, usually a mother and other close family members, as well as through his or her own immature cognitive capacity. It comprises *both* the basic *biological* and biochemical makeup of the child *and* the effects of early *learning* and *experience* in the first few years, including patterns of stimulation, reward, punishment, attachment, and separation, as well as trauma (LeVine 1982:116–117).

This mixing of biological and learning variables under one label is where LeVine gets into trouble: he uses a term lifted directly from biology—"genotype"—and uses it for something that is partly biological and partly social and experiential. At the very least he should have chosen a different term, because analogy or metaphor is emphatically *not* identity; similarity is not equivalence. It is important to stress, however, that the term, not the idea, is the problem. By employing this term and by lumping certain biological and experiential variables together, LeVine is saying something very important: that biological endowments and first experiences are *functionally* equivalent. Their deep embeddedness in the brain and their effects on behavior are unitary and inseparable. I believe that he chose the term "genotype" to stress that even the learned components might as well be biological, since the results are essentially the same.

Continuing with the biological metaphor, LeVine posits a personality phenotype, which is essentially behavior (personality indicators, remember), although not just any behavior. It is consistent, observable individual behavior that characterizes adults moving through and acting in all the typical settings of their cultural world (LeVine 1982:121–122). Unlike the personality genotype, it is responsive to change and can be, and often is, modified. In a sense it can be thought of as the personality genotype modified by later experience, analogous to the biological phenotype as the genotype modified by the interaction with the environment. In biology phenotype refers to observable characteristics, so one can understand why LeVine chose the term, but again the choice is problematic. Behavior is far more malleable than phenotypes are, and the relationship between personality and behavior may be quite indirect (we don't really know). But the analogy, if we always bear in mind that it *is* an analogy and no more, is a good one.

The third of what LeVine refers to as his "basic" concepts is "deliberate" socialization, "the intentions or actions of the parents (or substitutes) in training the child" (1982:124). This socialization includes, among other things, parental purposes, values, intelligence, and so on, and is affected in addition by the child's own actions. For the purposes of my argument here, I will ignore LeVine's qualifying adjective "deliberate": the effects of the socialization experience, intentional or accidental, are identical; whether a particular action is deliberate or not would seem to be irrelevant. Socialization, then, is fundamental in the creation of the integrated self and is the primary avenue for the cultural shaping of the self and personality.

Utilizing these assumptions and concepts, LeVine suggests that psychosocial adaptation is a continuous process in culture operating in several key areas accessible to field research. For example, early child-rearing practices must be adapted to the environment (LeVine 1982:132). Take the case of Liberian Kpelle mothers (or older sisters) who nearly always carry their child on their backs, secured by a length of cloth tied over the mother's breasts. To a Westerner it seems very limiting to be encumbered by a heavy child, even when working. I frequently saw women applying clay to the external walls of their huts while carrying (sometimes sleeping) babies on their backs. The rain forest environment, however, is a dangerous one for infants and toddlers: there are open fires, snakes, scorpions, driver ants, and animal feces, to name just a few of the more obvious hazards. The custom of tying babies on mothers' backs is an adaptation that enhances the odds for children's survival.

Cultural-evolutionary processes are also at work during the first few years of life when the child begins to adapt to societal norms through its responses to the child-rearing practices of parents and caretakers (LeVine 1982:133). The child is preparing, and being prepared for, entry into society. Its parents serve as cultural brokers or agents, gradually introducing learned cultural norms into the child's family environment. Through early socialization the child acquires some behaviors that facilitate later adaptation. For example, in North America, Europe, Japan, and many other places, some children learn to sit still and maintain attention before they are five; this prepares them for the school environment, which facilitates learning, which in turn increases the chances for cultural success. Aggression is encouraged in very small boys among the Yanomamo of Venezuela and Brazil; this early socialization helps prepare them for an adult life of frequent war.

Third, individuals control and manage their behavior, selectively expressing or suppressing aspects of their selves, to match appropriate norms in the range of social settings (LeVine 1982:132–133). People try to fit into their environments; they want to be accepted and valued. Individuals learn about their environment(s) and shape their behavior accordingly. American high school students try to be "cool" to be accepted and liked. Persons who are new employees of a business firm will generally keep major criticism to themselves until they reach the point where they believe their position is secure enough that criticisms and suggestions will be accepted without career damage. In the Kalahari Desert of Botswana, a !Kung hunter suppresses his hunger, sharing even meager kills with others in his camp. Stingy people are despised among the !Kung, and stinginess is very broadly defined; in that culture, virtually all Americans would be considered extremely stingy (Lee 1979).

Finally, LeVine argues that adaptation occurs in the gradual adjustment of the typical behavior of members of a culture to the demands and norms of their society (LeVine 1982:134–135). I remind you of the earlier examples of the assertive American traveling in Europe and the ostracizing of angry Inuit by their fellows. There are indeed modal or typical personalities associated with particular cultures, at least in a statistical sense. If behavior, as LeVine suggests, is taken as an index of personality and is carefully observed, measured, and statistically analyzed, the results, if significant, comprise a profile of the Trukese, Hopi, Tupinamba, Arunta, or Bena Bena personality. Where do these "group" personalities come from? According to LeVine, they arise from the adaptation of external behavior "to normative environments through the selective pressure of social sanctions" (LeVine 1982:134; emphasis omitted).

In other words, society rewards appropriate behavior and ignores or punishes inappropriate behavior. Through this adaptive process behavior in the aggregate gradually drifts one way or the other as people struggle for success and satisfaction, culturally defined, in their social lives. So competitiveness is a frequently observed (albeit not universal) American personality trait since competition is valued in school, business, and politics. Christopher Lasch (1979) has suggested that even "narcissistic" behavior—calculated, manipulative, what's in it for me?—is rewarded in many sectors of American life. If a personality type is rewarded, it persists and spreads; gradually parents begin to produce children with the culturally desired traits. Ask yourself, does the solitude of the American middle-class baby, alone in its own room, a custom unique among world cultures, have anything to do with individualism? I think it does, and I believe LeVine would agree. By contrast, a Chinese peasant is rarely alone from birth right through to death, and is not surprisingly more sociocentric than an American.

LeVine (1982:138) demonstrates that public behavior is a stabilized balance or compromise between an individual's inner self with all of its urges, goals, desires, and motives based in the personality genotype, and the general social consensus on appropriate and proper behavior in a given setting or role. A mother might strongly want to flee from a screaming baby to her friends at the local tavern, but the public definition of the role of "mother" prohibits such behavior, punishing it with sanctions ranging from shunning by friends and family to legal prosecution for child neglect. A compromise is reached: this time the mother stays home. Perhaps in the future she will trade child care duties with a friend who is also a mother for a few hours a week to lessen the burden. Perhaps not. But it is in these vignettes of everyday life that psychosocial adaptation takes place. Willing conformity of everyone to cultural norms is the hypothetical "ideal" of all societies—a perfect fit, albeit one that is never achieved in the real world. In my example the willingly conforming mom stays with her child and devises ways to make her days less stressful: trading duties with her husband or friends, visiting people and places, and so on. But if her conformity is unwilling ("coerced" in LeVine's terms), child abuse could easily result: she angrily stays home, but drinks too much and hits the infant.

Coerced conformity is common where a particular role (such as father, teacher, etc.) forbids the expression in behavior of feelings that the role itself creates (LeVine 1982:139–142). Cultures often provide defenses along with this coercion. In the last example, alcohol is such a defense. A strong belief in life after death might help alleviate the misery of poverty, a condition to which few are "willing" to conform.

Culture change is also an important part of adaptation in LeVine's (1982:153–161) scheme. For example, when a society industrializes, wholly new patterns of behavior, representing new personality configurations, are required. The seasonal time frame of a West African rice farmer must be replaced by the hectic daily schedule of the industrial worker; this new life pattern permeates the inner self within a generation. Another example of culture change is the transformation of local sovereign clan-communities in a place like New Guinea into dependent localities integrated into an emerging nation-state, drastically altering "the scope and complexity of [the] selective" environment (LeVine 1982:155).

These latter examples represent change originating on the *society* side of the compromise between society and the self, but change can also stem from the *self* side. Nearly imperceptible changes in taste, preferences, and behavior from generation to generation bring about change. Today's white-collar employee is less comfortable with an authoritarian style of management than the "organization man" of the fifties—some change in the corporate self that has occurred over the last thirty-five years has in turn changed corporate management style. Some innovations by individuals really catch on and eventually alter institutions. For example, during the eighteenth century in western New York, a Seneca named Handsome Lake experienced a series of visions concerning how to maintain and revitalize the culture of the Iroquois nations, declining rapidly in the face of the onslaught of European expansion (Wallace 1972a): today, many New York Iroquois worship at Handsome Lake churches. Gorbachev's innovations in the Soviet Union have already brought about dramatic change in phenotypic behavior *and* institutional structure both inside and outside the U.S.S.R.

Cultural adaptation theory has a long history in many areas of cultural anthropology but has not generally been applied to studies of individuals or to research that is dependent on the observation of the behavior of individuals. Robert LeVine's theory, while not without problems and no doubt not to everyone's liking, has paved a new road for the field of psychological anthropology to follow. Other anthropologists and a few psychologists have been following parallel paths.

Other Adaptational Models of Behavior

Robert Edgerton (1971a) and Walter Goldschmidt (1971, 1986, 1990) are particularly important in the study of human behavioral adaptation. They focus on the effects of ecology on personality, self, and behavior. One of their best-known projects was the Culture and Ecology in East Africa Project as reported in *The Individual in Cultural Adaptation* (Edgerton 1971a). This was a study in cultural microevolution involving four East African cultures, the Hehe, the Kamba, the Pokot, and the Sebei, each of which was divided into a herding sector and a horticultural sector. The idea was to establish whether basic subsistence activity shaped behavior more powerfully than ethnic identity did. Environmental and economic factors were the independent variables, while institutions and behavior were the dependent variables. They reported that herders are more emotionally open and expressive, whereas farmers' emotions are "closed" and somewhat hidden from the community. Herders prefer direct action and confrontation when faced with a problem or conflict; farmers prefer indirect action such as witchcraft. Herders are able to confront conflict because they are mobile and can escape if necessary; farmers on the other hand are tied to land and closer living in villages, and so must develop ways to avoid conflict (Edgerton 1971a:279). Thus the environment, broadly conceived, is a powerful selector for behavior: the self, in other words, is adapted to the environment.

Goldschmidt has continued his work with the Sebei of Uganda, further refining his adaptational paradigm. As in the earlier work with Edgerton, he systematically compares the behavior of persons in Sebei communities with different ecologies, different subsistence strategies, and/or different histories. He documents the disappearance or transformation of various institutions (cultural environment) as well as the introduction of new institutions from the outside or from within, and shows how these changes in the environment alter "the sentiments and feelings of the people by creating different kinds of tension and concern" (Goldschmidt 1986:145, 148). In other words, people adapt to changing circumstances. Attempting to generalize theoretically from the Sebei data, Goldschmidt argues that the process of evolutionary adaptation is orderly. Environmental change forces individuals to assess the situation and then behave in new and different ways, albeit ways that differ as little as possible from previous custom. As LeVine also argues, the new behaviors are not perceived by the actors as transforming society but transform it they do. The new behavioral repertoire sets up a new set of conditions which "creates a new basis for further change" (Goldschmidt 1986:148).

The late Charles Valentine (1968), in an important critique of the "culture of poverty" concept, argued that each new generation of urban poor *adapts* anew to the same or similar stultifying and deadening life conditions. It is this continual repeated "situational adaptation," not the intergenerational transmission of bad values (as "culture of poverty" theorists used to argue), that accounts for such problems as educational and economic failure.

The Nigerian-born educational anthropologist John Ogbu elaborated greatly on Valentine's thesis in two brilliant monographs that focus on social inequality and minority education (1974, 1978). His work is very compatible with LeVine's and Goldschmidt's and their colleagues. He argues that urban poor minority children fail in school in disproportionate numbers simply because they are *adapting* realistically to limited future opportunities (Ogbu 1974:13–15). African-Americans, for example, obviously do not have the same access as a group to meaningful, well-paying careers as do whites; they therefore responded historically "more or less unconsciously, to this limited postschool opportunity partly by reducing their efforts in school tasks to the level of rewards they expected as future adults of American society" (Ogbu 1974:254–255). He later generalized his argument, refining its applicability to African-Americans and emphasizing adaptation to what he calls the "job ceiling," and also applying the adaptational theory to several other "castelike" minorities in other societies around the world and in the United States: Native Americans, Mexican-Americans, and Puerto Ricans in the United States, West Indians in Great Britain, Maoris in New Zealand, low castes in India, Buraku in Japan, and Oriental Jews in Israel (Ogbu 1978). In all these diverse multicultural cases, Ogbu convincingly demonstrates the utility of the concept of psychocultural adaptation. "Specifically, the ability of a group of people to maximize their cognitive and academic skills depends on the opportunity they have to use these skills in the world of work" (Ogbu 1978:364). When the environment changes, as when the socioeconomic barriers to equality are removed, performance in school and associated behaviors will change in an adaptive fashion. Other anthropologists and psychologists who study cognition and cultural adaptation will be reviewed in Chapter 6.

Certain other psychological anthropologists also view adaptation as central in the understanding of the relationship between self and society, or personality and culture, but in a manner somewhat different from that of LeVine and the others just discussed. Spindler is representative of this approach: he focuses on social change due to contact between Western culture and less powerful cultures.

He employs the phrase "psychocultural adaptation" to refer to those features of culture and personality that affect the process of acculturation (the process of learning a new, dominant culture), especially the acculturation of Native Americans to "Whiteman" culture; he is especially interested in the emotional and motivational factors involved in such adaptation (Spindler 1968). Culture and personality are viewed as independent and inseparable systems: one does not follow or have primacy over the other. So, for example, the Blood Indians of Alberta, while retaining many important features of their tradition, including language, have adapted successfully to white culture because they already possessed traits valued by the white middle class, including "the controlled use of aggression for personal achievement," and a "high value upon personal success displayed in part through the acquisition of material goods" (Spindler 1968:332). The Menomini of Wisconsin, on the other hand, are less culturally and/or psychologically homogeneous than the Blood; they can be divided into five categories, each representing a "unique adaptation" to a harsh culture contact, ranging from conservative "native-oriented" and peyote cultists to "elite acculturated" (Spindler and Spindler 1971:2–6). Only the latter category are truly successful in "Whiteman" terms, but their success was made possible by a complete in-depth psychological adjustment: they learned "to stop being Menomini and . . . how to be middle-class achievement-oriented Americans" (Spindler 1968:330). A search for a satisfying *identity,* the construction of an integrated self, is an important part of Spindler's scheme, so "failure" in economic terms might not mean failure at all in terms of self-identity; the reverse is of course true as well.

DeVos (1973) similarly argues that Japanese personality, self-identity, and culture, while dramatically different from Western culture, has facilitated adaptation to a world structured by capitalist industrialism. They are "socialized for achievement," but the achievement is one of the family, the corporation, the group—not at all the individual as in the West. The Japanese self is continuous with the family—and other groups such as corporations are conceived as familylike—and possesses a strong need to belong and to work and play cooperatively with others. This sociocentric self and the cultural arrangements that sustain it predate European contact. Yet psychocultural adaptation to modernity has occurred with stunning rapidity: "The sense of validating the self through sustained work is transmuted into modern goals instead of ancient purposes" (DeVos 1968:362). Such adaptation is not without costs, and DeVos discusses a host of social and psychological problems. For example, many Japanese are obsessive about standards of excellence to the point that their self-esteem is threatened if such standards are not always maintained. Such standards in the social realm, internalized in the self as a preoccupation with proper role behavior, leave people poorly prepared for the inevitable social failures (DeVos 1978:248–256).

Finally, Marvin Harris and his cultural materialist colleagues and followers are adaptationalists who are thoroughly antipsychological: he opposes studying anything not directly observable, so one cannot study the mind or a self; rather, one studies observable *behavior* and only behavior (Harris 1964). Lest the reader wonder why Harris should be discussed here at all, I suggest that by treating psychological issues as end products of material forces he is in effect offering an *explanation* of the same issues. For example, the Yanomamo of Venezuela are famous in anthropology for being "fierce," aggressive, and violent, as documented by one of their ethnographers, the sociobiological anthropologist Napoleon Chagnon (1983). In other words, the Yanomamo self is, among other qualities, aggressive. Both Chagnon and Harris would agree that Yanomamo are violent because they are engaged in virtually constant warfare. Harris (1987:195–197) argues that the warfare is an adaptive response to an imbalance between population and available animal protein; essentially, there isn't enough meat to go around, so people move into each other's territories, resulting in fighting. Implicitly, then, Harris suggests that certain Yanomamo personality dispositions are adaptations to material imperatives.

In a recent study closer to home, Harris (1981) traces deeply psychological phenomena, including Gay Liberation, neofeminism, and the appeal of wild religious cults to changes in the material (technological, ecological, economic, demographic) conditions of American life. Again he is in effect explaining group psychocultural behavior through cultural evolutionary adaptation. I believe that a "LeVinian" approach to these issues is far more congenial to materialists such as Harris than earlier psychological reductionist approaches, and that a productive synthesis could be on the horizon.

In sum, I am convinced that patterned human behavior in groups and the cultural codes and selves underlying that behavior evolve and persist because they promote the survival of the group and of the individuals in the group, help maintain a satisfying lifestyle, and enhance the quality of life for members of a given culture. Culture, and the personalities and selves that sustain it, are maintained only when they continue to do these things. When they do not, when a culture becomes anachronistic and maladaptive, people will search out and explore other ways, other techniques, to answer life's questions and solve life's problems, and the old culture, the "traditional" culture, will wither away, sometimes forever, sometimes to resurface on special occasions involving the affirmation of ethnic identity, and even sometimes to be revived, albeit in drastically altered form, as part of a newly adaptive strategy in a modern pluralistic society.

Critiques of Adaptational Theory

The concept of cultural adaptation enjoys wide acceptance in cultural anthropology, but there are important criticisms. It should be stressed, for example, that not all human behavior is adaptive. All human beings are creative in the broadest sense and develop new strategies that might replace the tried-and-true ones. It would be a serious mistake to suggest that every specific custom in any given culture is adaptive and thus irreplaceable. Cicatrization (ritual scarring) can be replaced with tattooing, circumcision with tests of bravery, polygamy with monogamy, or beef with chicken! It is the *pattern*—the *whole structure*—that maintains culture, not a specific practice. The ethnographic literature is replete with customs that are maladaptive or at least not adaptive: Fore treatment of the degenerative neurological disease *kuru*, Dani amputation of little girls' fingers to memorialize a death, Nuer ritual treatment of smallpox before eradication, Western women's clothing and footwear styles, and so on. An important reservation about psychocultural adaptation therefore is that not all behaviors, not even some behaviors shared by entire groups, promote survival or enhance life. Adaptation is, however, a primary concern in the cultural analysis of group behavior, since so much of culture is made up of standardized adaptive strategies.

Christopher Boehm cautions that "cultural evolution is too different from biological evolution for us to operate so heavily in terms of biological concepts" (1982:105). As noted above, analogies and metaphors from biology are useful but should not be reified. Boehm argues too that the group-versus-individual debate over which is the fundamental unit of selection might be very different for cultural than for biological evolution since clearly a culture is far more than the mere sum of its members. But his primary critique of adaptational theory in general is that such theories generally deny or ignore conscious, rational adaptation by both individuals and cultural collectivities (Boehm 1982:114–116). LeVine emphasizes the largely unconscious nature of adaptation. But unlike biological evolution, cultural evolution is not completely "blind" since it involves the mind and learning at every juncture (Boehm 1978). Americans obviously tailor their behaviors to their work environments in a conscious, sometimes even calculated way. On a cultural level, a certain amount of planning and associated change are effected through science, perhaps the most perfect example of conscious rational decision-making and information-gathering.

A more global critique is offered by C. R. Hallpike in *The Principles of Social Evolution* (1986). As an anthropologist trained in the British tradition, he is interested in groups rather than individuals, in "society" rather than "culture," and is suspicious of theories relying on adaptation as an explanatory principle. He is nevertheless relevant to this book's concerns because of one extremely important point: the fact that a particular custom or behavior exists and persists is not necessarily a demonstration that it is the best, or most efficient, or least harmful. I have argued elsewhere, for example, that while genital mutilation such as clitoridectomy "works" to perpetuate valued gender roles among the Kpelle of Liberia and their neighbors, it is obviously neither the best nor the only way to do so, ignoring for the moment the desirability of maintaining these roles in the first place (Erchak 1979a). I have heard the felicitous phrase "survival of the adequate" employed in anthropological discussions to replace the erroneous and abused "survival of the fittest." Hallpike (1986) refers to the survival of "the mediocre," emphasizing that many allegedly adaptive customs are very far from being the best in *any* sense. "Crude and inefficient" forms of anything will work well enough to persist (Hallpike 1986:372). We should keep these criticisms in mind as we proceed.

SUGGESTED READINGS

Robert LeVine's *Culture, Behavior, and Personality* (1982) is subtitled *An Introduction to the Comparative Study of Psychosocial Adaptation* and so is a good starting point for learning about the adaptational approach to psychocultural study; it is a large part of the inspiration for this book. However, it is dense and difficult, requiring a great deal of effort. I particularly recommend Chapters 1–3 and 7–10. A condensed and somewhat simplified version of LeVine's theory appeared as Chapter 8 in David Goslin's (1969) *Handbook of Socialization Theory and Research.*

Walter Goldschmidt's introduction to Robert Edgerton's *The Individual in Cultural Adaptation* (1971a), entitled "the Theory of Cultural Adaptation," presents a concise version of another, parallel model. His 1986 *The Sebei: A Study in Adaptation* is a very readable ethnography, written especially for undergraduates, which utilizes this model to understand changes in behavior for several Ugandan communities. Finally, his new (1990) and wonderful *The Human Career: The Self in the Symbolic World* places the self squarely in the center of cultural theory. He shows how the self and its symbols are central to human biological as well as cultural evolution, and traces the self's development throughout the human life cycle.

2

Socialization:
The Formation
of the Self in Culture

The human life cycle from birth to death is ideal for both cross-cultural comparison and for illustrating adaptation. First, it is universal: every person in every culture passes through a life cycle. While this point is obvious, it should still be stressed, since many other facets of human life seem to be universal but in fact are not. For example, doesn't everyone everywhere have a family? Well, yes and no. Everyone has a mother, and at least a biological father, but that's all. There may be no *social* father at all, as in many Caribbean societies and among many impoverished African-Americans in U.S. cities. In addition, there are several very different types of human families found around the world; the North American nuclear family is in fact rather uncommon as the primary family group. Other cultural institutions are equally diverse: not all human groups recognize political leaders, not all have social classes, not all use markets, and so forth. But all have precisely the same life cycle.

Second, the life cycle is biological and therefore anchored for comparison. The biological growth, development, and aging process provides a series of independent variables which can then be related to a variety of psychological and cultural dependent variables. Finally, the life cycle is also cultural; that is to say, it is culturally managed. Nowhere is it simply allowed to run its course without cultural interference, and it is here, in this cultural shaping of individual development, that psychocultural adaptation occurs.

This cultural interference results from the fact that the life cycle is disruptive for social groups. Constant growth means constant change, which means constant challenges for each culture. Birth is disruptive, radically transforming the routines of a family. Puberty is threatening: a neuter child is becoming a highly sexed man or woman. Marriage transforms relationships. Old age disrupts communities, especially if economic self-sufficiency is lost. And death threatens the kin group with dissolution and extinction. Each stage presents society with an existential crisis, which must be managed in such a way that the general welfare is maintained. In this chapter I will focus only on the early part of the life cycle, from infancy to middle adolescence, since it is only in this period of life that the self is actually *formed*, although it is of course *trans*formed throughout life.

Socialization and Adaptation

Perhaps because it is both universal and at once biological and cultural, the socialization process is studied by several disciplines, including but not limited to anthropology, sociology, and psychology (LeVine 1982:61). A welter of terminology has emerged to describe essentially the same process: child-rearing, child-training, child development, informal education, cultural transmission, enculturation (cultural learning), and so on. However, the term "socialization" has emerged over the years as the most widely used, and so I will adopt this usage. Socialization is the social process through which a developing individual forms a self, learns cultural rules, and becomes a member of a society. It is convenient to conceive of socialization as consisting of two consecutive stages: primary socialization, which takes place in the first five or six years of life generally within a family context; and secondary socialization, which extends roughly from age six to anywhere from sixteen to twenty-one (culturally variable) mainly outside the family (Parsons 1949). In reality, of course, socialization is one unitary process, particularly from the "socializee's" vantage point. But there are solid analytical and heuristic reasons for splitting it, as you will see shortly.

Many anthropological studies of socialization emphasize adaptation, whereas the psychological approach emphasizes the family environment, child-rearing techniques, and, increasingly, biological issues such as birth weight, sibling order, and cognitive capacity of the child. Earlier anthropology, along with sociology, emphasized parental values; the latter also stresses the learning of role behavior.

I contend that an adaptational approach has significant advantages over other conceptualizations in at least two important ways. The family is placed firmly within a cultural context, avoiding the common mistake, especially prevalent within the field of educational psychology, of treating the family, the child's initial learning environment, as the ultimate starting point and the sole causal agent of a child's development. The family does not and cannot exist in a vacuum but rather within a culture and a society. Family structures, values, and child-training patterns have evolved for generations to respond appropriately to the realities of life conditions. Personality and self are indeed forged in a family context, but the family is adapted to, and part of, a culture; so socialization is a process whereby personality and the self are formed *in culture*. Second, the adaptational view stresses the active interaction between the developing individual and the society rather than the simple absorption of a passive being into an omnivorous society. Socialization is a process of compromise between the needs of a growing person and the needs of society.

Human beings reproduce biologically through intergenerational genetic transmission. Genes provide the variation necessary if a population is to meet the challenges of a changing environment. Individuals whose genetic structure does not provide adequate phenotypic fit with the environment suffer a decreased chance of survival through offspring-bearing age; gradually, those genes die out or mutate. The environment continually selects organismic structure and behavior—and the genetic combinations that underlie them.

With the reader's indulgence, I suggest that the socialization process is analogous to intergenerational genetic transmission, especially with regard to the formation of the self and personality. The processes are emphatically *not* the same in any sense: socialization goes on for years, but genetic transmission is virtually instantaneous; socialization is partly biological and partly cultural, but genetic transmission is biological; consciousness is important in socialization, but has nothing to do with genetic transmission. Yet certain parental personality features are passed to the next generation through socialization. Through interaction between the developing child and the environment, which includes parents or other substitute caregivers who act as cultural agents or proxies, a new personality and a new self are produced.

These new personalities and selves should fit well enough into the culture and physical environment because the socialization process has prepared them to do so. If a person has something wrong with him or her biologically, or if the socialization process itself was damaged or dysfunctional, the resultant psychological system may be incomplete and/or maladaptive, with negative consequences for both society and the individual. But if the process proceeds normally (as normality is culturally conceived), the end product should be an adult self capable of functioning successfully in the normal range of circumstances provided by the culture, including economic self-sufficiency, reproductive success, and the attainment of personal satisfaction as defined by the person's particular culture.

This self will have much in common with many others within the same culture but will also be unique in many respects. People within a bounded population share many genetic features, but no two people, other than monozygotic twins, have the same combination of genes. So it is with the self, and it is precisely this variation of selves and personalities within a culture which allows that culture to survive in the context of an ever-changing environment. It is almost as if a culture has a creative reservoir of varying selves to draw upon when the environment is altered. The narrower the range of variation, the less capable is a culture of surviving change. This is a part of the reason that small-scale, technologically simple cultures often become extinct as separate cultures, even though the actual population of people survives: the personality reservoir is too shallow (of course, there are other powerful factors operating as well).

Extinction or diminution is especially likely if change is very rapid, occurring in less than one generation. If the environment alters slowly enough, the culture may be able to adjust gradually. For example, gradual industrialization of a previously agrarian area creates a need for very different behavioral profiles in the local population. A few individuals who deviate from the norm adjust fairly readily, but most do not. Slowly, more and more persons engage in industrial wage-labor of various sorts and abandon full-time horticulture. Eventually family structure changes to accommodate new ecocultural pressures; perhaps the nuclear family begins to supplant the extended family, and postmarital residence becomes neolocal (living separately from either the husband's or the wife's parents) instead of patrilocal (living with the husband's kin). The child's learning environment is transformed, and child-rearing practices follow suit. In the end new behaviors, the outward signs of new personalities and new selves, replace the old, which now linger mainly among the elders, who bemoan the loss of the old ways. Adaptation is never so neat, of course, but this is a reasonable example of how the process might work.

Primary Socialization

A child enters the world as a human animal, a natural being; it must become a cultural being. Without primary socialization by other caring human beings, the child would probably not survive, but if it did, it would remain an animal, an acultural human. If this child received some minimal socialization, it could survive but would probably be culturally damaged—and headed for trouble in society later on. As products of evolution, children are born with the cognitive competence for language and culture acquisition as well as the capacity for the acquisition of personality and self. However, they need adequate caretaking to trigger whatever biological basis exists for the acquisition of language, culture, self, and personality; the essential learning that builds on this cognitive foundation is also totally dependent on caretaking by other human beings. The more adequate the caretaking, the better the acquisition.

Even though caretakers other than parents might be the primary socializers—surrogate parents—this discussion assumes that parents occupy this role. It is important to recognize that the parent in question is almost always the mother; to simplify further, I am going to assume that the biological and social mother are the same person although this is obviously not necessarily true. While fathers may participate in secondary socialization, primary socialization is usually left to mothers; even in secondary socialization, fathers often participate only with boys. Among the Kpelle of Liberia, for example, fathers can be seen playing briefly with toddlers but take no part in the actual labors of child care. I stress this simply because many Americans are used to seeing fathers change diapers, feed babies, and so on. In fact, American gender roles regarding parenting are probably more similar than those of any other existing culture, but this is most unusual cross-culturally.

The mother, then, is the baby's first social contact. From the infant's point of view, she is merely an extension of its omnipotent self. The early interaction between mother and infant is foundational in the most literal sense; all later social interaction and behavior are built on it. The mother is an agent of her culture, and she begins to impart the symbolic knowledge of her culture to the infant from "day one." Since she imparts cultural rules and notions where none previously existed, the mother's culture forms the bedrock of the child's enculturation and self formation. This culture will be with the child always, even if he or she "joins" an alien culture; the "new" cultural knowledge is laid on top of the "old," but the old remains. The growing child takes over, *incorporates*, the cultural world already occupied by the parents and others (Berger and Luckmann 1966). The mother filters the world for the infant, blocking or ameliorating some stimuli, selecting and magnifying others. The infant's world is culturally constructed as it is acquiring a distinctive self, one which is inextricably intertwined with the surrounding culture.

Primary socialization and the early learning environment are adapted to material realities. For example, North American parents "child-proof" their homes to minimize danger to infants and small children. Electric sockets are plugged, oven knobs are out of reach or difficult to turn, cooking is done on the back burners, playpens restrict movement at certain difficult moments, and so forth. For the same reasons—to minimize risk to children—African mothers carry their babies on their backs, out of danger. To ensure adequate nourishment as well as to replenish fluids lost through diarrhea, African, Melanesian, and many other of the world's mothers give their infants the breast virtually on demand, or at least very frequently. They sleep with or very near their youngest children, facilitating night feeding, protecting babies from danger, and providing them with the social security and sense of being-in-community that is consistent with their later adult life. Children in these societies develop very early an orientation toward dependency, or more accurately, social interdependence, which is adaptive in kin-based preindustrial societies.

LeVine (1974) has suggested that where infant mortality rates are high, as in most Third World tropical cultures—indeed, in most societies lacking pure water for drinking—deliberate primary socialization will mainly reflect parental concern for the actual physical survival of the child. Other concerns, such as teaching the child to talk, are remote. Customs that might decrease infant mortality rates, such as those mentioned above, are an adaptive product of cultural evolution. A parallel adaptation is the withholding of extensive parental emotional investment in the child for the early years. In many West African societies, for example, children are not given real names until age five or so, when their survival seems more likely, nor are they properly buried (although mourning by the parents is evident, as I can attest). Spiritual beliefs rationalize infant death and associated behavior: perhaps the ancestors were jealous and took the baby back.

Secondary Socialization

Somewhere between the ages of five and seven, children move, at least a little bit, into the wider community. They are still very much a part of the family, but more and more of their day is spent away from the family, even if just a few meters. Secondary socialization, that later period of education and personality and self formation involving social persona outside the immediate family, begins with the peer group. The timing is interesting, for it seems to be recognized everywhere. In the West, formal schooling begins at about five or six. We say that children have reached the "age of reason," by which we mean that they have attained Jean Piaget's stage of concrete operations (Ginsburg and Opper 1969:121). At this age, a child first begins playing structured games with rules (Piaget and Inhelder 1969:119). Also recognizing this cognitive shift, the Kpelle say that at about age six (they do not know children's ages), a child is beginning to "get sense." In Liberia, children now begin to take more of a part in the daily routine, are qualified to assist in the care of younger siblings, and are for the first time sexually segregated in various ways. Girls perform many chores, whereas boys spend more and more time playing with peers. Boys' chores begin in earnest at about age eleven or so. Age six also marks the introduction of corporal punishment; Liberian Kpelle parents believe that it is pointless to strike younger children since they won't learn anything because they "don't got sense yet."

The socializing influence of the peer group at this age seems to be a cultural universal. They introduce the child to the world beyond the family, along with new norms, rules, and behaviors and dominate children's lives, especially for boys, until puberty.

Socialization within the family, of course, continues apace. With concern for the physical survival of the child somewhat relaxed, child-training by parents shifts focus a bit but continues to reflect adaptation. For example, American middle-class parents emphasize school achievement, believed to translate into success in adult life. LeVine (1974) has suggested that in societies with an unreliable subsistence base parental goals during the "secondary" phase should strongly emphasize the future (adult) attainment of "economic self-maintenance." As stated earlier, most simple horticultural societies, especially those in the tropics, have food supplies that fluctuate from year to year or even from month to month. Many African groups, for example, experience an annual "hungry time" for some weeks before harvest when they may be reduced to one meal a day of undesirable food. Crop failures can lead to widespread starvation. In such cultures people are psychologically conservative regarding technological or economic innovation; traditional tried-and-true ways of farming are "safer" in that they do not worsen the odds for systemic disaster. The cultural emphasis is accordingly on replicating the preceding generations', the "ancestors'," customs. In turn, the secondary socialization emphasis is on obedience above all, the unquestioning following of tradition (LeVine 1974).

When queried, Kpelle parents state without hesitation that the best children are obedient children (Erchak 1977; 1980). Gender and age differences in children's behavior and training also reflect this delicate subsistence base, as will be shown in the Kpelle case study at the end of the chapter. But the emphasis on obedience (the Kpelle call it "full respect") is very striking and is consistent with the timing of the introduction of corporal punishment. Curiosity, along with the questioning of adults, is viewed as lack of respect and disobedience in many cultures around the world, especially horticultural societies. Obedience as an adaptation is not confined to rural nonliterate societies, however. Melvin Kohn (1977) has cogently shown how in modern nation-states, the lower the social class level of families, the greater the likelihood that parents will value and emphasize obedience, to themselves and to authority figures in general. This value-orientation is adaptive because it prepares children for a class-based work world, where lower-class workers follow the directions of others, while middle- and upper-class individuals are allowed a great deal of self-direction in their occupations. The findings have been replicated repeatedly in several nations (see Kohn 1977:xxviii).

One of the most central events during the process of secondary socialization is also the culminating event: the cultural management of the onset of puberty—the transition to adulthood and sexuality. Forests have been felled to supply all the paper that has been used to discuss and analyze the rituals surrounding puberty. A small portion of these studies will be discussed in the next chapter, which concerns gender and sexuality issues.

In this chapter I am concerned only with early adolescence as the end of secondary socialization. Every society must face the disruption and conflict generated continually by the end of childhood, although each society goes about solving the problem in a different manner. Dependent boys and girls must become independent men and women in this final stage of secondary socialization. The purpose of this stage is to induct children into adult society. Some complex cultures like the United States seem to skirt the issue, warehousing children in institutions known as schools, and treating them as adults in some respects, and children in others; this confusion may continue until as late as twenty-two years in the case of college students. At the present time (1991) American "adult children" may purchase caffeine without restriction, nicotine at age eighteen, and alcohol at age twenty-one; they may enter into legal contracts and serve in combat at age eighteen. Thus a person can buy a house at age eighteen but cannot have a beer in that house for three more years! By taking the "in between" period, when a person is neither an adult nor a child—a period anthropologists call *liminal* (Turner 1967)—and stretching it out for several years, U.S. culture has created serious confusion about self-identity, along with numerous social problems for the entire community.

Most preindustrial societies compress this liminal period through ritual management or through common agreement on role transition. In other words, some cultures employ *initiation ceremonies* of various sorts which in effect announce to the community that a certain person, or group or class of persons, is no longer a child but has become a man or woman. It is usual for male rituals to be conducted in groups, whereas those for females are often individual, although this generalization is by no means universal. Rituals may vary from a few minutes to several years of seclusion and tests. Many simple cultures do not carry out formal initiation ceremonies, but share such a tight consensus on proper behavior and roles for each sex at various life stages that they do not experience the disruption and confusion of complex pluralities such as the United States. It is perhaps worth noting that many North

Americans and Europeans still practice vestigial initiation ceremonies such as *bar mitzvah* and Confirmation, symbolically conferring adult status; sometimes there are family traditions, such as a boy's killing his first buck, which similarly mark a transition. Most often the only markers are rites devised by peers along with the graduation ceremonies of educational institutions.

Becoming Prosocial

The entire process of socialization from birth to adulthood is a process of becoming prosocial, "for" society rather than exclusively "for" self. The self and the personality must be harnessed for the community at large. Infants are born as what psychiatrists call primary narcissists; they are perfectly selfish because they just do not know where they end and others begin. Without boundaries, they are psychologically omnipotent—quite a paradox considering their actual helplessness. Gradually each child develops a sense of self distinct from others but still remains dedicated to self-indulgence, blithely unconcerned about the needs of others.

The prosocializing process of socialization begins in the family and gradually takes in first the local community and ultimately the society as a whole. Societies cannot function without the contributions of their members, while individuals cannot survive without their societies. The two entities must mesh in an adaptive process of socialization. When children behave in inappropriate or antisocial ways, they are censured by others: perhaps shunned or ridiculed by peers or punished by parents. But when they behave prosocially, they are rewarded, sometimes directly, but far more often subtly and indirectly through friendship, family harmony, and the like.

Self-esteem grows along with social esteem. An egocentric being becomes a sociocentric being, but paradoxically the individual self becomes stronger and healthier, more clearly bounded, in the process. While the "mix" of sociocentric and egocentric components of the self varies from culture to culture with the socialization process, the process itself always involves adapting individual egoistic behavior to adult social roles, creating a prosocial self. This development will be clear in the case study of the Kpelle that concludes this chapter.

Studying Socialization

Some of the earliest studies in the field of psychological anthropology were studies of socialization, so its importance in understanding the cultural foundations of the self, personality, and behavior is fundamental. Anthropological studies of the socialization process can be roughly divided into two categories, the "Mead school" (after the late Margaret Mead) and the "Whiting school" (after John and Beatrice Whiting). Margaret Mead was the first anthropologist to study socialization. Her second and third books, *Coming of Age in Samoa* (1928) and *Growing Up in New Guinea* (1930), set the tone for other studies of this sort. While valuable, insightful, and provocative, these studies are humanistic rather than scientific in method and style. These books and scores like them are unsystematic in data collection and intuitive and impressionistic in analysis. Mead viewed anthropology as a clinical discipline like psychoanalysis: the ethnographer takes notes while the culture is "on the couch." Many social scientists, myself among them, would not consider psychoanalysis a science and therefore would not consider Meadian ethnography scientific. I stress that this characterization does *not* denigrate her studies or others like them, any more than a dismissal of an essay on medieval art on the grounds that it was not "scientific" would lessen the value of that essay for the discipline of art history—it simply identifies them as being in a particular tradition so that they can be properly evaluated and compared with others.

Meadian studies are of two types, those that seek to solve a particular intellectual problem and those that are purely descriptive. Mead's own studies were of the former type. Margaret Mead was a student of Franz Boas at Columbia, an anthropologist who was atheoretical and a proponent of the modern notion that learning and experience were more important than biology in shaping culture. Accordingly, Mead's *Coming of Age in Samoa* shows how adolescence, especially female adolescence, was not necessarily a biologically determined period of acne and agony; in Samoa, it seemed to be a relatively pleasurable, carefree time. In *Growing Up in New Guinea,* Mead argues that the children of Manus believe less in spirits than their parents do, reversing the stereotypical Western sequence. She was trying to show that animistic beliefs in childhood (devils, monsters, etc.) are not biodevelopmental but rather culturally determined. Later studies in this tradition either use a case study to challenge a received notion, as Mead did, or are purely descriptive accounts, often contained in a chapter of a larger ethnography.

The Whiting-school approach to studying socialization is diverse but is oriented toward cross-cultural comparison, with an eye on generalizing about *humans* rather than a particular ethnic group; the approach is social-behaviorist, with a liberal dose of Freudian theory. Whitingesque studies fall into two broad categories. The first comprises large-sample cross-cultural statistical studies using established data sets such as the Human Relations Area Files or the Ethnographic Atlas. Correlations are established between independent and dependent variables, followed by arguments concerning causality.

For example, in *Child Training and Personality* (1953), John Whiting and Irvin Child, using ethnographic reports from seventy-five societies, hypothesized that the way children are trained by caretakers in such areas as nursing and weaning, "toilet" training, sexual matters, dependence, and aggression should ultimately be reflected in the culture's beliefs about disease causality and cure. For example, if a culture dictates very harsh weaning practices such as the use of hot pepper or slapping, then children should become "fixated," or unconsciously preoccupied, with oral matters, and the prevailing belief concerning illnesses should be that they are caused by ingesting something evil or sickening. In fact, the oral hypothesis just mentioned is the only one that received strong support by the data, although some correlation was also found between dependency and aggression training and later belief systems. The study is important, however, for its attempt to utilize the scientific methodological canons of replicability and falsifiability, rather than for its specific findings.

The next thirty-five years saw scores of similar studies, many of which concerned socialization. In 1957, Herbert Barry, Margaret

Bacon, and Child surveyed gender differences in socialization in 110 societies and found significant differences in cultures, depending on whether they hunt or raise large animals, they are nomadic or sedentary, they cultivate grain or root crops, and their households consist of extended or nuclear families.

In 1959, Barry, Child, and Bacon studied the relationship of socialization to subsistence economy, using data from 104 societies, and found that agricultural and pastoral cultures stressed *compliance* in child-rearing, whereas foraging societies stressed *individual assertion*. The explanation emphasizes adaptation: departure from established routines and methods in farming and herding might jeopardize the food supply for an entire season, but innovation in hunting or gathering would cause food supply problems for only a day or two (Barry, Child, and Bacon 1959).

Several other statistical cross-cultural studies followed these and dealt primarily with aspects of initiation ceremonies; these will be discussed in the next chapter. Such studies help discern cultural patterns and generate novel hypotheses and provocative syntheses which can then be tested in the field. For these and other reasons, cross-cultural comparative studies continue to be done and should be welcomed by the research community. For scientists not directly involved in cross-cultural research, however, the problems associated with comparative statistical work are perceived as outweighing the benefits. The biggest problem is simply the quality of the data: many of the sources used were written long ago when methods were less refined, or were written by ethnographers not particularly interested in socialization; the information might therefore be quite unreliable. Another difficulty is that simply establishing a correlation between variables does not establish causality: a third, perhaps unnoticed factor may underlie the others. This problem will be taken up in more detail in the next chapter.

John and Beatrice Whiting were themselves acutely aware of these limitations. One solution was to focus on more limited comparisons of smaller samples of societies using truly comparable data: the result was the well-known Six Cultures Project. This type of comparison represents the second category of studies by the "Whiting school"; I also include under this label the many ethnographic studies of the Whitings' students and colleagues which, while carried out individually in one particular culture, as are the

"Meadian" studies, are designed to be comparable, as part of a larger cross-cultural data set. In the original phase of the Six Cultures Project, six teams, each consisting of one man and one woman researcher, collected data on socialization using comparable methods; each pair employed the same field manual. Everyone looked at the same variables and had the same basic theoretical orientation (social learning theory; see, e.g., Bandura 1977). Some of the teams included a psychologist as well as an anthropologist. The six field sites were an American suburb in New England, a barrio in the Philippines, a community in Okinawa, a village of the Rajput caste in India, a Mixtec Indian village in Mexico, and a Gusii settlement in Kenya (B. Whiting 1963).

While ethnographic interviewing and participant observation provided much of the general information on each society, the primary method of data collection for socialization was the innovative technique of *systematic behavior observation* (B. Whiting n.d.; 1968; B. Whiting and J. Whiting 1973). With this method a selected sample of children (of both sexes and grouped by age) is observed for fifteen to thirty-minute periods across the range of times of day, settings, types of social interaction, and activities commonly found in a child's world in each culture. The researcher thus accumulates thousands of behavior bits on a sample of children. These interacts are then coded into categories of social behavior which the Whitings and their colleagues call *mands,* as in *de*mands, *com*mands, *repri*mands, and so forth (see Whiting and Edwards 1988:12 for a version of their code); after coding, the data can be analyzed statistically for *intra*cultural differences and patterns, and compared with similar data from other cultures for *inter*cultural contrasts, trends, and patterns.

The Six Cultures Project produced many publications. The first volume, entitled *Six Cultures: Studies of Child Rearing,* consisted of the six original ethnographies but did not include any systematic cross-cultural analysis (B. Whiting 1963). Leigh Minturn and William Lambert (1964), in *Mothers of Six Cultures,* wrote that children are more strictly punished for disobedience as well as for fighting with others when families live in crowded conditions. Beatrice Whiting and Carolyn Edwards (1973) investigated differences in the behavior of three to eleven-year-olds in the six cultures, finding that girls seek help and physical contact more than boys, and are a bit more sociable; boys tend to be a little more attention-seeking. By age seven, boys often react to parental aggression with counter-aggression, whereas girls remain compliant; in fact boys are more aggressive overall. An important interpretive conclusion of their study is that the nature of tasks assigned to children is the best predictor of the types of behavior—the behavioral repertoire—a child will exhibit in general. In an important earlier study among the Luo of Kenya, Carol Ember (1973), another member of the Whiting group of researchers, demonstrated that boys, usually boys without older sisters, who performed tasks generally assigned to girls were more prosocial in their overall behavior than boys who did not perform "feminine" tasks in the household; they made significantly more responsible suggestions concerning matters such as child care, etiquette, and household hygiene, falling slightly behind girls on this measure. Her study was the first that really emphasized task assignment as a predictor of child behavior.

The final volume that utilizes data from only the original six cultures is *Children of Six Cultures: A Psycho-Cultural Analysis* (B. Whiting and J. Whiting 1975). Findings concerning the impact of culture on children's behavior are perhaps the most interesting in the book: children in the least complex societies were more likely to be responsible and nurturant, while children in the more complex societies exhibited more dominant and dependent behaviors. The Whitings believe that this trend is due to the use of child labor in the household: the simpler the society, the more likely are children to be used for infant-sitting, sweeping, fetching, and the like, and their overall behavioral profile then reflects the habits inculcated by these tasks. On the other hand, dependent behaviors such as attention-seeking and dominant behaviors such as competing are rewarded more in complex societies where children's contribution to the household is minimal, while schooling is more common.

Children's behavior is adaptive in the six cultures. Findings related to other aspects of culture such as household and family type were similarly consistent with functional adaptational needs. Culture is shown to be very important in shaping the behavior and thereby the personality of children. Psychologists should place great importance on this conclusion, although given the history of their discipline, it is unlikely they will do so. The most general conclusion of *Children of Six Cultures* can be stated succinctly: *societies produce the kinds of people they need;* the socialization process within a culture shapes behavior and personality in children in order to produce the kind of behavior and personality in adults that will serve the general welfare while providing satisfying lives for members of the culture.

More recent work by the Whitings and their associates continues in the Six Cultures tradition, but with new samples augmenting the original six. In the most recent publication, *Children of Different Worlds: The Formation of Social Behavior,* Beatrice Whiting and Carolyn Edwards (1988), along with ten other collaborators, report on findings of a comparative analysis of thirteen cultural samples, including the original six; six additional communities, studied through very brief "spot" observations rather than the lengthier and more elaborate systematic behavior observation, also figure in some of the analyses presented in the book. Their thesis is that social behavior is shaped primarily by the settings children occupy while growing, recognizing that the most important feature of any setting is the other people in it (Whiting and Edwards 1988:4). They report that girls spend more time with babies and with mothers than do boys, and are assigned more work in general. Maternal responsiveness to their children declines as children grow, while training increases. Mothers are more controlling with boys, possibly because boys exhibit a lower level of immediate compliance, especially to verbal commands. The cultural sample divides fairly neatly into three categories based on mothering styles: the "training" mothers of sub-Saharan Africa, the "controlling" mothers of India, the Philippines, and Mexico, and the "sociable" mothers of the U.S. sample. The heavy workloads of the first group necessitate the use of their children's labor, which in turn shapes the interactions of mothers and children. The second group has a relatively lighter workload, and so mothers seem to focus their training on minimizing children's annoying or obtrusive behaviors. The final sample has the lightest workload and the least amount of contact with other adults during a day, permitting and even promoting a greater degree of sociability with their children (Whiting and Edwards 1988).

All hypotheses purporting to be about humans in general *must* be tested cross-culturally in order to become scientific principles of human behavior. The Whitings have pointed the way to a cross-cultural science of child development. In addition, their group's comparative work underscores the importance of adaptation in socialization and in human social behavior generally.

A Case Study in Adaptive Primary Socialization: The Kpelle of Liberia

The Kpelle are a group of about 750,000 in Liberia and Guinea in West Africa. They are slash-and-burn cultivators of upland rice and other crops; many adults also tap rubber or do other sorts of labor for cash. Their major kinship group is a shallow patrilineage, a group of kin related through male blood lines to a common ancestor; they are polygamous and patrilocal (residing with the man's patrilineage) although in recent years there has been a marked shift toward monogamy and some neolocality (setting up an independent household away from parents). They are politically divided into several small chiefdoms. Traditional religious life is dominated by sacred (or "secret") societies which, among many other functions, initiate children into adulthood (Gibbs 1965; Erchak, forthcoming).

In this section I focus only on primary socialization, leaving initiation for the next chapter. Kpelle children do not receive their permanent adult names until initiation; until then, they make do with a series of what we would call nicknames. These names are often humorously negative—Dirt and Old Man are typical—to fool jealous spirits who might want to steal the child. Both the avoidance of permanent naming and the use of negative naming reflect adaptation to a high childhood mortality rate (about 50 percent in the village I studied most intensively).

A newborn is given the breast nearly on demand. It sleeps with its mother and at about three weeks is put on her back for the first time, supported by a length of cloth tied over the mother's breasts. This close physical contact allows the mother to anticipate the infant's needs right away and promotes the development of social interdependence so valued by the Kpelle and other similar cultures. The first year of life is one of almost complete indulgence, with the exception of force-feeding, or "stuffing." Babies are forced to choke down rice water while their noses are plugged and they are securely held down. Even this apparently cruel practice has adaptive value: it facilitates the introduction of supplementary foods; this eases weaning later on and also makes baby-sitting by older siblings or other relatives much easier. The rice water is replaced by rice mush or premasticated rice at about nine months; a child is expected to eat most regular foods by about one year. Early childhood is a time of "casual nurturance" (see LeVine 1963), where mothers carry their babies on their backs and nurse them frequently but do so without really paying much direct attention to them; they continue working or perhaps socializing while caring for infants.

After the first year the child learns to walk and is no longer considered a baby; it is now called a "little girl" or "little boy." A far more difficult period of life is beginning. The child can no longer count on sleeping with mother since the postpartum sex taboo has ended; and weaning, often harsh, occurs anywhere from age one to four, depending on whether another sibling has been born. Children are expected to be able to feed themselves by age three. The loss of the high nutritive value of mother's milk, combined with the drinking of contaminated water, results in a heavy loss of life among children in the age group roughly between two and six. Beginning at about age four, children learn to dress themselves and may leave the hut to play with peers. Boys are able to wander farther and farther as they grow; girls, however, may rarely go far, since they are assigned useful and necessary chores at a much younger age than are boys.

Children's behavior and training throughout the preadolescent period of primary socialization are marked by adaptation to both the natural and cultural environments. For example, apparently religious warnings to children by parents concerning the need to avoid playing in or even near streams and rivers because of dangerous water spirits serve to promote the health and survival of children by reducing the incidence of sickness and death from water-related causes (Erchak 1979a).

Overall, Kpelle children learn subsistence skills that enable them to become productive adults, along with social skills that enable them to behave appropriately and participate in Kpelle culture;

they do not learn skills that are completely extraneous to Kpelle culture, even though such skills may be valued by other cultures. For example, they do not learn the conceptual and problem-solving skills required in the classroom, skills which are acquired through noncontextual verbal teaching and learning as well as through the encouragement of relevant behaviors. Kpelle technical and social skills (and indeed most skills of most people throughout the world) are learned largely through observation, imitation, and trial-and-error experimentation, with gradual improvement as the child grows. Kpelle subsistence and cultural survival depend on the acceptance of things as they are; intellectual curiosity, innovative tampering, and related attitudes and behaviors threaten the productive system and endanger lives and are therefore not tolerated, especially in children. Kpelle parents discourage curiosity and exploratory behavior on the part of their children. I found that children were in general kept rather still and subdued when in the vicinity of adults so that the adults could get their work done.

Child-training practices and associated child behaviors become increasingly based on economic factors with the advancing age of the child, as reflected in developmental trends. There is clearly increasing responsibility in task assignment along with greater self-reliance, increasing productivity within the household, and noticeable progress toward the adult economic role, even in preteen years. Children become less egocentric, less nurtured, and less mother-oriented, and at the same time more prosocial, sociable, and peer-oriented. Certain other trends in overall rearing apparently stem from mothers' or other caretakers' needs in performing required tasks, as when children are prevented from playing around the family drinking water. And as I mentioned earlier in the chapter, the Kpelle strongly emphasize respect and obedience in socialization, consistent with LeVine's (1974) hypotheses. All these findings were statistically supported and could, I would hope, be replicated by others; the data are reported elsewhere (Erchak 1977; 1980).

The material exigencies of Kpelle life also shape important gender differences in child behavior and child-rearing practices. Kpelle adult gender roles are sharply differentiated and closely related to subsistence and economic concerns: childhood is an adaptive harbinger of adult gender role. For example, girls have less free time and greater responsibility and so play less than boys do. Girls are more self-reliant and responsible in general, primarily because of their task assignments (see also Ember 1973) and the greater importance of women in the Kpelle economy (Erchak 1974; Bledsoe 1980). Girls are also more obedient to adults. While girls are being trained to be productive, boys, it seems, are being trained to stay out of the way and out of trouble. Girls, especially older girls, are more nurturant and more prosocial than boys, presaging their future roles as caretakers of children and domestic managers. In fact girls' behavior is very like their mothers', since girls remain around their mothers and other adult women helping with chores and receiving training. They are on a more familiar basis with adult women than boys are and accordingly tend to respond in kind to their mothers' social interaction with them, "giving back" much of the same behavior that mothers direct at them initially. Kpelle girls are more compliant to adults' wishes than boys are and receive more attention from adults. Adults seem to treat boys in a less tolerant and more aggressive style. These and other findings on gender role socialization among the Kpelle are also supported statistically: the interested reader can find the analyses in various other publications (Erchak 1976, 1977).

In sum, Kpelle primary socialization is well adapted to the Liberian rain forest environment, to swidden rice cultivation, and to other features of Kpelle socioeconomic life.

Conclusion

Socialization as an adaptive process subsumes at least five facets: (1) since caregivers often must simultaneously take care of children *while* performing essential economic tasks, the learning environment must be adapted to this balance; (2) children at different stages of development will be assigned different tasks; (3) boys and girls will in general be assigned different tasks; (4) the training of children for responsibility, for domestic work, and for contribution to the subsistence of the group will anticipate the adult economic role; and (5) children direct and shape their own behavior according to their own anticipation and perception of the adult economic role. For the Kpelle as for every culture, this process results in a learning environment that is a survival mechanism in local cultural evolution, helping to produce the selves, personalities, and patterns of thinking needed to maintain a particular culture. There is never a perfect "fit" among personalities, selves, patterns of thinking, cultures, and environments but rather a continuous "striving" toward such a fit; because environments change with history, the match remains elusive, for the Kpelle and for Americans as for every other culture.

SUGGESTED READINGS

Peter Berger and Thomas Luckmann's discussion of socialization in their classic *The Social Construction of Reality* (1966) remains one of the best concise theoretical outlines. Robert LeVine's brief article, "Child Rearing as Cultural Adaptation" (1977), presents an overview close in outlook to that of this chapter; other articles in the same volume, *Culture and Infancy* (Leiderman, Tulkin, and Rosenfeld, eds.), may also be of interest.

Margaret Mead's *Coming of Age in Samoa* (1928) should be on every socialization student's "must" list. Urie Bronfenbrenner's *Two Worlds of Childhood: U.S. and U.S.S.R.* (1970) is an interesting and readable comparison. John Hostetler and Gertrude Huntington's *Children in Amish Society* (1971) is a look at a group of communities struggling to raise their children in a manner very much at odds with the way of life in the rest of the United States; in some ways, it is also a peek into an older and more rural United States. Colin Turnbull's magisterial *The Human Cycle* (1983) is an around-the-world tour of the developmental process, treated as a series of case studies from Turnbull's own life as well as from his extensive field research; cases include the Mbuti of Zaire, India, Tibet, England, and the United States.

Children of Different Worlds (1988) by Beatrice Whiting and Carolyn Edwards is a good entry into the Six Cultures-type comparative work pioneered by the Whitings. Robert LeVine and Barbara Levine's *Nyansongo: A Gusii Community in Kenya* (1966; reprinted 1977), one of the original Six Cultures, is a particularly good example of an ethnography using systematic behavior observation.

For those who wish to learn more about the Kpelle, the best ethnographic introduction is James Gibbs' "The Kpelle of Liberia" (1965) in his *Peoples of Africa.*

3

Gender,
Culture, and Sex

Everyone is sexy. With the rare exception of hermaphrodites or biological transexuals, all human beings are biologically assigned male or female sex at conception. The degree to which sex, sexual behavior, and sexuality *remain* biological phenomena throughout the life course is, however, a topic of great controversy in academia, with various positions, sometimes scientific and sometimes ideological, staked out by social constructionists, feminists, cultural determinists, and sociobiologists, to name only the leading players. But no matter what the degree of biological input, it is well-established and undeniable that everywhere in the human world, culture shapes sexual expression and role of every kind (see, e.g., Nanda 1990) and that the many facets of sex, gender, and sexuality are adapted to the historical, material, and cultural environment.

Sex, Culture, Biology, and Ethnocentrism

The self is refracted through a sexual prism. Since there is no escape from sex and gender and since these, along with the self and behavior, are culturally shaped and expressed, behavior/self cannot be separated from sex/gender. This is *not* to say that boys and girls, men and women, do not share personality traits or features of self or that they do not exhibit similar behavior. Of course they do; they are far more alike than different (ask yourself why men have nipples if you do not agree), and it is very important to keep this closeness firmly in mind while reading this chapter and thinking about the issues involved.

It is rather to say that no matter how close males and females might be in behavior and/or personal psychology, society codes, labels, and interprets them differently. In the United States, highly aggressive behavior on the part of a woman in the office is often perceived as unseemly in some way while the identical behavior by a male co-worker might elicit neither notice nor comment. Boys who play with Barbie and Ken dolls are viewed with dismay by many parents, as are girls who prefer camouflage and G.I. Joe "action figures." Culture exaggerates and manipulates what biology provides. How many men shave their armpits and legs? What is the purpose of women's shaving these areas? Most Americans think that underarm and leg hair on a woman is "gross" because it is "like a man"; shaving makes one somehow more feminine. Yet in many other cultures, including several quite close to the United States in other respects, women manage to remain "feminine" without shaving a thing.

The term "sex" refers to physiology: the division of a species into male and female categories based on reproductive function. For many years, it was the only term employed in both biological and social research concerning human beings. Phrases such as "sex roles" and "sexual stratification" were common in the social science literature. This usage is still found and is still perfectly proper but is no longer the preferred usage. In the last decade the term "gender," formerly referring to a property of language and only colloquially to sex in the social realm, has become the preferred word in the social and behavioral sciences.

This new use of an old term arose in order to differentiate biological from social aspects of sex. A person's sex is ascribed at conception, whereas a person's gender is shaped by society. Gender refers to aspects of "sex" such as role, behavior, and identity, which are not directly related to reproduction or genital function (see, e.g., Mazur and Money 1980). The situation is not a black and white one but a matter of gradation, since biology and learning interpenetrate in all matters of sex (and gender). Although the distinction is unsatisfactory in some respects and followed only erratically in the literature, it does serve to underscore the arbitrary stretching and bending of sex/gender that goes on in all societies so it is certainly better than using simply the one term "sex." I will strive to maintain the distinction wherever possible.

"Sexuality" is another matter. While a neologism such as "genderality" is a possibility for referring more precisely to the non-biological aspects of sexual behavior, pleasure, excitement, and preference, at present only the single term "sexuality" is employed for all uses, biological and sociobehavioral. Here two terms would be very helpful in avoiding the common confusion of the biological and psychocultural features of sexual experience: this confusion usually results in *all* of sexuality being treated as purely biological, as in the famous studies by William Masters and Virginia Johnson (1966, 1970, 1979) of American sexual behavior.

Masters and Johnson's biologism is an example of ethnocentrism, albeit of a type confined mainly to the scientific community. Ethnocentrism is simply the naive assumption that the way *your* culture does things is the natural (or God's) way to do things and the morally *right* way to do things. The customs and behaviors of people in other cultures ("aliens") thus become evil, pagan, barbaric, and immoral, or perhaps incomprehensible, bizarre, inscrutable, and just plain amazing, or just dumb, stupid, odd, or funny. Every culture exhibits ethnocentrism; mild forms contribute to ethnic pride, social integration and cohesion, and a sense of community and "belongingness," qualities associated with a healthy and exuberant patriotism, but extreme forms such as nationalism and racism can lead to war and even genocide.

No one is immune, not even scientists: an ethnocentric peculiarity of American scientists (excluding some but not all social scientists) is the notion that behavior, whether normal or abnormal, is an essentially *biological* phenomenon. This paradigm, or explanatory model, has become an article of orthodox faith among American scientists, with important ramifications in fields as diverse as medicine, psychology, jurisprudence, and education. I will return to this subject later in this chapter, as well as in Chapters 4 and 5, but mention it now only to illustrate a type of ethnocentrism. The ethnocentrism found in Masters and Johnson's work and the work of other biologically oriented sexologists takes received banal notions of the educated middle class about sexuality, liberated from the moral constraints in which it is usually embedded among the more conservative (scientists would say "ignorant") sectors of society, and treats these notions as biological. That is, these sexologists transform psychological, cultural, and sociological phenomena into biological phenomena even *before* beginning research: the assumptions themselves are ethnocentric.

Another form of ethnocentrism pervades the social and behavioral sciences. In the last twenty years, feminism has transformed the study of sex, gender, and sexuality within these disciplines. The overall result has been positive, with earlier male-dominated sexist (and ethnocentric) analyses giving way to more balanced treatments. On occasion, however, feminism as an objective analytical posture gives way to feminism as an ideology, with questionable results. It is obvious that feminism has an important place in the American social and political arenas; and feminist discourse and analysis are an important part of contemporary scholarship. Nonetheless, feminism is an ideology of the Western elite, a Western belief system like capitalism or existentialism. Its vocabulary, assumptions, and epistemology cannot be applied directly to other cultures without serious qualification. When they are applied willynilly, the results can be dismaying: African village women turn into sharp New York investment brokers in ethnographic portrayals, the difference seeming to be more one of degree than kind; clitoridectomy as part of initiation into womanhood becomes just another example of the (male?) oppression of women, even when women carry out the operation in secrecy and in isolation from men. Female initiations in general have been characterized as brutal examples of male oppression, even though *male* initiation ceremonies are far more painful. It is better to view such customs as neutrally as possible.

Ethnocentrism always distorts attempts to understand other cultures no matter how well-meaning the researcher and no matter how beneficial the beliefs underlying the ethnocentrism might be to the researcher's own society, or even to the society under study. If *truth* is the goal, ethnocentrism must be reined in, replaced by cultural relativism, the position that each culture should be studied on its own terms, free from the value judgments of outsiders. This is particularly important and particularly difficult to implement in the area of sex and gender research and even more so in sexuality research, which is why I emphasize this point here rather than in an earlier section.

We in the United States find it very difficult if not impossible to separate sex from morals; but if we do not, objectivity becomes impossible and therefore the scientific cross-cultural study of sex, gender, and sexuality also becomes impossible. I do not believe that it is impossible to separate the two, but it is extraordinarily difficult. Not only biological imperialists, or feminists, or moralizers, but everyone, including yourself, must cast aside preconceptions in order to fully appreciate how other cultures construct and express sex and gender if we ever hope to achieve a true scientific understanding of the subject.

The Early Acquisition of Gender Roles

Gender roles are largely culturally defined. No one knows for certain what, if any, sex differences in behavior would exist between boys and girls if left to their own devices—without culture. Such an experiment would reveal the extent of the biological basis of sex differences in behavior but, alas, is completely impossible since no humans grow without culture. All cultures exaggerate the differences between the sexes and stereotype gender roles; the process begins very early. I remember my dismay when one of my sons went on a field trip to a hospital with his preschool. The preschool was progressive and operated by feminist teachers and an administrator who were nonsexist, as were most of the parents. My son's teacher, clearly appalled at what she had discovered that day, told me after school that at one point during the trip, the kids were all offered a choice of a doctor's "hat" and a nurse's cap to wear and keep. In spite of studious noninterference by the teachers, *every* boy chose the doctor's and *every* girl chose the nurse's hat. I do not have the impression that things have changed very much in the thirteen years since that event. So gender role and gender identity begin very early and, as illustrated in my preschool example, are well under way by age three.

The differentiating process picks up speed with advancing age. The reasons for this strong bifurcation are not difficult to ascertain. The training and treatment a child receives from parents or other caretakers differs by the sex of child, although the difference is generally inconsequential during infancy. In our own society there are even some noticeable differences in infancy, beginning with the assignment of the color pink to girls and blue to boys; sometimes there is also the ludicrous spectacle of a football being presented to a male infant. Decorating schemes for the child's room, as well as clothing, are often sex-specific from the earliest months. Later on, task assignment reflects anticipated adult gender role with greater differentiation as children grow older.

I have already shown that child-training differs by sex crossculturally and that the difference is adaptive to the economic and subsistence needs of families. Peer group pressure is a second important factor shaping the behavior of boys and girls; the peer group can be cruel and relentless in the administration of rewards and punishments for appropriate and inappropriate behavior. Children want to conform and be well-liked, so naturally few are able, or care to, buck the childhood cultural norms.

Since children learn most things through observation, imitation and practice, the adult division of labor is a third major factor in gender development. The division of labor by gender is universal and in many societies sharply marked. Children observe this, eventually imitating same-sex role models, although at first both boys and girls patterns themselves after their mothers.

Comparative research on gender differences in primary socialization and in children's behavior were already reviewed in the preceding chapter, particularly in the discussions of the Six Cultures and Kpelle research; to avoid redundancy, I refer the reader back to those passages. That research was based on social behavior, but gender differences are evident in solitary, nonsocial behavior as well.

The Kpelle data, for example, indicate that children practice manual skills, imitate, observe the world around them, play with everyday objects, show frustration and anger, and explore at about the same rate whether boys or girls. However, there are several significant differences in behavior. Boys play with toys more than girls do, probably because boys have more free time and fewer responsibilities. In Liberia the usual toy is some type of homemade car, which requires a lot of movement and space; since girls are more frequently limited to the hut and yard, they are less likely to play "driver." Boys also play with and abuse animals, including dogs, goats, and snakes, more than girls do, perhaps because men care for domestic animals other than chickens, and also do all the hunting. In playing with animals boys are simply familiarizing themselves with animals, a type of role play; in beating animals, they are rehearsing for one of their first meaningful chores, driving birds and other animals from newly planted or ripening rice. Solitary girls behave in a more self-reliant and responsible fashion than boys probably because of the greater role of women in productive work (Erchak 1974; Bledsoe 1980); they begin responsible housework as early as age six or even five, sweeping the house and fetching water. Boys have no major responsibilities until at least the age of ten. Adults in the vicinity, if they notice nonsocial behaviors, tend to support the gender-appropriate behavior and ridicule inappropriate actions (Erchak 1976). In both nonsocial and social behavior, then, Kpelle children's behavior primitively mirrors adult gender-typed behavior in significant ways; it is a sort of rehearsal for the parts they will play later in life. Child-training is also consistent in directing children toward productive work and future economic self-maintenance.

Initiation

The cultural patterning of gender is nowhere more evident or more intense than in the process of secondary socialization during the transitional period from childhood to adulthood, the period we know as adolescence or puberty. This period is always and everywhere a time of *initiation* for both males and females whether or not a given culture marks the transition ritually. Many students of social process restrict the use of the term "initiation" to rites of passage at puberty, but such a restriction is unnecessary and misleadingly limits the accompanying psychological changes to people in those societies that have such rites. Initiation, however, refers to *any* commencing, or to an induction into a society. The acquisition of physiological secondary sex characteristics, along with gender-typed behaviors and roles, indeed marks the beginning of adulthood, specifically manhood or womanhood, and the ending of childhood, especially in simple preindustrial societies where they do not prolong childhood as western societies do. The novice adults are also being inducted into society as citizens with full rights and duties; in a sense children are not really considered members of society, but are "minors" with limited rights; often they are little more than property until adulthood. Initiation, then, is a term that may apply to every culture.

Initiation *ceremonies,* however, compress the entire social and intrapsychic transformational process into one discrete event or series of events. Because they clarify and concentrate what still goes on in societies without them and because they are intrinsically fascinating and dramatic, they have been thoroughly studied. Only a few of the most prominent analyses can be discussed here.

The classic text on initiation rites is the Belgian anthropologist Arnold Van Gennep's *The Rites of Passage* (1960; originally in French, 1908). Van Gennep's comparative study showed that initiation rites were just one of a series of ceremonies occurring throughout life that serve to publicly mark the "passage" from one status to another. Some of the most obvious times of passage are birth, puberty, marriage, and death. Note that in American society each of these is usually marked by some sort of ceremony, even if vestigial. Van Gennep argued that it is important to distinguish between biological puberty and social puberty. Only the latter is marked by ceremony; biological puberty may coincide with the rites, especially in the case of girls, but it is often separated from the time of ritual by years. Finally, he proposed that rites of passage are always tripartite: there are first rites of separation where the child (in the case of initiation) is removed from childhood contexts; then rites of transition that occur during the "in between" liminal period; followed by rites of incorporation wherein the individual or group is welcomed back to society in his, her, or their new status. All subsequent studies take their cue from Van Gennep.

Victor Turner elaborated on Van Gennep's theses in his studies of ritual among the Ndembu of Zambia in many books and articles, especially *The Forest of Symbols* (1967). Regarding initiation rites, Turner is perhaps most famous for his detailed discussions of the symbolism of liminality. For example, the child "dies" and remains invisible to the community during liminality but is then "reborn" as a man or a woman, often with a new name, new adult garments, and permanent marks on the body.

Male Initiation

An important early psychological analysis of male initiation was put forth by the neo-Freudian psychoanalyst Bruno Bettelheim in his classic study *Symbolic Wounds* (1955). Noting the frequency of themes of rebirth and the imitation of female physiological processes, Bettelheim argued that men are anxious about and envious of female procreative power. This "vagina envy"—a switch on the old Freudian "penis envy" supposedly suffered by girls and women—is what underlies the painful genital surgeries that are often part of initiation; modification of the penis, including supercision (cutting but not removal of the foreskin), the very common circumcision (removal of the foreskin), and the radical subincision (slitting the penis open to the urethra; practiced in aboriginal Australia), serves to impress the individual through trauma that he is now a completely new person. The blood is male "menstrual" blood, and boys are reborn as men *from* men, a rebirth culturally valued above the mere biological birth of "neuter" children from women. Men are attempting ritually to acquire the mystical procreative powers of women.

The apparent cross-cultural relevance of this theory is quite striking. Many cultures with rugged initiation ceremonies for boys do indeed seem to possess symbolism concerning envy of women, insecurity regarding male dominance, or outright fear of women and their power. The widespread existential nature of these anxieties can be seen in the frequent use of phallic flutes and other priapic symbols of male power as part of a men's cult and boys' initiation in widely scattered cultures.

These cults and their symbols seem to emerge independently

wherever they are found, suggesting a quasi-universal basis. In West Africa, among the Kpelle and their neighbors, phallic horns are an important part of Poro (Men's Society) paraphernalia. The Mundurucu of Brazil use flutes to symbolize masculinity, keeping them secret from women, and express fear that women might attempt to steal the flutes and thus their power from the men (Murphy and Murphy 1974). In the New Guinea Highlands in Melanesia masculine cults and flutes kept secret from women abound: two of the best descriptions are of the Gahuku-Gama (Read 1965) and the Bena Bena (Langness 1974), both of which suggest that they use the flutes and other items such as bullroarers to intimidate women and fool them into submitting to male dominance. The Sambia (a pseudonym) of New Guinea along with several other Highland groups not only possess the flutes, along with a painful and prolonged initiation process, but also have a myth that recounts how *women* originally possessed them until the men seized them; men must be forever vigilant to avoid losing them to the women once again (Herdt 1987:186). The mythological symbolism refers to the psychosocial power of women: all men issue from the vaginas of women and are cared for by women in their early years, giving women tremendous power over boys; men seize this power through the initiation process and must never let women take it back.

Many of the major attempts to understand initiation rites in psychological anthropology have been psychological—or, more accurately and more consistent with this book's themes, psychocultural—combining psychological effects with cultural symbolization. John Whiting, Richard Kluckhohn, and Albert Anthony (1958), for example, hypothesized that cultures with exclusive mother-child sleeping arrangements along with a lengthy postnatal prohibition of sexual relations between husband and wife would be more likely to practice male initiation ceremonies. The close psychosexual attachment of a boy to his mother and his self-identification with her must be psychologically severed for entrance into manhood.

A more sophisticated and elaborated argument was presented by Roger Burton and John Whiting (1961) in "The Absent Father and Cross-Sex Identity," perhaps the most well-known psychocultural treatment of male initiation ceremonies up to the present. Their argument rests on what they call the "status envy hypothesis," the idea that children envy adults, who occupy a privileged status in numerous respects, and identify with adults by rehearsing adult roles in fantasy and play. Furthermore, children envy and identify with adults who have easy access to resources that the children also want but do not have access to. For example, a child might want to stay up late and watch television but is not allowed to, although parents stay up as late as they like. When male babies sleep with their mothers while father sleeps elsewhere, they identify with their mothers, a *cross-sex* identification; when they sleep with both parents, they identify (nonsexually) with adults. An initial cross-sex identity conflicts with the ideal adult same-sex identity; the conflict is especially intense in strongly male-dominated societies, indexed in the study by patrilocal postmarital residence patterns, a situation where a group of related males bring in stranger wives from elsewhere who obviously have no power base in the new community.

It is this cultural pattern—exclusive mother-son sleeping arrangements along with patrilocality—that should promote painful male initiation ceremonies complete with genital operations, according to the authors. The "initiation rites serve psychologically to brainwash the primary feminine identity and to establish firmly the . . . male identity" (Burton and Whiting 1961:90). The hypothesis was strongly confirmed statistically.

William Stephens offered support for the Whiting hypotheses in *The Oedipus Complex* (1962), a cross-cultural examination of the alleged mother-son sexual attraction and accompanying father-son rivalry popularized and named the Oedipus Complex by Freud (1916–17). Stephens mustered support for the argument that a lengthy postpartum sex taboo indeed intensifies the complex since it both engenders resentment and jealousy of the son by the father and strengthens the emotional bond between son and mother; initiation rites in essence replace the maternal bond with a paternal bond and a masculine identity.

Others were not impressed with the analysis (e.g., Cohen 1964; Young 1965). The disagreements stem from two primary problems: an affinity for or antipathy against psychogenic explanations; and the ambiguity of cause versus correlation. The first is simply a mind-set stemming from the researcher's own training and background.

The second problem, mentioned briefly in the preceding chapter, comes with the territory of cross-cultural statistical comparison: correlations can be established where adequate data exist; but causality can only be proposed, never proved, through logical argument. So many intervening variables always occur that alternative logical pathways are always possible. In the case under discussion, it is undeniable that initiation ceremonies for males are more likely to be painful and to include genital surgery (64 percent of a world sample) than those for females (33 percent) (Schlegel and Barry 1979). It is also well-established that males are more subject to gender identity confusion than are females (e.g., Money and Wiedeking 1980), perhaps because girls and boys are *both* reared by *women:* for girls this fact presents no problem, but for boys it might well promote confusion of gender identity, especially where other sociocultural conditions exacerbate this confusion (also see Chodorow 1974, 1978, 1990 on this important gender difference in socialization experience). One might say that there is a *correlation* between male initiation rites with painful genital operations and male gender identity confusion, but one may not say that male gender identity confusion *causes* painful initiation rites to occur. This could be logically argued, and in fact makes a great deal of sense, but causation simply cannot be proved. Gilbert Herdt (1989) argues, for example, that in many Melanesian societies where painful initiation rites for males occur, there is little evidence of boys' identifying with their mothers; the causal chain is more varied from culture to culture than the Whiting theory suggests.

Male Initiation among the Kpelle

The Kpelle of Liberia have initiation ceremonies for both males and females. They and several societies around them in West Africa are culturally centered on quasi-religious associations which are socially more important than any other group, even including kin groups. Most of these sacred, secret societies are exclusive in membership and dedicated to specialized cults. Two, however, are universal in membership, excluding membership on the basis of sex only. These are the Poro Sale (*Sale* means "medicine" or "magic") or Poro Society for men and the Sande (Bundu among some neighboring groups) Society for women, associations based on gender solidarity. Everyone must join, although with modernization it has become much easier to avoid initiation—at the price of ridicule and abuse from initiates who find out. Poro and Sande serve several important functions for the Kpelle which need not concern us here; I am interested at present only in their educational function as initiators of boys and girls. Kpelle initiation rites for boys will be treated here; those for girls will be discussed later in the chapter.

The ceremonies attempt to modify and exaggerate physiology through surgery and symbolism. They take a neuter being and transform him (in this case) into a man. The ceremonies are actually rituals of admission into the Poro Society, but this amounts to the same thing as admission to manhood. In the past boys entered Poro School and girls entered Sande School (both referred to generically as "bush school") somewhere between the ages of seven and sixteen. Boys would remain in the bush camp, completely secluded from all females and all noninitiates for one to four years and girls for up to three, depending on when they were admitted (they are not all admitted at once, but in an irregular stream). Nowadays initiation is expected to take place in a few weeks during government school vacations, but in very rural areas children still stay in seclusion for one or even two years.

The entire ritual cycle of initiation takes fourteen years to run its course: men have sole ritual control of the forest for eight full years, during which time women must not hold ceremonies there. Poro is in session for four of these eight years; the forest is then ritually "fallow" for four more years. A major ceremony follows during which the women symbolically wrest control of the forest from the men: now women control the bush ritually for six years. Sande is in session for the next three years and for three more, the forest is fallow. In the concluding ceremony, men regain symbolic use of the forest and the cycle is completed.

Boys must be circumcised *before* admission or else are circumcised on the spot at the time of entrance; in other words, circumcision, while required, is *not* part of the initiation rites. Boys are captured, terrified, from their huts, and hurled over a thatch fence in the sacred Poro grove in the forest; on the other side of the wall, terrible frightening sounds can be heard. Once over, the boys are surrounded by fearsome masked and costumed figures, ancestral spirits, called "devils" in English. One of them holds each boy while another carves deep cuts in a design on his back, chest, and stomach. The cuts are treated to make them swell and heal in permanent raised scars. This pattern of cicatrization is called in English the "certificate" of membership in Poro and entitles each man to attend and participate in Poro ritual anywhere, even in the territory of non-Kpelle.

The scars are the "devil's teethmarks," for they are made by the "Country Devil" or the "Forest Thing," the masked spirit (actually, the spirit inhabits the mask) who heads the Poro Society. It is he whose horrendous growls were heard on the other side of the fence; and it is he who "eats" the boys, killing them. The teethmarks are the evidence; childhood has been swallowed up—those little boys will never be seen again.

After this trauma the boys spend months or years being tested and learning the ways of men. At the closing of bush school the general secrets are revealed, the secular identities of the masked figures are learned, and the boys take a solemn oath to uphold Poro and to never disclose its secrets, under pain of death. The boys don special raffia skirts, a symbol of their new manly status, and apply white clay to their skin, a symbol of their spiritually charged liminal state. When they triumphantly dance through the village at the end of their long, trying ordeal, they are older, more confident, have new names, and behave very differently, especially toward their mothers: they are men. They are symbolically reborn as men, having been killed as little boys. In some areas the clay of liminality is washed off before the procession into the village; in others, including the area of my own research, the clay is washed off after graduation.

Female Initiation

Initiation rites for girls (37 percent of a worldwide sample) are more common than for boys (30 percent) (Schlegel and Barry 1979) but have not been nearly as well-studied and analyzed.

Where they do occur, they are often carried out on an individual basis within the immediate group (87 percent), resulting in a ritual more low-key and less spectacular than that for men (48 percent initiate boys in groups in society-wide ceremonies) (Schlegel and Barry 1979). Only a few societies, including the Kpelle, hold large-scale group ceremonies for females. The reason for this gender difference seems to be that for boys there is no obvious physical marker for puberty, whereas for girls menarche is evident and unmistakable and so a specific event rather than a slow physical change can be symbolized.

Girls' initiation rites are less likely to feature painful genital surgery (33 percent do) than boys' but sometimes include cicatrization, tattooing, fattening, filing of incisors, or other corporal modification. Genital surgery, if performed, could be female circumcision (removal of the clitoral hood), labiadectomy (removal of external labia), clitoridectomy (removal of clitoris, especially common in sub-Saharan Africa), or infibulation (sewing the vulva nearly closed, a practice in some Muslim societies in the Middle East and North Africa). Ritual seclusion is the most widespread feature of female initiation at menarche; seclusion and the observance of food and behavioral taboos are then usually observed during menstruation throughout reproductive life.

Judith K. Brown (1963), in a limited nonstatistical comparative look at female initiation, interprets the rites sociologically: she argues that such rites do not occur in cultures with patrilocal residence rules, since the departure of the young woman from the village serves the purpose of announcing her new status as a woman. But in societies with matrilocal residence, where husbands joins their wives' households after marriage, the girl remains in her home village even after marriage and so initiation rites for girls are performed, dramatizing the status transition.

Alice Schlegel and Herbert Barry (1980), in a statistical cross-cultural study of 186 societies, analyze both male and female studies; their report attempts to document the functions initiation rites perform for society rather than for the individual and is thus more sociological than psychological. They find that female ceremonies are especially prominent in foraging societies, whereas simple horticultural societies tend to have rites for both boys and girls, emphasizing gender solidarity; complex societies are unlikely to have any formal ceremonies. Female ceremonies are most likely where women contribute to the economy in significant ways.

Michio Kitahara (1984:135), noting that female initiation rites are based on more personal, individual factors than those for boys, suggests "that such rites are conducted in order to let the young girl realize the seriousness of her existence brought about by her genital maturation." This argument is in accordance with the Kpelle data, to be discussed shortly. Using a data set of sixty-two societies, Kitahara (1984:137–141) demonstrates that female initiation rites are associated with strong menstrual taboos and that the stronger the menstrual prohibitions, the more likely the rites will be: (1) held at menarche or thereabouts; (2) performed individually; (3) performed by women only; and (4) intended to culturally stress the girl's bodily, social, and behavioral changes.

Her argument is basically adaptational: feminine physiology, associated with pregnancy, lactation, and child care (see also Ortner 1974 on this association), is undesirable or threatening at times from a collective point of view; childbirth, pregnancy, and so forth limit productivity and mobility and thus threaten the survival of the group, particularly in those societies that live on the subsistence edge. These cultures in particular, Kitahara asserts, emphasize the serious implications of female physiological adulthood by means of initiation ceremonies. Of course other interpretations are quite possible; for example, female initiation rites in these cultures may be a symbolic celebration of the mysteries of reproduction and the mastery over men that this procreative power bestows on women— a more positive interpretation.

Female Initiation among the Kpelle

The Kpelle are among the one-quarter of the world's societies that perform initiation rites for both boys and girls, although they are somewhat unusual in that the girls' ceremonies are carried out in groups by all the women, going well beyond the domestic group, just as boys' rites are. In some parts of Liberia girls depart for the sacred Sande grove via a long thatched tunnel that extends from a Sande medicine woman's (*zo* in Kpelle) or "priestess's" hut into the forest. There they are seized by masked ancestral figures, one of whom performs the operations of clitoridectomy and labiadectomy on each girl. Symbolically, external "male" genitalia are excised in the surgery, emphasizing the novice's femaleness. As adult women, the altered girls are now participants in the Kpelle social order. Their bodies, products of nature, are now forever marked by culture. By removing the primary source of physical pleasure, sexual relations are culturalized, separated from mere biology. Since men are viewed as the masters of culture in Kpelle ethno-ideology, and since intercourse is a male prerogative in this polygynous society, the surgery in effect symbolizes women's submission to men, even though it is women who perform the actual operation (Erchak 1979b).

After healing, the novices learn and study Sande and Kpelle traditions along with everything women need to know. After one to three years (traditionally and in some remote areas, but a few weeks in many places nowadays) they dance into the village, wearing white clay, special grass skirts, and other special accoutrements, amid great feasting and rejoicing. After three days the clay is washed off and the young women take their places as women; they are now considered marriageable.

It is very difficult for Westerners to understand how the Kpelle or any society can snip away bits of genitalia, no matter what the reason. But when we point the judgmental finger we conveniently forget the millions of painful and unnecessary circumcisions we perform on male babies each year—as well as the frequent use of clitoridectomy on adult women in the United States in the nineteenth century to "cure" "nymphomania," masturbation addiction, and other alleged female disorders (Barker-Benfield 1976). Health faddist and cornflake-inventor John Kellogg, typical in those Victorian times, advocated "the application of pure carbolic acid to the clitoris" as a means to prevent masturbation (cited in Chapple and Talbot 1989:75).

Rather than eliminating imagined vice, Kpelle male and female initiation rites serve instead to maintain and preserve established gender roles, which in turn are part of Kpelle general adaptation. These roles have helped promote group survival for generations: their rough form must have been adapted to some recently past environment. I must emphasize that only the structure or framework is adaptive, not necessarily the content; clitoridectomy, for example, could be "replaced" by incisor-filing. Stereotypical gender roles and correlative behavior in a given culture probably have cultural survival value or they would have been modified. A cursory glance at gender roles in the United States over the last thirty-five years as they changed to meet a changing economic environment illustrates this point.

The Kpelle woman's role is adapted in part to the demands of bearing and rearing children. As Kitahara (1984) suggests, repeated pregnancies, prolonged nursing, and the demands of infant and child care limit adult women's productive activity, including farming and travel. They can engage in neither the prestigious activity of warfare, a prominent feature of life until the 1940s, nor the closely associated politics. So at the very least, Kpelle gender roles are adapted to female physiology, simple horticulture, the need for child care, warfare, and, by extension, politics.

The initiation rites serve to impress Kpelle girls with this pragmatic reality and to create a new adult self. The symbols and beliefs surrounding the rites are themselves adaptational, functioning to increase awareness of each girl's complete dependence on others— on society; I call this the *prosocializing* function of initiation symbols, because the girls' (in this case) selves are becoming less egocentric, and more sociocentric, a process reinforced by the ceremonies. "The genital surgery . . . dramatically, and painfully, associates Kpelle (gender) roles with the girls' own physiologies" (Erchak 1979b:93). The linkage of the surgery with formal instruction in womanly matters makes the connection explicit; before initiation little girls (and little boys) are considered literally stupid regarding anything really important. The religious nature of initiation ceremonies has the effect of making adherence to proper gender role behavior a *moral* issue for the rest of life.

All societies strive to maintain social order and to promote the survival of the community and the people in it. Initiation rites are part of this cultural-evolutionary process, as are established gender roles. The rites and roles of gender are backed by a cultural ideology that provides powerful motivations to adhere to them since they have been handed down for generations and have evolved as survival mechanisms in years past. Initiation ceremonies are most vigorous in those cultures where they are most necessary—where they perform the most important functions; as these functions become less central to the society, the ceremonies change, becoming *only* ceremonial, with watered-down symbolism. They are abbreviated, as when Kpelle Poro initiation is crammed into Christmas vacation from school, or may die out altogether. Whether or not a substitute for initiation is needed in societies like the United States that are normatively pluralistic, with loose gender roles and rules, is an open question. Are students in North America of high school and college age satisfied with being neither children nor adults? Is the placement of these young people in the relatively new cultural categories of "teenager" and "student" an adequate substitute for ceremonial transition from child to adult? Are gender roles so unimportant and undifferentiated in the United States that we can move generically from "child" to "adult" rather than from "boy" to "man" or "girl" to "woman"? Indeed, has anything been lost in this regard in modern society? What kinds of adult selves result? The reader must answer these questions—no one else can.

Hetero and Homo

Sexual orientation is an integral part of one's self, part of one's identity in culture. There is nothing "wrong" or "abnormal" about homosexuality; there is nothing "wrong" or "abnormal" about heterosexuality. There is nothing "moral" or "immoral" about homosexuality or heterosexuality: they are not moral issues until they are made into moral issues by society. Heterosexuality is not "better" than homosexuality; nor is the reverse true.

In fact, as I will show, it is difficult even to define the two adequately enough to differentiate them in a culturally meaningful way. Since heterosexual intercourse can result in children while homosexual intercourse cannot, that would seem to make one "natural" and the other "unnatural" from a biological-evolutionary point of view; in fact many Americans use precisely this distinction to accept and celebrate one while condemning the other. Unfortunately, even this apparently natural evidence does not hold up to scrutiny and sheds very little light on the cultural shaping of hetero- and homosexuality.

Very little sexual behavior has to do with intercourse for the purpose of reproduction: masturbation and oral and anal sexual practices, for example, are performed for *pleasure,* not for the continuation of the species *Homo sapiens.* In addition, only a tiny percentage of copulations are performed with the intent of pregnancy in mind: what about sex with birth control, sex with infertile people, sex with postmenopausal women, sex while already pregnant, and so forth? In other words, heterosexual intercourse has, statistically speaking, about as much to do with reproduction as homosexual intercourse does; both are done for the pleasure of contact, excitement, orgasm, and psychological satisfaction. Furthermore, many so-called homosexuals in the United States enjoy heterosexual pleasure, even including reproduction.

If thought rather than behavior is considered, the picture becomes even more muddled. It is safe to say that many men and women who are exclusively heterosexual in behavior have some thoughts that could be considered homosexual, and that otherwise homosexual men and women likewise have heterosexual thoughts. If one adds "bisexuals" to this mess, the confusion becomes hopeless. Clearly, U.S. culture, growing in large part from a Puritanical tradition, attempts to derive sharply defined categories from a loose continuum of sexual behavior.

Lacking any sexually free culture to use as a comparative anchor, we can never know what everyone would do without any pressure, moral stricture, or stigmatization from socialization or society in general. Humans have the capacity for orgasm, an intensely pleasurable sensation which evolved to "encourage" us to reproduce: that much we know. But we must *learn* how and where to achieve orgasm (or suborgasmic sexual pleasure), and it is this learning requisite that mucks up any tidy biological point of view.

People must learn the best way for them to achieve sexual pleasure; this learning occurs during the socialization process and through other experience. Some grow up preferring certain practices and positions, others different ones; some prefer to engage in sexual behavior with members of the same (Greek *homo*) sex, whereas others prefer the opposite (Greek *hetero*) sex; some enjoy sexuality with either sex; and some people are barely interested in sex at all. Sexual orientation is, then, a preference or taste rather than an inborn trait. In no culture, however, does this preference develop without cultural intervention.

Is the concept of adaptation relevant to the study of homosexuality? Yes, on both the biological and psychocultural levels. As one of many different and normal expressions of the sex drive, itself a product of biological evolution, homo- and heterosexual behaviors co-evolved along with other aspects of human sexuality (although homosexual behavior predates *Homo sapiens*). As far as psychocultural adaptation is concerned, it must first be stressed that it is a mistake to examine *one* custom or set of behaviors in order to determine how it is adaptive. No tradition, custom, or behavior exists in isolation but is always part of a larger cultural network and process: sexual orientation is no exception.

The socialization process produces individuals who prefer certain forms of sexual release; the society then generally (not always) provides some outlet for sexual expression and satisfaction. Ancient Greeks institutionalized homosexual relations between men and boys as part of the educational process. Plains Indians allow homosexual men to be *berdaches,* intergender "men-women" who perform women's tasks and may engage in sex with warriors. The Zande of Zaire and the Sudan permitted homosexual behavior in their young men's military dorms (Evans-Pritchard 1970). In the United States, homosexual preference can be more readily expressed and accepted in, for example, the entertainment industry and the creative arts, rather than in, say, the construction industry or in the corporate world.

Marvin Harris has argued persuasively that homosexuality is well-tolerated in"antinatalist" societies, which need to reduce their birth rate, and condemned in "pronatalist" societies, which also ban abortion and infanticide. "The inescapable conclusion is this: The aversion to homosexuality is greatest where the marital and procreative imperative is strongest" (Harris 1981:108). Homosexuality is adapted to the cultural environment, as are personality and the self.

Where expression is difficult, as in today's Iran or in small-town America, individuals suffer psychologically: the self is damaged by being continually devalued and condemned. Such situations are maladaptive, examples of poor "fits" between culture and self.

Society *should* provide for the normal sexual expression and behavior of its members, or pay for its failure in other ways. Most of the neurosis associated with the gay experience in North American society comes *not* from homosexual preference but from the overwhelmingly negative *societal reaction*. No one anywhere in the world can endure rejection by the larger community without some psychological fallout.

Culture shapes sexual behavior—through socialization and social pressure. Humans possess a powerful need to conform and to be accepted; accordingly, they try to shape their own sexual behavior to fit into society. If a particular culture "wants" its members to be heterosexual and perhaps even punishes and ridicules homosexual acts, then its members will attempt to be exclusively heterosexual, repressing any homosexual urges. Any statistics on homosexuality are therefore unreliable since they must be matched with the degree of repression in each society, something very difficult to quantify. But since human beings are not animals subject to uncontrollable drives but are rather conscious beings who can, indeed must, repress and control drives, then the degree of cultural freedom and repression regarding homo- and heterosexuality are absolutely essential data if statistics are to be at all meaningful.

Because of these enormous qualifications, definitions and statistics must be treated only as very rough indicators. "Homosexuality" as a term should probably be discarded completely, as should "homosexual" as a noun rather than an adjective; the first implies an inner state, a personality disposition or feature of the self, qualitatively different from other people's. The noun "homosexual" suggests a person or self set off from other people as completely different.

Such terms, with all they connote, are erroneous; the problem is that there are no other agreed-upon terms. "Homosexualism" is better since it suggests a behavior or set of behaviors that one may or may not indulge in; a "homosexualist," then, would be someone who indulges in these behaviors on occasion or regularly. Similarly, one could speak of "heterosexualism" and "heterosexualist." Until these or other usages gain wide acceptance and successfully avoid stigmatization, however, we are stuck with the old terms. Accordingly, "homosexual" should be used exclusively as an *adjective* referring to sexual activity with a member of the same sex, never to refer to a person or category of persons since such persons or category do not exist in any semantically accurate sense. "Homosexuality" refers to sexual behavior between members of the same sex, *not* to some inner psychic state. "Bisexuality" is not a scientifically useful term in my judgment.

The statistics most commonly cited for the United States are from the famous Kinsey reports: 37 percent of American men report a homosexual and orgasmic sexual experience at least once in their lives while 4 percent claim exclusive homosexuality throughout life (Kinsey, Pomeroy, and Martin 1948). Alfred Kinsey rated homosexuality on a scale from zero to six, with zero indicating no homosexual behavior at all, and six exclusive lifetime homosexuality; 10 percent of men rated three to six on this scale. Similarly, 13 percent of American women report at least one orgasmic homosexual experience while about 1 to 3 percent claim exclusive lifetime homosexuality (Kinsey et al. 1953). The difference in incidence may well reflect the greater gender identity confusion of males, stemming from primary socialization, as discussed earlier. Interestingly, Kinsey too argues that homosexuality as an identity or inner state simply does not exist (Kinsey, Pomeroy, and Martin 1948). When one considers that these data were collected in the 1940s, and that underreporting is likely in a homophobic society like the United States, it is difficult to consider homosexual behavior abnormal in any sense of the word.

Clellan Ford and Frank Beach (1951), in the first cross-cultural survey on the topic, concluded that in 64 percent of the societies where information exists, homosexual behaviors of some kind were considered acceptable for at least certain persons. In a recent survey Edgar Gregersen (1983) found that about 69 percent of societies where clear-cut information was available (it usually is lacking) approved of homosexuality in at least certain contexts. There are virtually no data on female homosexuality; for example, in Gregersen's study of 294 societies around the world, there was no information at all on female homosexuality in 178. Perhaps it is simply a matter of lower incidence, perhaps a consequence of ethnography carried out by male anthropologists, or one of several other possible reasons: since it is futile to discuss a topic on which there is no information, I will confine the remainder of the discussion to male homosexuality only.

In the United States, homosexual behavior was first considered a sin, and later a crime. For many years, it was considered symptomatic of psychiatric illness: it was not until 1974 that homosexuality was declassified as a mental illness by the American Psychiatric Association, although the event was partly the result of political pressure and maneuvering (Conrad and Schneider 1980:204–209); in private, many psychiatrists continued to treat it as an illness. Of course it is obvious to the reader that many people still see homosexuals as "perverts" who are qualitatively different from "normal," "straight" people, as "bad" immoral people, and even as criminals who should be punished by law. Scientific facts show that these views are completely wrong.

Even though the liberal "preference" view of homosexuality has become the dominant intellectual view in American society, and is the view advocated here as well as by most social scientists, it seems to be denied in many circles. The usual competing theory of homosexual genesis is that a homosexual orientation is "inborn," consistent with the biological orthodoxy of American personality and behavior discussed earlier in the chapter. The columnist Abigail Van Buren ("Dear Abby"), for example, regularly puts forth this view, as do many gay liberationists. "I have known I was gay since I was six," and other equally absurd reconstructed recollections, are frequent in the media. Who has clear sexual thoughts about their gayness or straightness in first grade? If homosexuality is innate, it is an inner identity, a position rejected by Kinsey and most other social scientists and sexologists although supported by some psychiatrists. And if it *is* innate, it is not a socially learned preference—one cannot have it both ways.

One of the most important uses of ethnographic descriptions is to provide test cases for theories of human behavior. For example, until fairly recently most political philosophers, including Aristotle, argued that leadership of some sort, if only a "headman" or chief, is essential for society and social order; but in the 1930s, ethnographies of African societies began to appear which showed unmistakably that many tribal societies function quite well without political leaders of any sort (see, e.g., Fortes and Evans-Pritchard

1940; Middleton and Tait 1958). Some Western economists argue that the profit motive is intrinsic to humankind, as natural as the weather; yet cultural anthropology has documented many cultures, particularly foragers, whose economics are based exclusively on reciprocity, with no profit in sight. If there is a well-documented exception to any thesis, proposal, or assumption, the proposition is not true for everyone. It may be part of an important social principle for one society, or group of societies, or societal type, but it is not a panhuman principle—not a principle of *human* behavior.

Such is the case with homosexuality: is it innate or acquired through experience? Can a person be homosexual for years, and then be heterosexual? If so, what does this tell us about the notion of an inner homosexual identity or self? If we want to develop theories of human sexual behavior, we must collect data on sex from all types of societies, from as many cultures as possible, and take these data seriously.

Anthropologists have known about "ritual" homosexuality for decades: some societies tolerate or even require homosexual behavior between males in certain well-defined ritual contexts such as initiation. This information remained little known outside narrow specializations, however, and had no real effect on Western theorizing about homosexuality. A new and particularly well-documented case has been published recently which should permanently alter received notions about homosexual behavior: Gilbert Herdt's (1981, 1987; Herdt and Stoller 1990) brilliant portrayals of the Sambia of Papua New Guinea. Not only does Herdt graphically depict the role of homosexual behavior—fellatio, to be specific—in the cultural development of maleness among these Melanesian mountain people, but he also addresses the implications for theories of homosexuality in general, and does so in numerous articles as well as in books written for other researchers (Herdt 1981, 1982, 1984) and for undergraduates (Herdt 1987). As Robert LeVine states in his Foreword to the first book: "No future discussion of gender identity and its development as a *human* phenomenon will be able to ignore the contents of this book" (in Herdt 1981:ix, emphasis added).

The ethnography is challenging, even shocking, to a Western audience. The Sambia believe that, while the physical growth and development of girls is a natural process, needing no cultural assistance from human beings, the growth of boys is not at all natural: without cultural assistance, they would not grow at all, but would in fact wither and die. Therefore all boys must be initiated in a complex, multistage series of rites. In effect, the physiological birth of boys from women is negated: not only is that birth insufficient as the beginning of a growth process, but even worse, it is a source of terrific female pollution, a sort of "original sin," which is actually inimical to growth to manhood. Only men can give (social) birth to men, and only they can ensure the healthy development and transformation of boys into men (note how closely Sambia initiation matches interpretation in previous sections).

Semen is the key to male essence and strength (*jerungdu*) and must be ingested if a boy is to become a man. Although there are many other important parts of initiation, including beating, whipping with nettles, and shoving cane forcefully down the throat, the most important is daily fellatio, including the swallowing of the donor's semen. Controversially from a Western point of view, oral insemination begins anywhere from age seven to ten and continues for from ten to fifteen years (Herdt 1981:2; 1987:6). During the first half of this period, the boy is exclusively fellator; during the second half, exclusively fellated. So until age fourteen or thereabouts, a boy sucks an older boy's penis every day; from about fifteen to around twenty-one, he is in turn sucked by a little boy. Absolute homosexuality is enforced during the entire period; no contact with females, sexual or otherwise, is permitted. Such contact would literally defeat the purpose of semen ingestion, depleting *jerungdu* and stalling growth.

I am sure it has not escaped your notice that Sambia initiation does more than just challenge Western ideas about homosexuality: from our point of view, the rites involve the emotional abuse of children (they are seized from their mothers and terrorized), the physical abuse of children (hazing, beating, and torture), and the sexual abuse of children. Ask yourself, "Is it morally different (from Western culture) if an entire community engages in these practices? If all boys and men have a common experience with friends and kin?"

One of the most fascinating aspects of the Sambia initiation ritual cycle, and the reason I am including it here, is that at the end of the rites, when boys become men, boys also become lifelong heterosexuals. The entire initiation process, in fact, is associated with a macho and *heterosexual* attitude toward women which cannot be expressed until graduation. In the final stages of initiation they learn rites of purification that will enable them to have genital intercourse with women without becoming permanently and dangerously contaminated from the dreaded female pollution. Typically, marital relations begin with fellatio as well as a brief period of bisexual practice. But once a baby is born, heterosexuality is the social norm (Herdt 1981:3, 321; 1987:166–167). "Most men feel that homosexual activity after fatherhood is immature and unimportant" (Herdt 1987:166); in fact, men who have become fathers but nevertheless continue to prefer homosexual oral intercourse are considered deviants or "rubbish men," the lowest form of adult male. Occasional encounters are acceptable, but a preference for boys along with an avoidance of sex with women is threatening to the entire social order and is therefore stigmatized.

To review: all Sambia boys and men participate in daily homosexual fellatio for many years while completely suppressing all heterosexual activity. The purpose of this homosexuality is to produce a strong heterosexuality; the end product is a fierce virile warrior who views women lecherously and derogates the rare "gay" man.

The Sambia case and other less well-known but similar cases strongly suggest that homosexuality, and by implication heterosexuality, are *culturally constructed* rather than biologically innate. It also refutes the popular notion, "Once a homosexual, always a homosexual." Clearly one *can* engage in exclusively homosexual activity to orgasm for many years and then become exclusively heterosexual. Perhaps this is why Herdt's *Guardians of the Flutes* enjoyed a brief "underground" popularity in a maximum security prison where I was teaching in 1981 and 1982, even among students not in my courses: its message was comforting to men who thought of themselves as heterosexual but who had engaged in homosexual acts on occasion in prison. Engaging in erotic acts with someone of the same sex, whether male or female, does not mean one is a "homosexual," but that one is simply "sexual"—and merely human.

Sexuality

All sexuality, not just homosexuality, is culturally shaped. Sexual beliefs, attitudes, expression, behavior, and identity are culturally constructed. The Sambia case suggests that in some cultures sexuality as well as homosexuality is considered normal behavior for children, an idea that many Americans find morally repugnant, but nevertheless undeniable. Solving this moral dilemma by dehumanizing the practitioners as "primitive" or "savage" is of course racist nonsense, objectively false, and itself morally repugnant. Sexual urges are obviously biological, but their use or expression in human behavior is not. Without culture, human beings can express precisely nothing, and this goes for sexuality as much as for anything else.

Early ethnographies often discuss sexuality as if animals were under discussion; primitive people, as they were called, were considered to be less evolved than Europeans, not as intelligent, and brutish like apes. Sex was discussed in coyly euphemistic phrases or in learned academic Latinisms. The great ethnographer Bronislaw Malinowski produced a remarkable monograph on sexuality in the Trobriand Islands called *The Sexual Life of Savages* (1929) which can still be read with interest in the 1990s, although he views much of Trobriand sexual behavior with undisguised disgust and holds the racist views typical of the early years of the century. The book is highly descriptive rather than theoretical, and emphasizes a license that contrasts with Western society. He describes sexual positions and attitudes, orgasm, ignorance of physiological paternity, standards of beauty, erotic dreams, and morals. The monograph is perhaps the first well-documented case challenging Western sexual norms, although the challenge was diminished by the racist and ethnocentric tone.

A few other later studies were almost "reverse-racist" in trumpeting a simpler idyllic life of sexual freedom. Scandinavian ethnographer Bengt Danielsson's *Love in the South Seas* (1956 [orig. 1954]), for example, is squarely in the Rousseauian "noble savage" tradition, emphasizing the allegedly halcyon sex lives of Polynesians. Like Malinowski, he catalogs a wide variety of sexual attitudes and practices. One important contribution of the book is his finding that Polynesians, unlike Westerners, do not conceive sexuality and religion as mutually exclusive, or even opposed, categories.

Gilbert Herdt's Sambia studies and such works as Thomas Gregor's *Anxious Pleasures: The Sexual Lives of an Amazonian People* (1985), a study of the Mehinaku of Brazil, are representative of current approaches to cultural sexology: psychologically learned, methodologically sophisticated, and culturally relativist. Herdt and Stoller's (1990) most recent examination of Sambia sexuality, *Intimate Communications: Erotics and the Study of Culture,* is especially path-breaking because they focus literally on what actually excites Sambia sexually; they do this through extensive interviews with a variety of Herdt's informants, including one woman. The interview data, reproduced in full, emphasize each person's subjective erotic experience; each interview is followed by a discussion between Herdt, the ethnographer, and Stoller, a psychoanalyst, presented in dialogue form. The result is a unique document that will undoubtedly influence the ethnography of sexual behavior for a long time to come.

While necessarily exotic from a Western perspective, Gregor's study also emphasizes the universalities of sexuality under the veneer of cultural difference, focusing on the widespread anxieties and fears of men. Mehinaku men, like the Sambia, have their flute cult as well as considerable antagonism and ambivalence toward women, a phenomenon dramatically documented in a psychosexual study of another Brazilian group, the Mundurucu, reported by Yolanda and Robert Murphy (1974). The Murphys too stress universality and shakey masculine identity rather than deep cultural difference.

Recently anthropologists have been turning their attentions to Western culture in increasing numbers. An example of this trend is Michael Moffatt's *Coming of Age in New Jersey* (1989), an ethnography of student life at Rutgers University. Two chapters concern student sexuality, a topic much dearer to students' hearts than academic matters. While Moffatt's account is heavily descriptive, spiced by very explicit student essays on experiences and fantasies, he does reach a few tentative conclusions, for example, American college-aged adult sexuality is to a great degree shaped by American mass popular culture. Students are quite homophobic, especially males, feminism is unimportant to them in matters of sex, and sexuality in general is biased toward men, who tend to call the shots. Sex is viewed by everyone as part of college "fun" (Moffatt 1989:229). It is clearly not coupled with marriage or reproduction, both of which are viewed as temporally quite remote by Moffatt's informants; this latter finding probably sexually separates young Americans from their peers in simple agrarian societies more than any other factor.

Although sexuality is biologically based, culture can affect some aspects that appear to be physiological. For example, poor nutrition and perhaps other as yet unknown factors can postpone first menses to as late as twenty in some parts of the world; I assume boys' sexual awakening is similarly delayed. The same factors might affect age of menopause as well as sexual interest and activity level. Karl Heider (1976) has argued improbably that the Dani of the Highlands of New Guinea, seemingly alone in the world on this dimension, are just not interested in sex: they do not practice it much, do not use erotic humor, do not talk about it, and do not flirt. Heider claims that their enormous priapic penis gourds are not at all sexual. If he is accurate, and I must confess to a certain skepticism, their "low-energy" sexuality could also be due to their very low protein diet or even to their unwieldy gourds (although this does not explain women's low interest), both cultural factors (Gregor 1985:5; Pontius 1977).

Aside from these somewhat problematic areas of interaction between culture and biology, the patterning of sexuality by culture is usually more straightforward: people learn cultural norms through socialization and then attempt to adhere to those norms to achieve a satisfying conformity and social acceptance. Most ethnological surveys have emphasized variation in cultural norms rather than universality, and description rather than theory and analysis (Ford and Beach 1951; Marshall and Suggs 1971; Gregersen 1983). In a hodgepodge article on the "anthropology of eros," Lawrence Fisher (1980) deplores such descriptions of sexual exotica as well as sexual studies that overemphasize biology, arguing that sexuality cannot be understood outside the context of the larger cultural system, and that in order to compare sexual practices cross-culturally it is necessary to compare whole cultural systems.

The poles of restriction and permission, especially concerning sexual intercourse, have received some anthropological attention. Nearly all societies restrict sexual behavior; Suzanne Frayser (1985:179–180) suggests that cultures restrict sexuality because orgasms are so uncontrolled that they are in effect a threat to social order. Her encyclopedic study of sexual experience intricately combines the findings of research in cultural anthropology, physical anthropology, biology, sociology, psychology, psychiatry, and sexology. She writes that foreplay varies cross-culturally from none at all to hours long, with Pacific Islanders being the most prolonged; foreplay might involve manual or oral contact with the genital organs or simple kissing and hugging. Positions vary cross-culturally, with the "missionary" position most common. Pacific Island and some Amazonian societies prefer the "Oceanic" position in which the couple sits or squats facing each other with knees flexed. The Kpelle of Liberia favor two positions, missionary and rear-entry. Premarital sex norms have been the subject of quite a bit of study, perhaps because of the widespread concern about teenage sexuality and pregnancy in the United States. One important study by George Goethals stresses cultural adaptation. In matrilineal societies (those that trace kin relationships through women only) with matrilocal postmarital residence patterns, men are interlopers from other villages or homesteads and therefore find it more difficult to regulate girls' sexual behavior than in patrilineal, patrilocal societies; in addition, in matricentric societies pregnancies are easily taken care of by the large numbers of related women, something far more difficult to manage in a patricentric society (patrilineal kinship, patrilocal residence). Accordingly, the latter tend to restrict premarital sex whereas the former are more likely to permit it (Goethals 1971). A sociobiologically adaptive explanation could be applied: men are especially concerned with knowledge of paternity in patrilineal societies.

George Peter Murdock (1964) concludes that the more complex the culture, the more restrictive the premarital sex rules, a finding confirmed, albeit weakly, by Gwen Broude (1975). Broude also reports a strong correlation between premarital sexual restriction and a high level of psychocultural anxiety about sex, as well as undependable or limited accessibility of caretakers, a factor which leads to anxiety about attachment to others. Frayser (1985) notes that some societies, especially Pacific Island cultures, permit and even encourage or actually train young people to engage in sex, considering it important training for life, whereas others, such as rural Egyptians, forbid it absolutely, at least for girls, and attempt to enforce the prohibition with clitoridectomy. Again, the more male-dominated patrilineal and patrilocal societies are far harsher and more restrictive than the nonpatrilineal societies.

Extramarital affairs are more widely restricted, running second only to incest prohibition; the punishments for violation are even more severe worldwide than those for incest (Frayser 1985:209, 215). Concern for proper paternity is even more important within marriage than premaritally. Sometimes adultery is permitted within a particular context, as during a ritual celebration or between certain affines. Important Kpelle men with several wives supplement their incomes with adultery fines, or might even allow a client to live with one of the patron's wives in exchange for labor (Gibbs 1963). Gender variation is also important: male violators are rarely punished as severely as female, perhaps because women rather than men might become pregnant. Frayser points out that men in patrilineal societies are "more concerned than those in matrilineal systems with keeping their wives and establishing paternity," an argument that is adaptational both culturally and sociobiologically. In patrilineal systems, men are more likely to regulate women's sexuality in order to establish clear relationships between men and their offspring, while in matrilineal systems, men are more invested in their sisters' children than their own, and are therefore less concerned about the sexuality of their wives or of women in general (Frayser 1985:343–344). Her hypotheses are strongly supported by the data.

Adaptation is important in the understanding of sexuality. All cultures attempt to manage sexuality just as they attempt to manage the biological growth process. Sexual expression is culturally constructed and consistent with other aspects of a cultural system. Look at American society: in the years following World War II, the United States urbanized at a rapid rate; simultaneously, public health improved. Both factors lowered the birth rate: it is more expensive to raise children in an urban than in a rural environment, and the greater assurance of a baby's survival to adulthood decreases the desire to give birth to several children. The result:

women were freed from the burden of mothering for longer periods of life and so could enter the labor force in greater numbers. High inflation in the 1960s and 1970s made it a necessity rather than an option for women to work for pay.

According to Marvin Harris (1981), the neofeminist movement is an adaptive response to these material imperatives. Gender roles loosened along with sexuality. At the same time rapid social change made it difficult for many people to adhere to seemingly outdated fundamentalist morals regarding sexuality. Birth control pills, contraceptive devices, and legal abortion contributed to a freer sex life for many. In retrospect American sexuality can be seen as adaptive to broader sociocultural and material trends and changes. Sexual behavior adapts to fit better into a changing environment. Currently a fear of sexually transmitted diseases such as AIDS and herpes, along with a distrust of the pill and IUDs because of the possible negative consequences of their use, may be resulting in further changes in sexuality, this time tightening and restricting rather than loosening and permitting.

SUGGESTED READINGS

Carol Ember's "Feminine Task Assignment and the Social Behavior of Boys" (1973), published in the psychological anthropology journal *Ethos*, shows how gender roles are learned during socialization. Serena Nanda's *Neither Man nor Woman: The Hijras of India* (1990), an ethnography of a eunuch sect, shows how deeply culture can pattern gender, in this case adding a third role. Sherry Ortner's wonderful article, "Is Female to Male as Nature Is to Culture?" (1974), in Rosaldo and Lamphere's *Woman, Culture, and Society*, is a provocative speculation on the symbolism of the female gender.

Arnold Van Gennep's *The Rites of Passage* (1960), even though written in 1908, is the essential beginning for any exploration of initiation rites. Victor Turner's "Betwixt and Between: The Liminal Period in *Rites de Passage*" (1967), a chapter in his collection entitled

The Forest of Symbols, is another classic piece. Roger Burton and John Whiting's "The Absent Father and Cross-Sex Identity" (1961), published in *The Merrill-Palmer Quarterly,* is an important psychocultural interpretation of male initiation. My own "Socialization and Subsistence, Symbol and Surgery: Women in a West African Society" (1979b), in the journal *Sociologus,* is one of the few attempts to analyze a collective female initiation process and its symbolism.

Several studies examine masculinity, along with its symbols and maintenance, focusing on universal questions as well as cultural particulars. Kenneth Read's *The High Valley* (1965), Lewis Langness' "Ritual, Power, and Male Dominance" (1974, in *Ethos*), and Gilbert Herdt's *The Sambia: Ritual and Gender in New Guinea* (1987) all deal with male initiation cults and symbolism in the New Guinea Highlands. Herdt's book is also important for its discussion of homosexuality. Yolanda and Robert Murphy's *Women of the Forest* (1974) and Thomas Gregor's *Anxious Pleasures* (1985) are similar in intent and analysis to the New Guinea ethnographies, but deal instead with Amazonian Indians.

Gregor's book is also one of the few ethnographies of sexuality available. Another is Gilbert Herdt and Robert Stoller's startling, almost voyeuristic, look at subjective eroticism among the Sambia, *Intimate Communications: Erotics and the Study of Culture* (1990). Suzanne Frayser's *Varieties of Sexual Experience* (1985) covers all the bases: it is a splendid introduction to the evolutionary and cultural aspects of sexuality, by far the best such study available.

4

Modal Personality,
Normality, and Deviance

Let us tread, very gingerly, onto thin ice. How does one tell the difference between a valid generalization about the behavioral characteristics of a certain people—and an ethnic slur? Is it just that the latter is invariably derogatory? Are all such attempts necessarily ethnocentric? Are there behaviors that are "typically Jewish" or "typically English"? How about "typically Jivaro" or "typically Sambia"?

Most, maybe all, human groups stereotype, sometimes insultingly ("they smell bad") and sometimes favorably ("they are good fighters"), the members of other human groups. Usually people generalize about the behaviors and personalities of people in groups with which they have some contact: occasionally more fanciful characterizations ("they are cannibals") are drawn of people whom no one in the local group has ever encountered. Stereotyping of others goes hand in hand with ethnocentrism: it seems to be a side effect of social solidarity and integration. Humans like to know what to expect from strangers so that they know how to deal with them. Rightly or wrongly, stereotypical characterizations are a part of this attempt to know the social environment.

There is often a grain of truth in such typologizing: many English *are* after all more reserved than many Americans. But the problem is that there also are many Americans who are more reserved than many English just as there are stereotype-defying boisterous Norwegians and taciturn Greeks. Stereotypes are folkloric, not scientific; they reflect the myths, history, and encounters of previous generations and as such, are often flat-out wrong. They may be rather good-natured and essentially harmless, but they can also be vicious and destructive. When stereotypes become slurs, and intersect with historical animosities, then war, racism, and even genocide can result: American and South African treatment of blacks, the slaughter of Native Americans in North and South America (continuing to this day in such places as Brazil), the Ottoman Turks' extermination campaign against Armenians, the Jewish Holocaust. The list goes on and on.

There *are* important group differences in culturally patterned behavior. But differences must never be condemned, ranked hierarchically, or used as a basis or excuse for discrimination. They should be learned about, recognized, and appreciated as an adaptive pool of vital diversity. An important task for the cross-cultural study of social psychology is to learn as much as possible about the similarities and differences among human groups. If selves and personalities are built upon cultural foundations, and adapted to cultures, and if cultures change continually to meet the requisites of an ever-changing environment, and if socialization is a process of forming selves and personalities *in* culture, then the self and the personality will reflect cultural adaptation, will be shared to some extent by group members, and will differ in the aggregate from culture to culture.

The scholarly effort to document and analyze cultural differences in personality and behavior is what underlies studies of "modal personality" and "national character," the most frequently used terms for such typological profiles. Unfortunately, the end product is sometimes neither scientific nor objective.

National Character and Modal Personality: The Concepts

"National character" and "modal personality," along with other synonymous terms such as "social character" and "basic personality type," have been employed in the social sciences almost interchangeably to label any study that attempts to characterize a human population on the basis of psychological, rather than, say, political or economic, traits. When these terms were in vogue, the word "self" was rarely used. "National character" is applied only to modern nation-states and usually has a psychiatric or psychoanalytic clinical flavor, whereas "modal personality" can be applied to studies of small-scale preindustrial societies as well as modern nations. The latter term, unlike the former, is—in theory at least—a more scientific statistical concept, a measure of the "mode" or central tendency of a group's distribution along a certain psychological dimension. In reality, "modal personality" has from time to time been applied to clinical, nonstatistical studies as well. In fact, no distinction has been consistently followed in practice over the last fifty years; I will try to use the same term employed by the researcher under discussion whenever possible.

Psychocultural Configurations

The earliest studies did not employ either term, but rather spoke of "cultural configurations": configurationalism was an attempt to ferret out the one or two dominant psychological traits that are allegedly central to every well-integrated culture. Such traits are said to permeate other aspects of culture, so that each culture is a configuration with these dominant psychological characteristics or tendencies at its core. The first to employ the concept were Franz Boas's famous students, Ruth Benedict and Margaret Mead. Although they wrote a number of early articles outlining cultural configurationalism, the first major work utilizing this framework and bringing it to the attention of both the lay and scientific public was Benedict's *Patterns of Culture* (1934b), an extremely influential book.

The configurationalist viewpoint is that cultures are simply a collective version of the individual psyches that comprise it, and so the culture will possess the same traits as its members. In *Patterns of Culture,* Benedict digs into an odd grab bag of cultures, the Pueblo, Plains, and Kwakiutl Indians of North America, along with the Dobuans of Melanesia, and characterizes them respectively as Apollonian, Dionysian, Dionysian with megalomania and paranoia, and Paranoid. Her choice of cultures was apparently dictated by convenience rather than any scientific comparative criteria: she had done some work herself on the Guardian Spirit complex among Plains Indians and had carried out field research at Zuni Pueblo in New Mexico; her mentor, Franz Boas, had carried out extensive work among the Kwakiutl of British Columbia; and her friend Margaret Mead's second husband, Reo Fortune, had worked on Dobu just off the coast of New Guinea.

Her selection of configurational labels was equally eclectic, with the terms Apollonian (repressed, controlled, mild) and Dionysian (expressive, wild, given to excess) lifted from the German philosopher Nietzsche's studies of Greek tragedy (Benedict 1934b:78), and the more familiar megalomaniac and paranoid from psychiatry. She writes with approval only of the sober, measured behavior of the Zuni, while adjectivally disapproving of the others in varying degrees. Benedict did not argue that all cultures could be typologized psychologically, or that her labels were static and unchanging, but rather that only a few exceptionally well-integrated cultures could be so characterized and that even among these, the tendencies toward psychocultural consistency could be disrupted and altered by history. Unfortunately, even here she did not follow her own criterion of integration, since few would label the fractious, leaderless, stateless, and lawless Dobuans "well-integrated."

All human beings, she argued, contain within them the same potentialities for paranoia, restraint, excess, and the like; certain cultures choose and stress one trait rather than others because of historical circumstance. She remains correct in insisting that psychological interpretations of cultural behavior are meaningless without taking history into account (Benedict 1934b:232–233).

A virtue of *Patterns,* in addition to being beautifully written, is that even though it has little scientific value, it is at least confined to very small-scale societies, about which generalizations are safer and, what is more important, can be easily tested by other observers. And Benedict's ideas were indeed tested, particularly in New Mexico, the site of her original fieldwork. This is not the place to review fifty-five years of Pueblo field research, but it is unfortunately true that a small army of ethnographers has found Benedict's analysis to be oversimplified, to use the most charitable characterization. Later on, when configuration metamorphosed into national character, as it did under the pressure of World War II, the relative ease of generalization about a small-scale preindustrial culture became preposterous overgeneralization about huge nations, and contrasting analyses became essentially matters of opinion.

The overall effect of the book, however, has been positive. Benedict wrote for a popular audience and so helped to educate the public about the role of culture in all human life and to engender some appreciation of other ways of life, or at least of the Pueblo people. Like Boas and his other students and colleagues, she stressed the plasticity and adaptability of human behavior and its shaping by culture. She also brought anthropological and psychological analyses together—a lasting legacy.

A Case Study of Modal Personality: The Alorese

Along with configurationism came another lasting legacy from the astonishing Department of Anthropology at Columbia University in the 1930s: the concept of modal personality. Abram Kardiner (1939, 1945), a neo-Freudian psychoanalyst with a strong interest in anthropology, introduced the concept which gave birth to modal personality, "basic personality structure": a society's "primary institutions" (child-rearing practices along with the socioeconomic structure) condition and produce a basic personality type that is an inner organization of adaptive mechanisms; this collective personality then goes on to produce the society's "secondary institutions" (myth, religion, and their symbols) (DuBois 1961 [orig. 1944]:xxi–xxii). Kardiner was perhaps the first to make adaptation a central concept in studies of culture and personality, an intellectual contribution which should have assured Kardiner a more central place in intellectual history than the fringes he occupies instead (Manson 1988).

His star student, Cora DuBois, traveled to the Indonesian (then Dutch East Indies) island of Alor in 1938 to field-test the concept in a non-Western "primitive' culture. By the time *The People of Alor* was published in 1944, DuBois had discarded "basic personality structure" in favor of "modal personality," as far as I know the first use of the term. She defined it as "central tendencies in the personalities of a *group* of people studied by means of more or less objective and cross-culturally applicable tests as well as by means of observation and autobiographies" (DuBois 1961:xix). DuBois carried out participant observation on Alor for one and a half years, a long time for fieldwork in the twenties and thirties. In addition, she collected life histories and administered the Rorschach and other psychological tests, decades before a "multimethod" research strategy became common. Whatever other faults it may have had, DuBois's study was clearly a scientific one.

She set out to test the very proposition upon which the book you are now reading is based: whether or not there is a direct relationship between modal personality and the cultural environment. In a preface written twenty years after her fieldwork, she self-effacingly denies having found such a congruence, stating that it was "doubtful whether any culture is fully integrated in this sense" (DuBois 1961:xviii). However, her undertaking laid an important theoretical foundation for future studies of the same relationship.

The book is more of a social psychological study (in fact, it is subtitled as such) than a traditional ethnography: she covers socialization, psychological aspects of religion, autobiographies, and the analyses of the projective tests. It is interspersed with psychological commentary by Kardiner and another psychiatrist, another analytical innovation. Her primary findings concern the effects of maternal deprivation and neglect on personality formation. Alorese mothers do most of the horticultural work and so are separated from their children for long hours each day. During this time, babies are indifferently cared for by siblings and other children. Analysis of the projective tests after DuBois's return indicated that the Alorese were emotionally shallow, insecure, suspicious, indifferent, and apathetic (Oberholzer, in DuBois 1961:588–640), findings that could perhaps be dismissed as products of the inappropriate use of Western testing in a non-Western setting except that they concur with DuBois's own field notes based on participant observation.

It is unclear whether the modal personality characteristics stem from maternal neglect or some other variable such as poor nutrition. The Alorese pattern of women's productive horticultural labor is a very common one in the tropical world, yet the negative personality features of the Alorese have not often been noted elsewhere. Furthermore, DuBois herself stresses that there is a wide variation in personality type, even in this relatively small society (she focused on a group of about 300 out of a total island population of 70,000). Anthony Wallace (1952) discusses this problem of significant variation in modal personality, and I will return to his research on the Tuscarora later in the chapter. DuBois's work was very influential and stimulated many others, often joint anthropologist and psychologist teams, to conduct similar studies in other parts of the world.

National Characterizations

Even though *The People of Alor* first came out in 1944, the field research on which it is based, like Benedict's, was carried out before the war. The coming of World War II shifted the focus of culture and personality studies away from small-scale societies and toward the nations, both enemies and allies of the United States, that were waging war. The result was a series of (in)famous national character studies; early configurationalist notions, which had some credibility in small tropical villages, were applied less credibly to modern nations, often without the benefit of any field research whatsoever. I will examine only some of the more well-known studies.

In her patriotic *And Keep Your Powder Dry* (1942), Margaret Mead was clearly preparing her readers for war rather than presenting an objective analysis. She argues that each American generation differs from the one before it in that parents expect their children to live differently than they themselves did. There is allegedly a high emphasis on individual achievement and a low emphasis on class membership, along with a Puritan ethic which requires Americans to be on the side of moral right if they are to be able to fight successfully. Many other equally dubious propositions are advanced, but, since it was clearly written to boost morale, it is probably unfair to take it further to task.

Far more significant was Ruth Benedict's *The Chrysanthemum and the Sword* (1946), a study of Japanese national character which is an attempt to "know thy enemy." The Office of War Information assigned Benedict to provide useful information on Japanese character in 1944 in order to help the war effort. Since she obviously could not go "to the field," she relied on the analysis of cultural materials such as literature and film, and interviews of Japanese-Americans who grew up in Japan. As in her earlier publications, her writing is compelling. The word "configuration" does not appear anywhere in the book, although the basic theoretical orientation is the same: Japanese culture is the Japanese individual "writ large." Japanese national character thus centers on psychological traits that could aptly apply to a single person. For example, Japanese value order in all things, a sense of knowing one's place in a great, all-encompassing universal hierarchy. Closely related is an emphasis on order in behavior, expressed in self-discipline and a tendency to serious ritual, even in the pursuit of pleasure. The spiritual side of life is valued over the material. Finally, great cultural stress is placed on respect and politeness and on honor and shame. Early childhood is a period of complete indulgence, followed by tighter and tighter constraints on the self and its expression through middle age, with increasing indulgence once more in the later years. Conformity and social acceptance are emphasized from early school age. While Benedict reasonably traces some national character traits to child-training practices, she does so in a soft, nondeterministic way, ostensibly leaving a door open for other interpretations. Her dominant metaphors, the chrysanthemum and the sword, express the sensitive intricacy of her thesis. Although they do indeed represent a conflicting dualism in Japanese character, it is not, as many suppose, the contrast between order and serenity on the one hand, and martial violence on the other, but something far subtler: the chrysanthemum symbolizes the beauty of individual restraint, lovely but imperfect if allowed to grow untended, but perfect and symmetrical if carefully tended and constrained by well-placed wire. The sword is a symbol "of ideal and self-responsible man" (Benedict 1946:296). The sword is one's body; it cuts and tarnishes. The idea is that one must bear the full consequences of one's behavior. Later on-site work contradicted some of Benedict's points while confirming others (e.g., Hsu 1975; DeVos 1978). All in all, this study holds up quite well and remains perhaps the best of the national character studies of the forties and fifties.

Geoffrey Gorer's national character work is heavily influenced by psychoanalysis, which may account for both insight and naïveté in his published studies. In *The American People* (1948), a study primarily of Northern urban WASPs, he offers his definition of "national character": "the concatenation of characteristics and patterns of behavior . . . exhibited by a significant number of the members of (a) group, and . . . approved of, or . . . assented to, by most of the remainder" (Gorer 1948:16–17). These characteristics are those that play the largest role in shaping social institutions in a particular society. Such a view is known as psychological reductionism or psychological determinism because he argues that individual personalities and behaviors create society, rather than the other way around.

The American People is a continuation of *And Keep Your Powder Dry* without the wartime morale-building agenda. Like Mead, Gorer emphasizes the lack of continuity between generations. He stresses the American mother's anxiety about the right way to raise a child, the central preoccupation with feeding in infancy (on a "schedule" in the forties) and throughout childhood, and the push toward independence, initiative, and physical activity. American men grow up to be homophobic, extraordinarily aroused by women's breasts, and addicted to milk. Americans are antiauthoritarian and therefore antimilitaristic. They value friendship, want to be loved, and fear rejection. Material success is important, as is novelty, innovation, "keeping up with the Joneses," and conformity. In retrospect, the book is a rather uneven blend of commonplace observations and psychobabble 1940s-style, along with some deep cultural analysis and acute psychological insight. At least Gorer in this case was able to live among the natives.

Such was not the case in his attempt to understand the psychology of the Russians under Joseph Stalin (Gorer 1962 [orig. 1949]): Gorer could not speak Russian; nor was he able to carry out research in Russia, although he had been there on two brief trips as a tourist in the thirties. Gorer's essay "The Psychology of Great Russians," included in a slim volume entitled *The People of Great Russia* (Gorer 1962), was then a return to wartime ethnography in absentia, only this time the war in question was the Cold War. In the essay, he introduces the much-maligned "swaddling hypothesis." Gorer states that Russian "peasants" (although he frequently switches to "all Russians") wrap their babies like little mummies, with their arms held tightly by their sides, for the first nine months of life, unwrapping them only for bathing and nursing. All of this is carried out in an impersonal manner. Gorer did not suggest that the practice of swaddling by itself produces Russian national character, as his more vociferous detractors aver, but rather argued that the study of swaddling practices led to the discovery "of the most important clues to the interpretation of Russian behavior" (Gorer 1962:129). In spite of the disclaimer, however, he does clearly give it central importance as the foundation of a configuration of customs and behaviors (remember, "national character" grew out of "configuration"). Swaddling causes "undirected rage and fears"; these in turn engender "unfocused guilt"; this guilt underlies the Russian Orthodox dogma of universal sinfulness as well as the alleged Russian mania for confessions, both public and private, including the confessions during Stalin's great purges (torture probably played a larger role than swaddling, I would think). Russian patience and stoicism have their origins in the long periods of swaddling, while adult devotion to orgiastic excess follows from the ecstasy of periodic release from the tight bands of cloth. Because of their "unconscious hostility and guilt," Russians develop a need for authority: their "psychological well-being" depends on the preservation of an idealized authority figure—a dictator—without fault or frailty (Gorer 1962:168–169). The essay presents many other connections and hypotheses, including governmental policy recommendations, all with swaddling at the epicenter, even if not technically considered to be "causal." Such a study could well be called one of "national caricature."

Victor Barnouw (1985:110–127) aptly labels such approaches to psychosocial analysis "childhood determinism," whereby the childhood experiences of a culture determine its social institutions. Many criticisms could be, and have been, leveled at Gorer's hypothesis. For example, dictatorships similar to the U.S.S.R.'s exist all over the world, in societies with radically different forms of child-rearing. Gorer pays scant attention to the causal roles of economy and history in the development of Soviet institutions. He does not address the genesis of swaddling and other aspects of Russian child-rearing; they are simply givens. Those who confessed during the purges of Joseph Stalin were intelligentsia, not peasants, and were probably never swaddled (Harris 1968:445). The sociologist and Sovietologist Alex Inkeles (1968) has shown that Russians do not idealize their leaders and in fact express a great deal of hostility toward them if they abuse power or govern poorly. How would Gorer, now deceased, explain Gorbachev's reforms? Well, swaddling is very rare nowadays . . .

Margaret Mead's *Soviet Attitudes Toward Authority* (1955 [orig. 1951]) is in my view an example of a more useful style of national character study because rather than attempt to characterize a nation of millions along a few psychological dimensions, she targets one problem, as the title expresses. Her analysis of Soviet authoritarianism, while more sensitive and diverse than Gorer's, nevertheless confuses Stalinism with the Soviet personality: a vicious dictatorship, imposed by force, is in no way dependent upon a culture/personality configuration, but arises from political history along with economic conditions.

Partly in response to critics, the group at Columbia responded with improved methodology. The remarkable volume *The Study of Culture at a Distance* (Mead and Metraux 1953) outlines in great detail the need and rationale for studying cultures even when fieldwork is impossible, through interviews with expatriates, written essays by informants, analysis of literature and folklore, film analysis, projective testing, and other methods. Certainly, a particular culture's inaccessibility should not necessitate a total anthropological and ethnographic "hands off" policy; this volume shows how some of the methodological problems inherent in such a venture can be overcome. Many interviews are reprinted verbatim in a spirit of scientific collegiality and openness. Past mistakes and misunderstandings are clarified or defended. French, Chinese, Italian, Polish, Russian, Syrian, Jewish, Thai, Japanese, and British culture and character are discussed at various points in the volume, always in the context of illustrating a particular method, such as projective testing or working with informants. It is a shame that this volume on method did not appear a decade earlier, because it seems to have appeared too late to defuse criticisms of the entire national character enterprise. The last one in this (the Columbia group) tradition is Gorer's *Exploring English Character* (1955), a vast improvement over his Russian work: of course, Gorer is English.

Although the particular type of study discussed up to this point fizzled out in the fifties, efforts to characterize populations psychologically continued apace. In anthropology, researchers saved their psychologizing for the somewhat safer rural preindustrial societies with which they had long been associated; I will review just a few of these later in this chapter. Psychological characterizations of the citizens of nation-states fell to scholars in other disciplines: history, sociology, and social psychology, as in the following examples.

American Character: Other Treatments

The sociologist David Riesman's (1950) *The Lonely Crowd* is a study of American national character, but of a different sort: Riesman's manipulative "other-directed" outwardly conforming individualist does not create society—society creates him. The essay seems more modern because he is writing on the self rather than personality. His analysis of the inherent conflict between American individualism and societal pressure to conform set the tone for later essays on the American self and character.

Another sociologist, Philip Slater (1970), argues that the much-vaunted American individualism is more myth than reality, and that we are essentially doomed if we do not develop more sociocentric and interdependent selves—in a sense, a return to "tribal" community. The French anthropologist Hervé Varenne (1977) studied a small midwestern American town and found that individualism, as understood by his informants, always implied community: people did not see themselves as individualists in the sense of being separate from their community but as an integral part of it. Fun, happiness, and love were categories he found to be most central in the expression of midwestern American individualism.

Arguably the most significant studies of American national character in recent years are those of the Freudian socialist cultural historian Christopher Lasch, *The Culture of Narcissism* (1979) and *The Minimal Self* (1984). For Lasch, the middle- and upper-class individualism so valued by Riesman and deplored by Slater has become perverted into narcissism, a dangerous lack of a strong sense of self. Narcissism is not, as commonly thought, egotistical self-love; in fact, it is closer to self-hatred but is most accurately an anxious preoccupation or obsession with self. Lasch's study is a configurationalist national character study of the finest sort: it avoids the simplistic reductionism of the postwar studies and focuses on self rather than personality.

Americans reach adulthood with diminished and blurry selves because they are raised by parents who all too often place their own needs and gratification before their children's; accordingly, these children are never certain that they are truly loved and valued by their parents. A healthy self is built on a foundation of such valuing and love; without it, children grow into narcissistic adults, always striving for the admiration and love of others, inevitably disappointed, never satisfied. Lest the reader spot this description as simple childhood determinism, I must stress that Lasch situates the family and its child-training styles firmly and adaptively in a historical, social, and economic context. The particular form of the American family is an adaptation to the capitalist mode of industrial production, which removes fathers from their homes, limiting their role in the socialization of their children; mothers themselves often have little or no experience with children and so rely on experts, failing "to provide the child with a sense of security" (Lasch 1979:176). Thus the family and its child-rearing practices are an *adaptive* response to a set of specific socioeconomic conditions. Furthermore, the selves produced from this familial environment are rewarded by the culture, in LeVine's sense (see Chapter 1). Narcissistic selves, according to Lasch, fit nicely into late twentieth-century capitalist society. "Narcissism appears realistically to represent the best way of coping with the tensions and anxieties of modern life, and the prevailing social conditions therefore tend to bring out narcissistic traits that are present, in varying degrees, in everyone" (Lasch 1979:50). National character studies like Lasch's are important and valuable: his theory combines the best of psychoanalysis, Marxism, configurationalism, and psychocultural adaptationalism; in addition, it provoked a spirited and productive debate about the nature of the American character which still continues.

National Character: Other Approaches

Modal personality and national character studies of the peoples of other modern nations also continue to be published. They range from careful scientific studies to glorified travel books. Social psychologist David McClelland (1961) is an unabashed psychological reductionist whose *The Achieving Society* is a comparative overview of what makes societies tick: societies achieve a high level of economic development if their citizens have a high degree of "n ach"—need for achievement. Americans score high on this personality characteristic, while Russians score low, but high on "need for affiliation." In still another study of Soviet modal personality, sociologist Alex Inkeles (1968) confirms McClelland's finding in his study of 3,000 former Soviet citizens, adding a strong need for dependence and low need for autonomy and approval; Inkeles, however, sees modal personality as stemming from social conditions rather than the other way around. Both McClelland and Inkeles employ an array of scientific methods to arrive at their conclusions, so their books are a great improvement over some of the previous studies.

Many modern statements of national character, however, are not based on any scientific research, but spring instead from the humanities; they are products of imagination and experience. For example, the writer and pan-Europeanist Luigi Barzini has written about the national character of the Italians (1964) and the Europeans (1983), focusing in the latter study on the British, Germans, French, Italians, Dutch, and Americans. Concentrating especially on history and politics, Barzini describes the British as "imperturbable," the Germans as "mutable," the French as "quarrelsome," the Italians as "flexible," the Dutch as "careful," and the Americans as "baffling"; of course, his elucidations of these labels are not so pat. Bernstein (1990) describes the French again as quarrelsome, increasingly fragmented, and fascinated with power. Such accounts appear with great regularity, and vary greatly in quality.

National character and modal personality studies of modern nation-states are probably necessary in spite of their faults; a few have clearly been valuable. In any case, they will continue to be written for good or ill, because they fill the need to understand the social environment. From an anthropological vantage point, however, they present such enormous methodological problems that they have been all but abandoned in favor of community studies or studies of specific settings, organizations, or occupations, along with the traditional ethnographies of non-Western preindustrial societies.

Modal Selves in Small-Scale Societies

Cora DuBois's research on Alor rested on much firmer methodological ground than, say, Gorer's work on the Russians: a year-long participant observational study of the entire population a village numbering 600 can provide the basis for generalizations far more easily and reliably if it is part of a culture of 20,000 people than if it is part of a culture of 20,000,000. When I visited the Micronesian islands of Yap, population about 5,000, I was struck by the boundedness of it; an interviewer working with enough assistants could interview almost everyone, ensuring a reasonable degree of validity for conclusions concerning Yapese modal personality. On neighboring atolls such as Ulithi, the problem is simplified even further.

However, even within such small-scale societies, there is still quite a bit of variation in modal personality, as DuBois herself discovered on Alor. For example, Anthony Wallace (1952) published an important treatise on the modal personality of the Tuscarora, an Iroquois group in western New York state. He analyzed the results of Rorschach tests from seventy individuals, and found that only twenty-six individuals, or 37 percent, fit the resulting modal personality profile on all relevant dimensions. This figure is often cited as a caution in studying modal personality even in compact, small-scale societies; partly as a result, anthropologists have since tended to confine their psychological characterizations to nonstatistical observations within a larger ethnographic context. But the cautionary note was misleading and unnecessary: if one adds to Wallace's modal core group another sixteen individuals who *almost* fit the profile, a very sound and realistic addition, then *60 percent* of his sample exhibit Tuscarora modal personality, a very impressive finding, with a very different methodological implication.

Many anthropologists characterize their informants psychologically, although the term "modal personality" is now rarely used within cultural anthropology. A quick look at some examples will show how unavoidable ethnographic psychologizing is. It is essentially impossible to describe human beings and their behavior without making some statements having to do with individual psychology; and when one characterizes the behaviors of a number of informants, deliberately or inadvertently, individual characterizations become group typifications at some level. Human behavior is at once sociocultural and psychological, always existing on two levels.

Some recent studies are designed as research in culture and individual psychology, and generalize explicitly about a group's modal personality. Such an ethnography is the cultural psychiatrist Robert Levy's (1973) *Tahitians: Mind and Experience in the Society Islands,* an innovative attempt to understand Tahitian life along the psychocultural dimensions of self, cognition, emotion, and morality. After sensitive examination of Tahitian sexuality, supernaturalism, friendship, drinking, socialization, adoption, and many other areas that bear on an understanding of modal psychology, Levy (1973:491) concludes that Tahitian selves "are smoothly integrated": individuals are adapted to the culture and the community; internally, ideas, feelings, motives, self-images, and the like, are well-integrated within an organized psychological system. Behavior is graceful, symptoms of stress and anxiety are infrequent, and people are comfortable in a variety of situations. Psychiatric probing, however, reveals anxiety regarding separation and dependency, along with anger and a fear of its consequences, and a little paranoia. Levy (1973:502–503) also speculates on the differing selves of men and women, given their different roles in the culture. Such a brief outline, of course, cannot begin to do justice to more than 500 pages of penetrating psychocultural analysis. *Tahitians* has influenced many subsequent studies and has had a substantial impact on ethnography itself.

Unlike Levy's book, Colin Turnbull's much-misunderstood book *The Mountain People* (1972) is ostensibly not about modal personality, but is nonetheless representative of much of anthropology in that, intended or not, it turns out to have quite a lot to say on the subject. Best known for his studies of the Mbuti Pygmies of Zaire, Turnbull was looking for another remote group of foragers, mountain and savannah hunters, to compare with the rain-forest Mbuti: such a people, he thought, were the Ik (previously and mistakenly called Teuso) of northern Uganda, never before studied ethnographically. Fieldwork was a disaster: the Ik had recently been prevented from hunting in their traditional area, which was now a game park for tourists. They were being forced to farm, even though they had little interest in farming, and even less knowledge about how to go about it; and all of this during one of the worst droughts of modern times. In short, they were literally starving to death, and this situation had brought about massive changes in culture and behavior.

Although *The Mountain People* is more of an essay about the human condition than an ethnography of a culture, the reader learns a great deal about the adaptation of self and behavior to culture, and the latter's adaptation to the ecology. Turnbull suggests that culture is a thin varnish, a papery exoskeleton, whose very existence depends on at least minimal satisfaction of the basic animal needs for food and water. Take these essentials away, and culture disappears along with them. The Ik had undergone a metamorphosis from a cooperative society based on reciprocity and ritual to a mere collection of mutually antagonistic self-centered individuals, lacking love, goodness, passion, or religion. Children were turned out at age three to fend for themselves in predatory packs; food was literally snatched from the mouths of the ill or elderly. The Ik had turned into a group "as unfriendly, uncharitable, inhospitable and generally mean as any people can be" (Turnbull

1972:32). This is how they *had* to be, for such qualities as friendliness and hospitality arise to preserve society but are dysfunctional qualities when society breaks down; then, *individual* survival is all that matters, and society be damned.

With some hyperbole, Turnbull sees in the Ik a warning for us in the West, with our individualistic pursuit of personal pleasure with little thought for the consequences for society, the environment, or posterity. More relevant to the immediate concerns of this book, however, is another message: selves, personalities, and behavior do not arise full-blown from individual physiologies, but from cultural foundations; if the culture is damaged and fragmented, so too will be the selves and personalities it supports.

I do not wish to leave you with the impression, however, that a particular sort of culture, for example, a tropical savannah cattle-herding culture with a small amount of maize cultivation, or a particular set of cultural variables, will produce a particular type of person. There is more to it than that, and anthropologists and others are just beginning to sort it out. History, ethnic tradition, microecology, and sociobiology are but four sources of variation out of many that might operate even when cultures appear to be quite similar. A comparison of two such similar cultures is most instructive in this regard; like Turnbull's study, these two ethnographic projects typify much ethnography in that they are not specifically about individual or group psychology. Yet they each include a near-configurationalist characterization in the very titles of their central monographs. I refer to Robert Dentan's *The Semai: A Nonviolent People of Malaya* (second, "fieldwork" edition, 1979) and Napoleon Chagnon's *Yanomamo: The Fierce People* (third edition, 1983), two of the most popular ethnographies for classroom teaching in recent years. While the "nonviolent" characterization of the Semai is not a self-characterization (although Dentan [1979:55] does note that the Semai do conceive of themselves as nonviolent), while the "fierce" characterization of the Yanomamo is their own, in both cases the usages of outsider (ethnographer) and insider (native) appear to be quite congruent.

The two ethnographers have very different theoretical orientations but are both meticulous in their fieldwork. Neither is a psychological anthropologist in the usual sense. Yet one of the principal "messages" embedded in each study, in fact a primary reason these books are selected as texts in undergraduate "intro" courses, is a message about modal psychology: these folks are "opposites," one very violent and the other not at all.

Both writers are careful to base their assessment on observable behavior, rather than on data concerning inner mental life. Dentan (1979:133) is clear: "Semai are not nonviolent because they have 'nonviolent personalities,' whatever that means." But they are definitely nonviolent within a purely Semai cultural context. Only one Semai murder, out of a population of about 15,000, occurred between 1963 and 1976, and that one involved a non-Semai shopkeeper. Semai do not hit children, pets, or one another. They run from potential violence. Their gentle manner is supported by the concept of *punan*, a condition of accident-proneness resulting from anything even remotely or potentially violent—even something as mild as turning down a request for a favor (the Polynesian word "taboo," or *tapu*, usually translated as "forbidden," comes from the same "pu" root).

The Yanomamo of Venezuela, on the other hand, engage in frequent observable violent behavior. At least 25 percent of all men die violently; one village studied by Chagnon was raided twenty-five times in just fifteen months (Chagnon 1983:5, 7). Men beat and even kill their wives; even their magic is violent, often concerning attempts to kill and devour the souls of their enemies and their children. Man-to-man violence is culturally graded in a hierarchy, moving from chest-pounding to side-slapping to club-fighting to raiding to the ultimate form of violence, *nomohori*, or treachery. Yanomamo value and reward aggression, fierceness, and hotheadedness in men. One cannot become a headman without being especially *waiteri*, or "fierce" (Chagnon 1983:5); furthermore, such headmen are likely to possess more wives and hence more children (think of the implications). Creation myths support this image of fierceness (Chagnon 1983:95).

Aside from this enormous character difference, the Semai and Yanomamo share many basic material traits, which would lead many, certainly an ecological determinist, to expect rather similar psychological traits, especially if personality is seen as straight adaptational outcome. Both groups are despised aborigines in emerging Third World developing nation-states dominated by other groups. Both groups are small: about 15,000 Semai versus about 12,000 Yanomamo. Both inhabit lowland tropical rain forest punctuated by mountains ascending to no more than 3,000 feet, although the Semai in general live a little higher up than the Yanomamo, partly to avoid the Malays and Chinese who live in the lowest elevations. Both groups are semisedentary and moved into their present locations from elsewhere (although they did not travel far), driven there by both internal and external pressures. Both rely primarily on slash-and-burn horticulture for their subsistence, the Semai emphasizing dryland rice, and the Yanomamo plantains, but both groups also invest a good deal of energy in hunting and gathering. The list of similarities goes on and on.

Clayton A. Robarchek (1977), an anthropologist who has carried out extensive fieldwork among the Semai, was also struck by the many similarities to Amazonian groups like the Yanomamo. As a result, he recently completed another stint in the field, this time among the very violent Waorani of Amazonian Ecuador, who "are perhaps the most violent society ever reported," enduring "a homicide rate on the order of 60%" (Robarchek 1989:916). The comparative conclusions should be most enlightening and challenging.

How did they evolve psychoculturally to be so different? Is cultural adaptationalist theory wrong? This apparent paradox cannot be resolved, but it does underscore the complexity of human psychology and culture. First, the violent and nonviolent images are emphases rather than absolutes. When Malays conscripted Semai to fight Communist revolutionaries in the early 1950s, the Semai warriors killed with abandon. Dentan (1979:58–59) argues that this violence was possible because the Communists had killed Semai counterinsurgents' kin and that Semai were removed completely from their familiar cultural environment and ordered to kill, resulting "in a sort of insanity which they call 'blood drunkenness.'" Many of the films about Yanomamo life made by Chagnon and his colleague Timothy Asch show Yanomamo men as loving, playful fathers and tender companionate husbands, a far cry from their violent image portrayed in his books and other films. People in both groups feel all human emotions, obviously, and at least have the potential for every sort of human behavior, but their cultures reward certain behaviors and styles, while denigrating others.

There are myriad possible reasons for Yanomamo violence. The men inhale powerful hallucinogenic drugs several times a week—could this practice bear on their violence? Or does it stem from conflict over hunting territories? Or from population increase? In turn, Semai nonviolence may have evolved as an adaptive response to the more numerous and more powerful Malays and Chinese. It must be stressed that *both* systems "work," both are adaptive; it is a mistake to think that broadly similar conditions will produce similar modal personalities, unless *everything* else is equal—and it never is. As I discussed in Chapter 1, Hallpike (1986) has argued that within a particular set of environmental and historical constraints, all sorts of arrangements will work well enough to persist, arrangements which might even be as different as those of the Semai and the Yanomamo.

Normality

To speak of national character or modal personality is to speak of normality, whether "normal" is taken to mean "ideal," "representative," "average," "typical," or statistically most common. Was not Ruth Benedict suggesting that it is "normal" for a Dobuan to be paranoid? A normal upper-middle-class American is narcissistic, with a high need for achievement. A normal, albeit starving, Ik is self-centered. Normal Semai are nonviolent, normal Yanomamo highly aggressive. And so on. The researchers who studied all these groups and reached their typifying conclusions were of course not really talking about normality at all. Benedict and Lasch, writing respectively about the Dobuans and upper-middle-class Americans, were in fact suggesting that these *cultures* themselves were neurotic, thereby producing neurotic individuals. We are left with normal neurotics, or neurotic normals, an oxymoron in either case. Turnbull's Ik were a sick, dying society, rendering questions of normality irrelevant. Nevertheless, it is extremely difficult to separate the concepts of national character, modal personality, or any other typification from the concept of normality.

The semantic connotations of normality include a moral dimension. Normal good, abnormal bad. We like normal people. Normality is healthy, positive, acceptable. We want our kids to be normal kids who grow up to be normal adults. Although the concept is a Western one, I suspect that the basic sentiment, however covert, is universal. Because the term "normality" is so imprecise, and because it is at least implicitly a value judgment, anthropologists generally eschew the label in their writings. I suggest that there is a proper place for normality as a concept in psychocultural analysis, however, and will return to this point shortly.

I hope I have shown thus far that there is a use for statistical measurements of central tendency with regard to psychological characteristics of a population. If one is speaking statistically, the term "modal" is perfectly accurate when employed to characterize a central tendency in a distribution of some measured quality, although it is not widely used outside the field of science. Alternatively, "normative" is a useful word when referring to behavior that follows widely accepted social norms (rules or standards).

If we take the lead from psychiatry, "normal" and "normality" can properly refer to behavior that is adaptive, and/or to a self that is well-adjusted to the environment. Psychocultural adaptation is the adjustment of individual selves, their behaviors and personalities, to their cultural environments and through their culture, to the physical environment. A culture provides satisfying lives to those people who willingly conform to its rules, norms, and standards. These hypothetical willing conformists are *normal* in the sense that they are well-adjusted, relatively satisfied—in short, adapted to their society and, indirectly, their overall environment. The moral connotations of the word "normal," in fact, probably stem from a psychocultural reality: persons who are not normal, or at least are not perceived by other social actors as normal, are felt at least vaguely to be threats. Since they are not well-adjusted to the sociocultural system, since they are poorly adapted to the culture around them, they threaten the viable functioning of the whole system, thereby threatening each observing actor in the community, who then labels them "crazy," "dangerous," "criminal," *not normal,* in whatever term or manner is culturally appropriate. At the very least, uneasiness, avoidance, or possibly amusement or even abuse might be culturally acceptable responses. Norms of tolerance and intolerance are relevant here. If a wide range of selves and behaviors can exist within a particular society without especially affecting the food supply or the viability of the social system, as in some tropical foraging societies and in pluralistic capitalist societies, tolerance will be broad. If unusual ideas or patterns of behavior threaten, or are perceived to threaten, the food supply and thus survival itself, as in rural Liberia, or the social system, as in communitarian religious communities or in, say, Communist North Korea, the range of tolerance will be quite narrow.

Conformity is at once a necessity and a danger. Adaptation requires a degree of conformity. On the other hand, if everyone slavishly and rigidly conformed within a given society, that society would extinguish, since no environment is unchanging, and a society of automatons would lack the mental and behavioral flexibility to adjust to external change.

Deviance

"Abnormality," then, is *positive*, not negative, in its cultural-evolutionary impact on society, although its impact on the stigmatized individual is generally negative. I am not referring, of course, to those individuals and traits at the very tips of the two tails of a distribution, extreme psychosis or serial murder, for example, but rather to behaviors and psychological dispositions outside the mode. Genotypic variation alone guarantees the existence of some "abnormality" in every society, at least in a statistical sense; factor in differing life experiences, and you can rest assured that there are plenty of abnormal people, exhibiting all kinds of abnormal behavior, in every society—fortunately for the human species. By definition, there is *always* a mode and always people (or personalities or behaviors) outside the mode, no matter how authoritarian, restrictive, or intolerant the society; every distribution has two tails and a middle. Recall a basic assumption presented in the first chapter: selves are genelike, in the sense that they are sources of variation within each culture, wellsprings of cultural vitality. For example, there is a world of difference between the ecologically based seasonal patterns of tropical slash-and-burn cultivation and the continual daily patterns of a factory assembly line. Wholly different attitudes and behaviors are required of individuals if they are to succeed in either "work environment." When factories are introduced into an agrarian society, only those individuals—those "abnormal" individuals—possessing "new" personality traits will last for very long in the factory.

Terminological and semantic problems are the flip side of those discussed above concerning normality. Unfortunately, parallel terms are not available in English. Two useful neologisms would help solve the problem. "Abmodal" could accurately refer to individuals, traits, dispositions, or behaviors statistically outside the mode or central tendency in a distribution. "Abnormative" could refer to behavior that does not follow social norms. I offer these wishfully, since they are not employed in the social science literature at this time. In fact, the usual terms, "deviance" and "deviant," come from sociology: they are just starting to be used in anthropology (see Edgerton 1976; Freilich, Raybeck, and Savishinsky 1991) and are rarely used in psychology, where "abnormality" remains the usual term. I will not utilize "deviant" to refer to selves, an unsatisfactory usage in numerous respects, but will use it to refer to behavior; "deviance" refers to patterns of deviant behavior. As in sociology, I will attempt to confine the deviant label to statistical deviation only, whether measured or simply implied.

Like "normality," the word "abnormality" connotes a moral quality, suggesting a negative attribute. No one wants to be perceived as abnormal; many persons even try to conceal from the community ideas, attitudes, emotions, and other private states that they themselves consider abnormal, or believe others would consider abnormal: homosexual lust, for example, or murderous rage. Unfortunately, the term "deviance" does not circumvent this problem, even though sociologists use it in a nonjudgmental and value-free fashion—or at least intend to. I have frequently encountered gay students, or students with alcoholic parents, who bristle at the suggestion that homosexuality or alcohol abuse is deviant. "I'm jut as normal as anyone." "My parents aren't bad; they just drink too much." To the general public, even the college-educated public, deviance apparently implies badness, sociological disclaimers notwithstanding. These pages are not the place to solve this problem, but I do want you to be aware of it. In the social and behavioral sciences, the use of the terms "deviant" and "deviance" implies no moral judgment whatever: it simply refers to behavior that is either *not* modal or *not* normative.

The astute reader has perhaps noticed a possible contradiction in the preceding paragraphs. I have argued variously that both normality and abnormality are adaptive. Normal people are well-adjusted to their culture. Abnormal or deviant behavior is functionally requisite as a source of variation which cultures draw upon in responding to change. There is really no contradiction here, because each usage refers to a different theoretical level. Normality refers to adaptation at the individual level, within personal biographies; deviance is a part of adaptation at the societal level, although as noted, much deviance is not at all adaptive. Deviance is not a unitary phenomenon and so cannot be characterized as adaptive or maladaptive in all times and places. But it is clear that certain forms of deviant behavior benefit society enormously, while other forms threaten to destroy it.

The classic anthropological statement on the subject of abnormality is still the last word, reflecting the cultural relativism that is such an important component of what cultural anthropology has to offer. I refer to Ruth Benedict's (1934a) famous article "Anthropology and the Abnormal," in which she argues for the cultural relativity of concepts of normality and abnormality. Her thesis is deceptively simple: certain behaviors, and the individuals exhibiting those behaviors, considered abnormal in one culture might very well be considered perfectly normal in another culture; conversely, actions and persons that are normal, appropriate, and positively functional in one society may be seen as deviant, pathological, and threatening in some other culture. A Western salesperson would be perceived as dangerously aggressive in Inuit society. Sambia initiation would be criminal child abuse in the United States. A woman hears voices. Should she be institutionalized as psychotic? In the United States she would be, or at least heavily drugged. But in many other times and places, she might be considered a religious visionary—or a witch. Benedict refers primarily to adjustment rather than deep, perhaps neurological, disturbance, although she suggests that even schizophrenics may occupy valuable roles such as becoming a shaman or religious practitioner. For Benedict, the key is whether or not the disturbed, or potentially disturbed, individual receives positive support from the culture: if not, suffering and dysfunctional behavior could result; if affirmative support is received, the "abnormal" might be able to contribute to the community and live a useful life. Not in every case, and not in every culture, but often enough to suggest a reexamination of our theories of deviance and disorder, the subject of the next chapter.

SUGGESTED READINGS

Ruth Benedict's *Patterns of Culture* (1934b) is the first major configurationalist work; in addition, the final chapter presents many of the same ideas discussed in "Anthropology and the Abnormal," written in the same year. *Patterns of Culture* is important in understanding the theoretical underpinnings of the later "national character" studies. Benedict's *The Chrysanthemum and the Sword* (1946), a study of Japanese national character, is the best of that series. Christopher Lasch's *The Culture of Narcissism* (1979), a withering critique of contemporary American character, is a modern national character study that shows just how significant such an endeavor, if done carefully, can be.

Ethnographic studies of small-scale non-Western societies that bear on modal personality are many and varied. Cora DuBois's *The People of Alor* (1961 [orig. 1944]) is a classic which remains very readable; I particularly recommend Part 2, which includes Chapter 9, an essay on the determinants of Alorese personality, by the psychoanalyst Abram Kardiner, although the entire study is fascinating and full of surprises. Robert Levy's *Tahitians: Mind and Experience in the Society Islands* (1973) is an intricate psychocultural account of a changing culture. Colin Turnbull's *The Mountain People* (1972), not intended as a study in cultural psychology, will probably be one of the most disturbing books you ever read: it is about you as well as the starving Ik. Robert Dentan's *The Semai: A Nonviolent People of Malaya* (1979) and Napoleon Chagnon's *Yanomamo: The Fierce People* (1983), neither of which is a study in cultural psychology per se, carefully depict two cultures that, while occupying very similar environments, nevertheless contrast starkly in character and behavior.

5

Disorder:
Mental and Behavioral

Early in Chapter 1 I mentioned that human beings apparently crave order and explanation, perhaps as a natural result of the evolution of consciousness and the brain. We seem to need some notion that there *is* an explanation, or a natural or social order, whether we personally grasp it or not. We crave *cosmos,* or order, and fear its evil twin, *chaos.* Perhaps this primordial inclination underlies some of the fear and loathing associated with behavioral disorder (culturally defined), a vast category subsuming various sexualities, so-called mental illness, and the use ("abuse") of feared "substances."

Confusion reigns supreme in matters of culturally perceived disorder, both "on the street" (the new home for many Americans with disorderly behavior), as well as in the groves of academe. Biomedical practitioners and pharmaceutical companies hawk psychotropic drugs like so many patent medicines. Craven politicians push for absurd jail sentences for users of ancient and widespread "substances" and "narcotics." Televangelists condemn "perverts" to Hell. A gigantic "addiction" industry springs up, long on righteousness but short on science. It includes "Twelve Step" and other self-help programs, which are generally overtly religious or at least quasi-religious ("spiritual") and paradoxically against drugs but in favor of medical explanation; programs abound for virtually every type of behavioral disorder, including alcoholism, drug "abuse," hyperemotionality, "sexaholism," "workaholism," obesity, and dozens of others. The United States sometimes seems to be a huge carnival of disorder and self-help, with shamans and prophets seeking new converts and rallying followers, all promising comfort, solace, and a better life.

Mental Illness versus Behavioral Disorder

Let us begin with some semantic difficulties that have important philosophical consequences. Knowledgeable individuals these days speak confidently of the "mentally ill," rather than the "evil," "possessed," "mad," or "crazy." But the word "mental" refers to the *mind,* something without a physical location or material substance. Like the self, mind is an abstract label for some aspect of brain function. The term itself, along with the concept of mental illness, reflects the medieval philosophical dualism of mind versus body, an opposition with theological roots. In theory the term "mental illness" applies to personality problems or behavioral disorder without known physical cause. Hence a disorder believed to be physiological in origin, Alzheimer's for example, is technically a *brain* disease, not a mental illness. In reality, neither etiology nor usage is clear. Many bodily illnesses and disorders have no known cause, yet are unambiguously labeled as physical. Why is the brain treated differently? On the other hand, many behavioral disorders without any known physical cause—"alcoholism" is one good example—are labeled as physical diseases, at least in the United States.

Put simply, we don't know what we're talking about; that is, we confuse mind, brain, personality, self, and behavior, all of which should be kept analytically and conceptually distinct. When physicians, psychotherapists, behavioral scientists, or laypersons speak of "mental illness," are they talking about deviant behavior, personality disorder, deranged thinking evidenced in deranged utterances, or brain disease of some sort? For consistency's sake and for the purposes of this chapter—and of course, because I firmly believe it to be the best approach—I will avoid the use of the meaningless term "mental illness" altogether, and employ the term "disease" or "illness" only if there is an established or at least implied physical cause, whether in the brain or elsewhere. If the cause is unknown, the terms "personality disorder" and "behavioral disorder" will be used, consistent with the "LeVinean" definitions of "personality" and "behavior" proposed in Chapter 1. Behavioral disorder, observable to members of the community, is an *indicator* of personality disorder or a disorder of the self, which is otherwise hidden from others. If personality organization serves as a symbolic encoding device that intervenes "between environmental conditions and behavioral response" (LeVine 1982:5), then personality disorder suggests a *dis*organization in the brain, a symbolic *mis*coding, that produces disorderly behavior. I should probably note at this point that, although disorders of the self certainly exist—Lasch's pathological narcissism, discussed in the preceding chapter, is a good example—no one of whom I am aware uses the term "self illness" or similar terms, but rather "personality disorder," and I will follow suit whenever necessary.

Just as culture cannot be disentangled from personality (or self) because of their coevolution and interdependence, neither can culture be separated from personality disorder and/or behavioral disorder, as Ruth Benedict (1934a) stated so persuasively nearly sixty years ago. Behavioral disorder, a little paradoxically, is not without order. Culture patterns disorderly behavior as well as orderly behavior; the most disturbed individuals of necessity express their culture, even if in bizarre ways. What else, after all, could they do? Furthermore, culture patterns the response of others—those whose behavior is ordered rather than disordered. Theory, labeling, response, treatment—all are shaped by culture. Our own approach to disorder, including science itself, is not immune to these powerful cultural forces.

The American Biomedical Model

I mentioned earlier that human beings appear to have some sort of inner need for order, both intellectual and behavioral, suggesting that this craving for order was an outcome of the evolution of neurological consciousness. People thus seek explanations for natural phenomena and life experiences: if a commonsensical material or empirical explanation is unavailable, insufficient, or unsatisfying in some way, other culturally patterned explanations are sought. Generally, these other explanations are of the sort we in the West label supernatural, magical, mythical, or religious.

Every culture provides for its followers a belief system that orders the social and physical universe. In small-scale nonliterate preindustrial societies, these belief systems are relatively unitary and shared for the most part by all members of the community. In normatively pluralistic societies such as the United States, however, various paradigms compete for intellectual allegiance in the understanding of phenomena. Science and religion dominate belief in the West, but magical, folkloric, and ideological (e.g., political) mental models also compete for intellectual dominance. Often different sorts of questions are addressed by different paradigms; in this case the various models coexist peacefully within an individual. If you or a loved one becomes seriously ill, for example, you seek a scientific, medical explanation. You learn, perhaps, that your friend or relative has an untreatable form of cancer. Science has thus provided you with a rational, empirical explanation: your loved one has a "disease" labeled "cancer." Upon request, lengthier explanations, along with literature and objective test results, can be mustered and presented to you. For some, all of this is sufficient, but for many it is not. Science does not tell you *why* your friend or relative, rather than someone else, is terminally ill—but religion does. It is her "time," it is "God's will"; she is going to "Heaven," and so on. Both types of explanation provide order for the inquirer; one explains "how," the other suggests "why."

In the United States, more than in any other society even among Western nations, the biomedical model has become the culturally preferred model for explaining disorder and deviance (see Conrad and Schneider 1980). Unusual behaviors are seen as "symptoms" of some deeper sickness, impairment, or disease, frequently biochemical in nature. Deviance is thus *rationalized*, brought under intellectual and, ultimately, practical control. It can then, the reasoning goes, be researched using the methods of the natural, rather than the behavioral or social, sciences. The deviant (behavior or person) can be diagnosed and treated, often with medication. Through this process of medicalization, slim girls are redefined as "anorexic," overweight people are treated by "bariatric" medical specialists, slow learners become "dyslexic," and so on. Many forms of deviance and disorder have already been medicalized, including behavioral disorder ("mental illness"), homosexuality (although it was officially demedicalized in 1974, as noted in Chapter 3), drug and alcohol abuse, gambling, and fidgetiness and attention problems ("hyperkinesis" or ADHD [Attention Deficit Hyperactivity Disorder]). Others, such as learning disabilities, are currently midstream in the process of being medicalized (Erchak and Rosenfeld 1989).

It is important to put aside for a moment your everyday received notions about medicine, doctors, science, disease, and so forth, and realize that such terms as "disease," "sickness," and "illness" are culturally defined. Each culture defines what is considered sickness and what is not. If a certain pattern or condition is very common, such as obesity in Polynesia, it is not considered to be deviant, and certainly not sick. The excessive consumption of alcohol is considered to be a symptom of the "disease of alcoholism" in the United States, but not in Europe. Even physical disease is a culturally defined category: from the point of view of "nature," or coldly rational science, certain diseases are purely natural process at work, a competition among organisms. The invading organism dwells within the host, without evil intent or indeed any intent at all, and breaks it down, perhaps killing it. The process is called disease.

The medicalization of physical conditions rarely presents a problem, however—at least not for behavioral scientists. It is the medicalization of behavior, disordered or not, that I am concerned with here. To paraphrase the notorious critic of behavioral medicalization, Thomas Szasz (1963), himself a psychiatrist: physical illness happens to us, whereas mental illness is something we do. In other words, it is *behavior* that is sick, since the "mind" cannot be seen. Such distinctions matter little, however, in the medicalized America of the 1990s: they essentially lose their meaning as medicine controls the way we think about the world, our lives, and our problems (Stein 1990). As biomedicine engulfs larger and larger areas of behavior, defining and ultimately treating problems both physical and "mental," it becomes harder and harder to distinguish real suffering from imaginary, or physiological from culturally shaped disorder.

Critics of the medicalization of behavior, deviant or otherwise, quickly learn that there is more at stake than the mere intellectual critique of a competing theory. The biomedical model has become dogma—moral orthodoxy. It is ironic that a paradigm originally adopted for behavior to destigmatize deviants by viewing them in a scientific, morally neutral, nonjudgmental fashion (as in the case of homosexuality, mental illness, or alcoholism) should itself become a morally righteous model. To disagree with the biomedical model is to be labeled a heretic: you are immoral, irresponsible, or just plain ignorant. Grant money is difficult to obtain if the "correct" paradigm is not followed. Scientific articles critical of the establishment view of deviance can only be published in the journals read by fellow heretics, never to be seen or read by those being criticized. For example, sociological critiques of the medicalization of deviance are published in various sociology journals, but rarely if ever in medical journals.

What is true in the scientific community is also true in large sectors of the general population, especially among the well-educated. It is nearly impossible to discuss seriously the notion that drug addiction, for example, is not necessarily a "disease" requiring medical treatment, although it is clearly a behavioral disorder. Liberal, progressive people generally will dismiss such a proposition impatiently, believing that the disease concept of addiction has been well-established by "science." This view has become "politically correct." Interestingly, the same people would be horrified at the suggestion that homosexual behavior *was* a mental illness, although such a notion was widely accepted, even in educated circles, only two decades ago!

Surprisingly, anthropologists have participated very little in the ongoing critique of the biomedical model of disorder and deviance, other than presenting accounts of various syndromes found in particular cultures, or lamely suggesting that physicians and psychiatrists should take "culture" more seriously into account in diagnosis and treatment. Most medical anthropologists, in fact, apparently embrace the paradigm to a greater or lesser degree, uncritically employing terms such as "mental health" and "substance abuse." However, some have begun studying American medicine as a cultural system and as part of the American belief system (DiGiacomo 1987; Stein 1990), or what Atwood Gaines and Robert Hahn (1985:3) call the Domain of Biomedicine: "Practitioners of Biomedicine assume as . . . true their own . . . 'science' which professes the cellular, even biochemical basis of pathology. Anthropologists . . . have been struck by this reductionism which excludes . . . cultural and social forces as wellsprings of human behavior." Sociologists, especially social constructionists, social psychologists, and—again, surprisingly—a few psychiatrists, have been the most vocal and persistent critics, although their voices, drowned out by the roar of the medical juggernaut, are rarely heard. I will review the critiques of a few of them at appropriate spots later in the chapter.

The culture of the United States and the subcultures of its major institutions, including biomedicine, can and should be studied critically and anthropologically, employing the same objective and relativist lens ethnographers use to study exotic faraway cultures. A study of the cultural foundations of self and behavior demands a critique of biomedicine along the way.

A case study will illustrate many of the points made in the preceding passages. When a "new" disorder or disease emerges from the firmament, as it were, and when this disorder is claimed by medical researchers and practitioners to have a biological basis, the chances are excellent that the disorder is socioculturally shaped. Biophysiological disorders that *affect or determine behavior* in general do not suddenly appear at a particular time and place. Anorexia is an alleged illness that can actually bring about someone's death. A search for a physical cause continues to this day; yet anorexia is a disorder of Western, primarily American, culture, affecting mainly girls and young women, with varying rates across groups (ballet dancers, for example, have the highest rate). It emerges only in a culture that defines appearance as extremely important and fat as ugly. Yes, newly discovered or at least newly labeled physical diseases do indeed surface from time to time: Human Immunovirus

(HIV) Disease (AIDS), for example, or Legionnaire's disease. But new behavioral disorders without known physical cause emerge from a changing sociocultural context and are likely caused by factors within that context, since human physiology cannot change overnight. In fact, certain factors that might at first glance appear to be biological—diet comes to mind—are actually part of the sociocultural environment.

Learning disabilities, especially dyslexia, are currently undergoing medicalization, and as such are quite instructive regarding our cultural emphasis on biomedical explanations and treatment of behavioral deviance. Richard Rosenfeld and I studied the process of the medicalization of learning disabilities. Dyslexia is not (yet) considered to be an illness or a disease, although it may be so considered in the near future; however, it *has* been redefined from an educational problem to a medical, specifically neurological, disorder. We do not deny that some people probably have an objective condition that impairs learning, especially reading; nor do we deny that this impairment might well be neurological in origin. But we do argue that only a small core of those currently labeled as dyslexic or "LD" are actually biologically impaired, and that, furthermore, there is no scientific evidence of a neurological or any other physiological basis for impairment for even the "hard core" dyslexics. But the absence of supporting data has not stopped or even hindered the medicalization of learning problems, just as it has not in the case of hyperactivity or alcoholism. Dyslexia might even be considered a "culture-bound syndrome" (see the discussion of such syndromes later in this chapter), since ultimately the disability concerns achievement *valued* in American culture (McGuinness 1985:235; Coles 1987). "We have created 'dyslexia' rather than 'dysmusica' or 'dysmechanica,' because we value reading ability over musical or mechanical ability and not because reading is more closely tied to the organization or functioning of the brain" (Erchak and Rosenfeld 1989:84).

The condition is very vaguely described. Few even agree on definition: while most specialists argue that dyslexia is a kind of learning disability, in fact the two terms are often used interchangeably. Symptoms of the disorder are also nebulous and often contradictory, including low activity, high activity, overattention, inattention, opthalmological problems, lack of coordination, poor recall, problems with math, and dysgraphia (poor penmanship). The original, or "classic," symptom is letter and word reversal, yet many medically diagnosed dyslexics show no signs of such perceptual reversal. Parents and dyslexics themselves often add many more ethnomedical symptoms, including greater sociability, problems with balance, and other unusual traits (these are taken from actual statements by parents). An anthropologist who has studied "LD" as a social construction sums up the condition nicely: it is simply "unexplained underachievement" (Carrier 1983).

Nevertheless, at conferences and in public talks for teachers and parents that we attended, various medical specialists continually hammered away at the alleged neurological causes of LD and dyslexia, in spite of the complete lack of evidence for their claims. Teachers we interviewed, perhaps swayed by the higher status and greater sociopolitical and scientific power of doctors, largely accepted this biomedical model of learning problems, as do many of the journals that they read, such as *The Journal of Learning Disabilities.*

But it is parental endorsement of this point of view that is especially strong. Parents clamor for written diagnoses or written certificates, which they can present to health insurance companies and especially to school personnel in order to arrange for special treatment for their "disabled" kids. In effect, we learned that parents would rather be told that their child has a permanent neurological disability than an environmentally based learning problem! Medicalization thus fits nicely with parents' desires for medical solutions for their children's learning difficulties. Teachers and parents alike hope to use the prestige of medicine to support self-interested, albeit well-intentioned, approaches to learning problems; they both receive government funding for "special ed," and they both obtain nonpejorative explanations for children's failure—and perhaps their own (Erchak and Rosenfeld 1989:90–91; also see Granger and Granger 1986).

One problematic consequence of the medicalization of dyslexia and learning disabilities is the overall medicalization of the classroom. If teachers and parents disclaim responsibility for the academic failures of children, how can they claim responsibility for their successes? By the very logic of the biomedical model, *high* achievement must be just as much a matter of neurology as low achievement, especially given the absence of data either pro or con.

The biomedical model oversimplifies psychological issues with an asocial unicausal paradigm that reflects American cultural folk beliefs and morality. As a human social activity, learning, deviant or otherwise, is an outcome of an interaction of cultural, social-structural, personality, and cognitive factors, just as behavioral disorders, alcohol abuse, and other examples of deviant behavior are, and cannot be reduced to a single biological source.

Psychiatrists Criticize Psychiatry

The biomedical model dominates American psychiatry and therefore dominates psychiatric discourse on personality issues. Psychology too has become increasingly biologized in recent years, and in any case has far less influence on psychiatry than psychiatry has on psychology; in addition, psychiatry—a *medical* specialization—has far higher occupational status and commands higher fees in American society than does psychology.

It may be surprising to learn, then, that some of the most trenchant critiques of the medicalization of behavioral disorder come from within the ranks of psychiatry itself (Starr 1982:409). Cultural-anthropological and sociological critiques, however well-documented and closely reasoned, have had relatively little impact on the medicalization of deviance; psychiatric self-criticism has exerted a little more influence, but even here the spread of biomedicine is so inexorable that many of these critics are summarily dismissed as "mavericks" and crackpots. I do not think it would be appropriate in such a brief volume to review all these "antipsychiatrists," but it is important for students to understand the general stance.

The late Scottish psychiatrist R. D. Laing was among the most famous of these critics. In a series of works in the 1960s (Laing 1960, 1967, 1969; Laing and Esterson 1964), he argued that insanity, especially schizophrenia, is really an adaptive response to an "insane" society. In effect, we can all learn a great deal about life and society by taking the hallucinatory experiences of schizophrenics seriously.

Thomas Szasz is probably the most vocal and prolific of the psychiatric antipsychiatrists. While he has written many books criticizing biomedical approaches to "mental illness" (Szasz 1970, 1974, 1976, 1978) and against the use of the insanity defense in courts of law (Szasz 1963, 1965), they all essentially restate the message of his most famous work on the subject, *The Myth of Mental Illness* (rev. ed., 1974), which is simply that there is no such thing as an illness of the mind. The use of labels and categories such as "schizophrenia" is scientism rather than science, since the term is a catchall category whose symptoms and diagnosis are rarely agreed upon by psychiatrists. He aptly characterizes the term "schizophrenia" as a *panchreston,* from the Greek "explain-all," at once explaining a condition by simply naming it, and thus explaining nothing at all (Szasz 1974).

Szasz argues that those labeled mentally ill simply have "problems in living" which might require voluntary reeducation, not medical treatment. As a libertarian, Szasz believes that no one has the right to interfere in others' lives; people must be free to choose a manner of living, no matter how eccentric or deviant, as long as they do not break any law. Of course, Szasz's critics question whether someone who is "mentally ill" is really capable of rational choice. The debate continues today with a focus on homeless persons with behavioral disorders: who decides how people should live their lives? When does care become coercion?

E. Fuller Torrey's (1972, 1974, 1980, 1986) critiques of his profession are less radical, subtler, and more complex; as a result, they appear to be taken more seriously by the psychiatric establishment. He does not oppose the imposition of a biomedical model on behavioral disorder categorically, only its inappropriate application. Briefly, Torrey argues that many diagnostic categories are spurious, and not diseases in any meaningful sense. "Nymphomania" (which today would be called sexual addiction or "sexaholism") is one of his more amusing examples (Torrey 1974:43–46): compulsive female hypersexuality labeled as a disease is little more than conventional middle-class Western morality draped in medical language. Like Szasz, Torrey is particularly incensed at the legal use of such ridiculous categories. But unlike Laing and Szasz, Torrey strongly believes that true "back ward" psychoses—the sort often labeled schizophrenia—*are* indeed actual diseases, specifically *brain* diseases, and so the biomedical model is quite proper for those disorders. He estimates that about 25 percent of those institutionalized for mental illness during the late 1960s and early 1970s, the years of institutionalization just prior to the current policy of deinstitutionalization, now about twenty years old, had psychotic brain disease; the other 75 percent had various problems in living which should be treated by education, not medicine.

The importance of these critiques is underscored by disagreement among the critics themselves, especially regarding the status of schizophrenia. All three discussed so far agree that emotional and behavioral disorders are often spuriously labeled, and that a medical model of classification, diagnosis, and treatment is generally erroneous in the extreme, but Laing treats schizophrenia as an inward journey to self-knowledge, Szasz feels that it is a residual grab-bag category of diverse problems in living, and Torrey argues that it is in fact a disease of the brain. Such disagreement is truly alarming and demonstrates the need for further research on, among other topics, cross-cultural versus culture-specific factors in behavioral disorder, an area where psychological anthropology has much to contribute.

One psychiatrist who criticizes psychiatry also carries out cross-cultural research and works closely with psychological anthropologists. Arthur Kleinman (1980, 1986, 1988a, 1988b; Kleinman and Good 1985) argues forcefully that behavioral and emotional disorders and their treatments must be seen in the context of culture, a position rarely taken by trained psychiatrists in the United States. In *Rethinking Psychiatry* (1988b), for example, he argues persuasively against the biochemical reductionism of American psychiatry in the last decade, insisting that all behavior is sociocultural as well as biological. This reductionist bias is so strong in American psychiatry that even pertinent developments in psychological research and theory are neither learned nor understood by psychiatrists, according to Kleinman (1988b:145). One can only imagine the reception of the findings of sociology or cultural anthropology in such an intellectual climate: they are dismissed as irrelevant and unscientific, if they are even read or discussed at all. Unlike some other critics, Kleinman is no radical; he is a sober-minded scientist who has worked in other cultures, China in particular, and therefore knows from personal practice that psychiatric problems have a cultural component which absolutely must be taken into account. He is just as critical of the extreme cultural relativism of some cultural anthropologists as he is of the extreme biological universalism of so many American psychiatrists. Whether his critique, along with others like it, will have any lasting impact on the profession remains to be seen, but any really serious or thoughtful response seems unlikely given the dominant paradigm.

Culture and Behavioral Disorder

A vexing problem that anthropologists can help solve—in fact they are the major players here, along with a minuscule group of cross-cultural psychiatrists like Kleinman—is the question of the universality of behavioral disorder. Are emotional and behavioral disorders (so-called mental illnesses) of the sorts frequently encountered by Western psychiatrists found everywhere in the world, varying only in surface, superficial ways in terms of cultural manifestation? Or does each culture produce its own peculiar neuroses and psychoses? Or perhaps some disorders are universal while others are culture-specific? If so, how can one tell which is which? Finally, if it could be determined with some certainty that such disorders were universal, or culture-specific, or both, what would such findings imply for the putative biochemical versus sociocultural etiologies of disorders? These are just a very few of the important issues raised by the juxtaposition of culture and behavioral disorder. As I have already pointed out, such a juxtaposition is rarely made by most psychiatrists or even psychologists, but remains for the most part a problem for psychological anthropologists alone.

Many of these questions, and other similar and corollary ones, are unanswerable. Each culture causes stress for some of its members; some individuals, either because of some biochemical predisposition or because of socialization experience, develop an emotional or behavioral disorder from this stress. Since cultures socialize their members differently, and since cultural environments obviously differ widely in any case, it seems likely that behavioral disorders will vary by culture *to the extent that they are culturally caused,* something very difficult to demonstrate scientifically. While all disorders will clearly be manifested in cultural ways, some disorders might nonetheless be universal or nearly so *to the extent that they are not culturally caused.* But universal incidence in and of itself does not demonstrate biochemical causality (although it does indeed make it more likely) since many of the problems of life are also universal: the stresses of parenthood, the temptations of illicit sex, the trauma resulting from the death of a loved one, and so on. What *is* indisputable is that all behavioral disorder must be understood, as Kleinman (1988b) notes, in a cultural context. Stripped of cultural context (all too often the case in psychiatry), behavior, whether normal or disordered, makes no sense.

Here are three hypothetical cases of human behavior essentially devoid of cultural context:

Case 1   A woman begins to fear going to town after a spooky encounter: earlier in the week a man she knew slightly stared at her for a few moments and then followed her briefly. The woman becomes anxious, sure that many people, including this man, are "out to get her." She feels weak, drained, and her head begins to hurt. She hears sounds outside her window and cannot sleep. She stops eating and begins to decline. Her own family is "in on it," she is sure, so she stops speaking to them.

Case 2   A young man brushes against a certain woman in a narrow alley. He studies his shirt anxiously. Hurrying home, he washes the shirt; but he still feels a vague dread and so washes his whole body. He avoids that alley for several months. He divides his dwelling into safe "male" areas and contaminated "female" areas. If he strays into a polluted zone, he must engage in vigorous washing and rigorous ritual purification. Hours each day are devoted to purification. He knows that these behaviors are essential to his well-being: something awful would happen if he did not keep himself pure; he would weaken, maybe even die.

Case 3   A woman hears voices. At first they are very faint, as if from far away; she cannot make out what they are saying. After a few weeks, they grow louder, nearer; she begins to hear her name and the name of a nearby stream. The voices become loud and demanding—something about a "sacrifice" and "salvation." She kills a dog and walks naked through town to the stream, and jumps in, immersing the bloody animal.

In an American cultural context, the first case appears, on the surface at least, to be paranoid schizophrenia or delusional disorder. But in many non-Western cultures, the unfortunate woman would be seen as the victim of witchcraft or sorcery; rather than being a deviant, she would be the object or victim of a deviant. The strange man gave her the "evil eye," and her resultant terror brought about psychosomatic symptoms along with exhaustion, starvation, and dehydration.

The second example looks like a case of obsessive-compulsive disorder in a U.S. context. The young man experiences extreme anxiety as a result of contact with this particular female. He tries to "wash her off"; he is contaminated by her "germs" or "cooties." Certain areas of his dwelling eventually become "danger zones" of female pollution. However, in the context of Sambia culture or that of some other group in the Highlands of Papua New Guinea, the entire behavioral sequence is absolutely normal. To brush up against a woman (who might be menstruating, for all the young man knows) in those cultures and then *not* undergo ritual purification would risk contaminating all areas and other men with whom he came into contact later. The repercussions would be extremely serious, both for himself (he would indeed go into a physical and spiritual decline) and for others (who would probably punish, perhaps even execute, the polluter).

People who hear voices, even following directions given by the voices, are represented by the third case. In American society, such an experience is often labeled paranoid schizophrenia (American Psychiatric Association 1987:197) or perhaps multiple personality disorder (APA 1987:270–272). This latter diagnosis has been employed fairly frequently in legal cases in recent years; for example, the claim might be made that a murder or series of murders, were carried out by a personality other than the one being tried, or that

voices from within—the voice of an emergent new personality, perhaps—ordered the murders. In Case 3, the woman is apparently
ordered by her inner voices to remove her clothing and then kill
and submerge a dog, achieving in this manner some sort of purification or salvation. But in many non-Western cultures, these
events would be a sign not of mental illness but of spiritual possession. The woman is possessed by a spirit who demands that she
sacrifice a dog and cleanse herself in the stream. If she can hold
herself together in the following weeks, she might be called upon
to serve as a healer or adviser to her people.

While these examples are deliberately extreme, they show that
the cultural context is always essential in order to grasp the full
meaning of any behaviors, whether peculiar or mundane. To treat
any of the above cases as simple manifestations of an underlying
neurological, biochemical, or in some other sense physiological disorder or disease is simplistic, naive, and even dangerous since
treatments based on such diagnoses often have harmful side effects
on the body and on behavior.

Culture-bound Syndromes in Non-Western Cultures

Much of the discourse concerning emotional and behavioral disorder in psychological anthropology and cross-cultural psychiatry
concerns "culture-bound syndromes," disorders that are apparently confined to a specific culture, or groups or types of cultures.
Discussion generally centers on questions of the putative uniqueness or universality of the disordered state. Scores of fascinating
studies have appeared with regularity for at least seventy-five
years: some of the most famous cases concern *latah* in central and
southern Asia (Yap 1952, 1969; H. Murphy 1976), a startle reaction involving involuntary and compulsive speech and actions;
amok in Indonesia and the Philippines (Guthrie 1973), a form of
extremely violent behavior often following some sort of public em-
barrassment; *susto* ("soul loss") in Mexico, a state of lassitude and
extreme depression (Rubel 1964; O'Nell and Selby 1968); *pibloktoq*
in northern Greenland (Wallace 1972; Foulks 1972), a form of violent hysteria; and *wiitiko* psychosis among the Ojibwa of Minnesota

and Manitoba, a complex category involving possession and cannibalism (Parker 1960; Fogelson 1965).

Many of these have been analyzed many times from several different perspectives—social learning, Freudian, biochemical—with little agreement. Neither is there much consensus on whether they are truly "culture-bound" or actually superficially varying manifestations of universal hysterical, depressive, or anxiety disorders. While most anthropologists take a somewhat cultural-relativist position, a few are unabashed universalists. One of the most outspoken of the latter group is Jane Murphy, who has conducted extensive cross-cultural research on mental illness (her term) among Alaskan Inuit, Nigerian Yoruba, and rural Nova Scotians. In an important article in the prestigious journal *Science,* she contends that Alaskan Inuit and Yoruba, and the literature shows that many other cultures around the world as well, all recognize and have a word for insanity (generally meaning schizophrenia) (J. Murphy 1976). Certain forms of mental illness, in other words, are common to all human beings and are not simply cultural constructions of abnormality. Nevertheless, the category of culture-bound syndromes is an important one; and it rarely includes behaviors we would label schizophrenic or even psychotic.

Latah, for example, is a set of behaviors often resulting from being startled which include, among other symptoms, compulsive repeating of others' words (echolalia), mimicry of others' gestures and movements (echopraxia), and outbursts of obscenities (coprolalia) (Yap 1952; H. Murphy 1976). Interpretations focus on *latah* as an outcome of various stresses on vulnerable individuals, but it also bears some similarity to Tourette's Disorder and related Tic Disorders, believed to be neurological in origin (APA 1987:78–79). But if they are indeed neurological, why would they vary in rate from one time period to another (H. Murphy 1976), or from one area to another within the same ethnic group (e.g., the Semai) (Dentan 1979:63)?

Pibloktoq, a variant of what is often called "Arctic hysteria," has also been interpreted both culturally and biologically by various scholars. This specific form is found among the Polar Inuit of Greenland, although related behaviors have been reported in Siberia, Alaska, and Canada. At first, the sufferer is withdrawn and sullen for a few hours or days; then he or she becomes manic and excited for a few minutes to a half hour; the excitement is followed by seizures and deep sleep or coma for as long as twelve hours; normal behavior follows the sleep (Wallace 1972:371). In an influential paper, Anthony Wallace (1972) argues for an organic explanation of the syndrome. A biological explanation appears to fit the conditions better than the psychoanalytic explanations that had held sway for some sixty years. Simply put, Wallace notes that the symptoms are consistent with those manifested by victims of hypocalcemia, or calcium deficiency disease. Although Inuit consume adequate calcium, it is not nutritionally available to the body in sufficient quantity due to a low level of Vitamin D, a nutrient essential to the metabolism of calcium. The low level of sunlight in the far north, particularly during the winter months, is the primary reason for the vitamin deficiency. The victim's behavior and subsequent treatment by the community are shaped by Inuit culture. Wallace emphasized that only field investigation could scientifically determine whether the psychological (hysteria) or organic (hypocalcemia) or some other hypothesis was correct. A cross-cultural psychiatrist studying under Wallace, Edward Foulks, picked up the gauntlet. He found that hypocalcemia could not account for *piblok-toq*, since calcium levels were generally within the low-normal range, although changes in calcium rhythms throughout the year could affect behavior (Foulks 1972:81). In summary, he concluded that a host of physiological, ecological, psychological, and cultural factors all contribute to the syndrome; no single factor predominates.

Some instances of behavioral disorder appear to be associated with particular cultures or culture-areas, but unlike *latah, pibloktoq,* and the others discussed above, they are unnamed. Two examples from the Kpelle of Liberia are worth mentioning in this regard. I observed a woman grab a toddler and run off with her down the path out of the village. Several women pursued her and caught her; they took back the child, and then one of the oldest women in town—an important midwife—lectured her, yelling, for several minutes. Nothing else was done, and I was told that she had stolen babies before because she was infertile. Some of the women pointed out that they had known of other women like this in the past. I assume that the extreme emotional and social emphasis West Africans place on women's reproductive function engenders a great deal of stress when a woman is unable to have babies, resulting in behavioral disorder in some women.

The Kpelle also report another type of disorder, a kind of "wild man" behavior, although I never witnessed such a case. Many Kpelle believe that each person has a spiritual animal double who lives in the forest, as I noted in Chapter 1; sometimes people change into their animal doubles. Occasionally a person, usually a man, enters a state of wild excitement similar to Filipino *amok*, in which he runs into the bush acting like his totemic animal: a man with a buffalo double, for example, will run straight through the bush, ferociously uprooting saplings; a man with a monkey double will wildly climb a tree, hooting all the while. In every case, the person returns to normal and no one speaks of the deviant episode.

Often a deviant behavior reported for a particular culture is obviously one that is well-known elsewhere as well, but seems to take on different dimensions in specific cultural environments. For example, the suicide rate for young men is very high in Micronesia, especially in Truk (Rubinstein 1983, 1985; Hezel 1985). The annual rate was 66/100,000 for males between the ages of fifteen and nineteen, and 101/100,000 for males between twenty and twenty-four, over the twenty-year period 1960–1979, but around 250/100,000 for Trukese males between fifteen to twenty-four in the 1975–1979 period, over fifteen times the U.S. rate for the same age group (Rubinstein 1983:659). The Trukese suicide rate appears to be associated with several cultural and psychological factors. Young men often feel hopeless and powerless in the face of the rapid changes that have swept through the islands in recent years; they don't want to fish and grow taro as their fathers do, but have no entry into modern sorts of occupation; this state of normlessness is known as anomie in the sociological literature. In addition, Trukese culture promotes the internalization of conflict and the avoidance of confrontation: a public humiliation of an angry young man can push him into a sudden suicide, especially if he has been drinking. Copycat suicides occur frequently as well. On Yap, another Micronesian island group with similar stresses and problems, I found that suicide is treated rather matter-of-factly: people are saddened by it, but "what can you do?" Copycat suicides are well-known there as well.

Whereas suicide is usually interpreted psychoculturally, homicidal violence is sometimes interpreted bioculturally. Ralph Bolton (1973, 1978), for example, studied the high rate of aggressive violence among the Qolla, a Quechua-speaking group in the high Andes of Peru, and found it to be related to hypoglycemia, or chronic low blood sugar levels. According to Bolton, Qolla men go out of their way to start fights, boasting about their own prowess and machismo while insulting and deriding others. Homicide rates appear to be very high: in one village Bolton studied he determined that half of all household heads were involved in some way in cases of homicide (Bolton 1978). Because Qolla claim that fighting makes them feel better, Bolton hypothesized that maybe it really *did* makes them feel subjectively better. Testing a sample of adult males for serum glucose levels, he found that 50 percent were low. According to Bolton, this chronic hypoglycemia may have its origins in their poor diet (very high in carbohydrates and very low in protein), low oxygen levels due to high-altitude living, and chronic ingestion of coca leaves and alcohol. Since engaging in violence does indeed raise serum glucose, Bolton (1973) argued that their aggressive behavior is an unconscious attempt to raise their blood sugar levels. His analysis is controversial, and unconvincing to some, but certainly illustrates the complex interplay of biological and cultural factors in the genesis of behavioral disorder.

Culture-bound syndromes in non-Western societies are certainly a mixed bag, including disorders that are possibly physical but are manifested in behavior, some behaviors that appear unusual from a Western point of view but which are accepted with equanimity by some other cultures, disorders that appear to be unique to certain cultures or culture areas, and others that may just be superficial variations on universal "themes" of behavioral and emotional disorder. In all cases, however, the disorderly behavior, whether locally recognized or not, and whether labeled or unlabeled, matches up with the local culture, expresses cultural patterns, or is shaped or promoted by the culture. Even if a disorder is one that occurs nearly universally, such as depression, aggression, or suicide, the local version of it, and the mode of expression, will be culturally unique—in fact it *must* be.

Culture-bound Disorders in the United States

I hope that you are now prepared to look at some possible culture-bound syndromes in the United States, having pondered the dominance of the biomedical model in American scientific and popular belief systems, and examined some culture-bound syndromes from other cultures. They do not occur only in exotic lands, but right here at home as well. I have already mentioned anorexia, nymphomania, and dyslexia and learning disabilities as candidates for this category of deviance and disorder. Later on in the chapter, I will discuss alcoholism in some detail; it too is a culture-bound syndrome peculiar to the United States in the way it is defined and treated.

Multiple personality disorder, kleptomania, and codependency are three alleged diseases that appear to be unique to American culture, or at least more common, or more frequently reported in the United States than elsewhere. The case of multiple personality disorder is particularly interesting and more than a little complex. In an important study, *The Passion of Ansel Bourne: Multiple Personality in American Culture* (1986), anthropologist Michael Kenny theorizes that what psychiatrists today label multiple personality disorder was actually spirit possession in an earlier America, and no doubt in other cultures as well. In essence, he is offering a universalist argument, suggesting that the basic underlying psychological phenomenon can be found in a wide range of times and places, but that its labeling, management, and treatment and reception by society are culturally relative. He insists, however, that neither possession nor multiple personality is a *universal* mental disorder, but rather each is a culturally appropriate metaphor, with "discernible cultural origins both as a medical concept and as a mode of behavior" (Kenny 1986:3). He argues that people create their selves through the concepts, categories, ideas, and beliefs provided for them by their cultures. So if people believe fervently in spirit possession, then persons hearing inner voices, entering fugue states, and so forth will believe themselves to be possessed, and so will those around them. But in today's United States, they will wind up diagnosed psychiatrically: the diagnosis may well be "multiple personality disorder," and they and those around them will believe and behave accordingly.

The condition has been removed from the realm of the soul and placed instead in the nervous system, a change that occurred around the turn of the century (Kenny 1986:134). From 1913 until 1957, the year of the publication of the multiple-personality classic *The Three Faces of Eve,* the condition was believed by psychiatrists to be extremely rare, and little attention was given to it. While it is not exactly common now, neither is it rare, and in fact is fairly regularly used as a legal defense in courts of law. Such a sudden renaissance of an obscure disorder would seem to point to socio-cultural causation, even though deterministic biomedical explanations are sought even as I write. Kenny (1986:164) notes that the phenomenon is at least in part media-driven: most "victims" of this disorder are very familiar with the books, articles, and films about multiple personality disorder. A few of the cases are probably fraudulent, either directly or indirectly. But all multiple personality phenomena, whether spirit possession or mental illness—in fact, *all self-experience* "is culturally and socially shaped. . . . The oppositional logic of multiple personality is derivative from Christian Euro-North American culture. Other places, other cultures and times—other demons, other psyches" (Kenny 1986:173, 181).

In a similar comparative study, Erika Bourguignon (1989), a respected anthropological authority on spirit possession, argues that the two may only be considered equivalent to the extent that healers as well as the larger community to which the subject belongs validate rather than reject the subject's experience. Since spirit possession is usually viewed as the entry of an entity into the subject's body and/or mind, whereas multiple personality is generally seen as dissociated aspects of one self, Bourguignon considers them to be analogous but not identical. But both scholars agree that both conditions (or the single condition) are culturally constructed.

Kleptomania is another Western culture-bound syndrome but, unlike multiple personality disorder, one without a non-Western analogue. *The Diagnostic and Statistical Manual of Mental Disorder (DSM-III-R)* defines it as "a recurrent failure to resist impulses to steal objects not needed for personal use or their monetary value . . . (when) the person has enough money to pay for the stolen objects" and notes that the diagnosis is made only if not due to Conduct Disorder or Antisocial Personality Disorder. (American Psychiatric Association 1987:322–323). Factors that predispose people to "contract" the "mental illness" of kleptomania are not known; family histories are also unknown. However, kleptomaniac shoplifting is believed to be more common among females (APA 1987:323).

Feminist historian Elaine Abelson (1989, 1990) shows convincingly that kleptomania is a culture-bound syndrome that appeared rather suddenly in the late nineteenth century, specifically among middle-class American (and sometimes European) women: the alleged medical condition is thus class- and gender-bound as well as culture-bound. An important precondition was the Victorian notion of women as innately nervous and unstable, given to hysteria and manias. Menstrual disorders, a sort of nineteenth-century "PMS" (another suspect mental illness), were especially important in medical diagnoses of unexplained shoplifting (Abelson 1989:132). Beyond this gender-based predisposition, the "invention" (Abelson's apt term) of kleptomania coincides with the rise of large department stores. "Within this highly restrictive model, women and department stores were seen in a symbiotic relationship in which the stores filled an elemental need for women" (Abelson 1989:135). Shopping was seen as a natural extension of female physiological functions, according to Abelson. Whereas in previous times one had to request products from a merchant at a counter, in the new department stores a woman could stroll freely about, handling merchandise with little restraint (Abelson 1990). Some women inevitably succumbed to temptation. As is the case with the use of many categories of mental illness today, these respectable citizens could employ the medical diagnosis of kleptomania in their legal defense; it was and is far less stigmatizing than plain criminal theft. Like anorexia, bulimia, dyslexia, and multiple personality disorder, once kleptomania was medically recognized and became part of the cultural belief system, numbers of cases ballooned.

So it is with one of the very newest mental diseases: codependency. Codependency as an illness has its origins in an early eighties self-help movement for so-called Adult Children of Alcoholics (orthodox groups are actually special-interest meetings of Al-Anon, itself an organization for those close to someone who is an alcoholic). As part of a larger study of alcoholism and its treatment, I attended over thirty meetings of an Adult Children of Alcoholics group in a small northeastern city from 1981 to 1983; in 1983 I also attended group therapy sessions for "adult children." I reviewed what was written for or about this population; it is in this literature that codependency first became an illness in its own right (Wegscheider 1981; Woititz 1983). In the groups I learned that spouses of alcoholics were "co-alcoholics" and that children of alcoholics were "para-alcoholics"; both of these were considered to be "just as sick as the alcoholic; in other words, the mere happenstance of having a heavy-drinking parent or spouse was itself a disease" (Peele 1989:123). Alcoholism was referred to as the "family disease" in these sessions. As many as eighty million Americans (including alcoholics and their codependents) apparently suffer from this insidious malady, according to its enthusiasts (Peele 1989:25). I will discuss this phenomenon as it pertains to alcoholism later on in the chapter; now I simply want to point out the origins of the new behavioral and emotional illness of codependency.

This new disorder has been called a "disease blamed for such diverse disorders as drug abuse, alcoholism, anorexia, child abuse, compulsive gambling, chronic lateness, fear of intimacy and low self-esteem"; it "is generally described as a failure to feel, or a failure to feel what's true" (Kaminer 1990; see also Peele 1975; Gil 1983). This disease is perhaps the ultimate American culture-bound syndrome, since it is an offshoot of other disorders that are *themselves* culture-bound. Since it is largely, although not exclusively, a female disorder, it is also gender-bound. Some *96 percent* of Americans may suffer from some form of codependency illness, if we accept such definitions as "being affected by someone else's behavior and obsessed with controlling it" (Melody Beattie, *Codependent No More*), or "a disease process whose assumptions, beliefs and lack of spiritual awareness lead to a process of nonliving which is progressive" (Anne Wilson Schaef, *Co-dependence: Misunderstood—Mistreated*; cited in Kaminer 1990:26). Try to figure out the meaning of these definitions. The recent American obsession with addictions—addictions as illnesses and addictions including almost every repetitive behavior—has produced a mental illness that finally includes virtually everyone.

Behavioral and emotional disorders, including culture-bound syndromes, project and express cultural themes, whether in a small-scale preindustrial, nonliterate non-Western society or in a complex postindustrial Western society like the United States. Many such disorders are in fact culturally constructed from cause to symptom, while even those that may be universal are clearly culturally adapted in the ways in which they are locally manifested. Treatment (and nontreatment) are also culturally shaped.

Treatment of Disorder

In the West, behavioral and emotional disorder is culturally believed to be treatable and, furthermore, to *require* treatment. Unless the deviant individual engages in criminal acts or is completely incompetent and antisocial, treatment is generally voluntary; in most states, laws preventing involuntary institutionalization, or at least making it more difficult, were passed during the last thirty years in order to prevent the casual incarceration ("commitment") of unpleasant or difficult family members by their relatives. Treatment usually consists of one or a combination of the following: medication, psychotherapy, institutionalization, or participation in a self-help group. While psychotherapy broadly defined (there are dozens of types) continues to grow as it becomes culturally less stigmatizing, the real explosive growth is in the use of drug medication and in the proliferation of various self-help and recovery groups. Long-term institutionalization is on the wane, except for chronic psychotics (usually diagnosed as schizophrenic), although short-term institutionalization is still widely used for a variety of disorders, including anxiety, obsessive-compulsive, and depressive disorders, to name just a few. In addition, short-term institutionalization is also used for detoxification and rehabilitation.

Psychotherapy is usually individual: the "patient" or"client" (this usage depends on the therapist's academic degree and self-concept) visits the therapist in the therapist's office; after fifty minutes, the patient leaves. If the therapist is a psychiatrist, the patient will leave with a prescription for medication; if not, the therapist either will not utilize pharmaceuticals or will contact a consulting psychiatrist who will in turn write a prescription. Note the cultural consistency: in the United States, disorder is believed to be located in the *individual* rather than in the community; hence, the individual is generally treated in isolation from the community by a lone therapist. In addition, the biomedical model of disorder, a peculiarity of American culture (in regard to its extremely wide application), also defines deviant behavior as an individual pathology. To be sure, family systems and group therapy approaches are also employed in contemporary treatment of behavioral and emotional disorder, but they are less widely used than individual psychotherapy; even when they are employed, it is usually as an adjunct to individual treatment. I am not necessarily criticizing the utility of these approaches, but rather underscoring the cultural shaping of treatment.

Medication, often with extremely powerful mood- and mind-altering drugs, is increasingly used in treating behavioral and emotional problems: Prozac and Anafranil for obsessive-compulsive disorders, Thorazine for certain psychoses, Ritalin for childhood Attention Deficit Hyperactivity Disorder, Xanax for panic disorders, Tofranil for depression, lithium carbonate for manic depression—the list is long indeed. In fact, the introduction of Thorazine and other so-called antipsychotics is largely responsible for the large-scale "deinstitutionalization" of mental patients during the seventies. If they took their "meds" regularly, they no longer needed to be kept in large state mental hospitals ("psychiatric centers") at public expense. The problem is that follow-up was and is very inadequate; in fact deinstitutionalization itself, along with the lack of economic programs for the poor of the eighties and nineties, is partly responsible for the large numbers of emotionally disturbed homeless people living on the streets of American cities today.

The use of drugs to cure disorder is a perfectly logical outcome of the individualistic biomedical model of behavior. Neurological and other related branches of medical and psychiatric research are very important and should be supported; and drug therapy based on controlled, falsifiable, replicable scientific research should of course be used. But all too often the near-religious faith in drug efficacy leads to a haphazard application of medication to conditions with social or psychological causes unrelated to physiological functioning. The sources of many psychological disorders are either completely unknown or subject to several competing theories; in such an epistemological environment treatment should probably be conservative and noninvasive, with drugs avoided unless there is a proven connection.

Overreliance on drugs further diminishes interest in other pathways to the treatment of behavioral disorder on the part of researchers, funding agencies, and sufferers themselves. After all, drugs are easier to see and much quicker-acting than the hard work of self-control, behavior modification, counseling, the practice of new behaviors, and so on. Patients can become dependent on the medication, fearful of stopping it, and its use might continue long after the original problem would have passed had drugs not been used. Alternatively, since drugs often (but not always) treat symptoms rather than underlying causes, they can mask a problem, in effect completely preventing real improvement. Social psychologist Stanton Peele (1989:15) has written "that medical and pharmaceutical breakthroughs on the level of the antibiotics . . . have not been forthcoming in dealing with our major mental illnesses" and that psychiatrists are uneasy about creating drug dependency in their patients. Yet their use continues unabated, growing dramatically with each passing year.

The horrors of patient life in large publicly funded psychiatric hospitals are well-known. While conditions have improved in some, and while many have closed or have had their patient populations severely cut back, they are still the only treatment available (along with drugs) for profound psychoses, especially schizophrenia. Surprisingly, although there have been many impressionistic studies and critiques (e.g., Goffman 1961), few have carried out systematic scientific research on the institutional treatment of "mental illness." A brilliant exception is the superb study of psychiatric treatment by Stanford social psychologist D. L. Rosenhan (1973), published in the journal *Science* under the title "On Being Sane in Insane Places." His premises were simple and clear: given that the mentally ill are diagnosed, labeled, treated with drugs, and often institutionalized, it should be assumed that medical personnel involved in this process know what they are doing, that their labels are accurate, and that they can distinguish sane from insane, normal from abnormal. If they cannot, we are in big trouble.

To test these premises, he had himself plus seven confederates, eight pseudopatients as he called them, committed to twelve different psychiatric hospitals. The pseudopatients were mixed by gender, age, and occupation, and the hospitals were similarly varied from old to new, public to private. Admission was gained through alleging phony symptoms purporting to indicate an "existential" psychosis, chosen strictly because such a condition does not exist. Major life experiences were presented factually. All but one were admitted with a diagnosis of schizophrenia (remember Szasz's characterization of the label of schizophrenia as an explain-all). After admission, which was alarmingly easy, the pseudopatients behaved perfectly normally and naturally at all times, even to the point of telling staff, when asked how they were feeling, that they no longer experienced the slightest symptoms. None of these pseudopatients was ever detected—nor was their evident sanity. Even when eventually discharged, they were "in remission"—not cured, not sane.

Real patients in the subject hospitals, by contrast, frequently recognized the obvious sanity of the researchers, occasionally even opining that the pseudopatients were journalists or professors. To further test whether psychiatrists could recognize mental illness, Rosenhan told the staff at one research and teaching hospital that some time in the following three months, a fake patient would attempt to gain entry. Out of 193 new admissions during this period, forty-one were said to be pseudopatients by at least one staff member, and twenty-three by at least one psychiatrist, but in reality no pseudopatients ever attempted to get in! Rosenhan (1973:252) suggests, with more than a little understatement, that "one thing is certain: any diagnostic process that lends itself so readily to massive errors of this sort cannot be a very reliable one."

He also learned that once a person is labeled schizophrenic, psychotic, or whatever, even routine normal acts are perceived as symptomatic and disturbed: humdrum life histories become transformed into biographical deviant psychodramas, note-taking for the experiment becomes "writing behavior," pacing the halls from boredom is seen as a sign of nervous anxiety, and so on. Patients were ignored and depersonalized, treated like animals or objects. Average daily contact by a pseudopatient with physician, psychiatrist, medical resident, or psychologist was just under *seven* minutes.

Rosenhan's group also commented on the extensive use of

drugs. During their stays at the various hospitals, stays that ranged from seven to fifty-two days and averaged nineteen, the pseudo-patients were given 2,100 pills of several radically different types (in spite of uniform symptomology); when they threw them in the toilet, they frequently found real patients' "meds" already there.

The conclusion seems inescapable: the American cultural belief system of biomedicine is incapable of distinguishing the "mentally ill" from the "mentally well." "We now know that we cannot distinguish insanity from sanity" even in psychiatric hospitals designed for precisely that purpose (Rosenhan 1973:257). Treatments based on such an uncertain foundation are not likely to succeed. Other than continuing deinstitutionalization, which few claim is successful these days, and the accelerating biologizing of psychiatry, the situation has not improved in the eighteen years between Rosenhan's report and the writing of this chapter.

The rapid recent proliferation of self-help and support groups of various sorts is a peculiarly American cultural trend that deserves some comment before I turn to treatment of behavioral disorder in non-Western and other Third World societies. American culture has a strong egalitarian antihierarchical streak which self-help taps. The very notion of *self*-help arises from this democratic egalitarianism along with American individualism: "I don't need a psychiatrist, but I don't mind hanging out with people with similar problems. They understand me better than any therapist ever could." Yet these groups promote a high degree of conformity to group norms and rituals. The combination of individual self-help and other-directed conformity to the group is strikingly reminiscent of the Americans portrayed forty years ago in David Riesman's (1950) *The Lonely Crowd*. In addition, the preoccupation with self fostered by these groups, the search for other selves like one's own, is perfectly consistent with Lasch's (1979) self-absorbed narcissists, also discussed previously. Participation in some of today's self-help groups seems to be a thinly veiled search for self and for validation of one's identity. Perhaps the oft-noted contemporary fragmentation of family and community promotes the substitution of groups based on shared deviance and disorder to provide the comfort and security of those older social collectives. There are other cultural consistencies as well; for example, many, though by no means all, of these groups are based on Alcoholics Anonymous's

"Twelve Step" approach, a religious approach based on fundamentalist Protestantism; this too is consistent with the religious values of a majority of Americans.

Behavioral and emotional disorders are treated very differently in other parts of the world, especially so in non-European cultures (although European rural peasant cultures are also very far removed from American and urban-European approaches as well). In a brief outline such as this, I can provide only a few examples and suggestions; the rich variety of treatments and approaches worldwide would take up several volumes by themselves.

I must remind you at the outset that, as Ruth Benedict (1934a) pointed out so long ago, since many actions and patterns of behavior that we would consider to be signs of mental illness would in some other societies be considered quite normal or even exemplary, it follows that the same behaviors would not be "treated" in our sense. They would be accommodated or perhaps ignored: a woman who hears voices might be respected for being in close touch with ancestral spirits, while a man with mild anxiety about traveling would simply not travel. On the other hand, a mildly aggressive or selfish Inuit would be shunned, and a young Cheyenne man who had never hallucinated and seen a Guardian Spirit would be considered abnormal and encouraged to continue attempting to have a vision.

When treatment is undertaken for a culturally defined disorder, it is rarely individual. Since most agrarian and nonindustrial societies are more communitarian than industrial societies are—their very survival depends on cooperation and interdependence—the treatment of disorder also involves the entire community. Healing ceremonies for the foraging !Kung of southern Africa (Katz 1982) and for the hunting and cultivating Yanomamo of the Amazon rain forest (Chagnon 1983), for example, are remarkably similar. Neither differentiates between physical and psychological disorder, and both employ very ancient spiritual shamanistic techniques. During lengthy and intense ceremonies, the shaman (or shamans) enters a deep trance state, aided by tobacco in the case of the !Kung and hallucinogens in the case of Yanomamo, draws the sickening agent from the body, and casts it out of the community. In an important sense, the whole community, rather than a single person, is cured and cleansed. This theme of community therapy runs through most of the accounts of treatment, particularly in simple non-Western preindustrial cultures. Community treatment, or at least community involvement in treatment, is beautifully depicted in Victor Turner's (1967) classic account of the treatment of Kamahasanyi, a disturbed individual of the Ndembu of Zambia. For the Ndembu, all behavioral and emotional disorders—indeed, physical disorders as well—in individuals are believed to be socially caused, by ancestors, by sorcerers, or by witches, who are punishing the victim for some sort of social failure or transgression. Diagnosis is made through divination. Cure is effected through several healing cults whose members have suffered similar disorders; interestingly, the patient becomes a candidate for membership in the cult. I am struck by the similarity to drug and alcohol abuse counseling in the United States; counselors are largely drawn from the ranks of "recovering" drug and alcohol abusers (more on this in the next section).

In the particular case described by Turner, the patient, Kamahasanyi, was clearly a deviant citizen who was under a great deal of stress from a series of setbacks. He was a conspicuous failure as a hunter. He lived in his father's village well into middle age, a sign of childish dependence in a culture that insists that a man go to live in the village from which his mother came when he reaches adulthood and marries. He was very effeminate and, to make matters worse, had failed to father any children, even though he had been married four times. He was frequently cuckolded by these wives; in fact, his fourth wife's lover blatantly treated her mother as his (the lover's) mother-in-law, a grievous insult to Kamahasanyi. In spite of his failures and humiliations, he maintained the airs of a conceited snob who could barely conceal his disdain for others in the community. He became ill with palpitations, pains, and lassitude, all of which Turner (1964:255) believed to be psychosomatic.

A doctor of the *Ihamba* cult, a cult primarily associated with hunting and its symbols, treated him. This medicine man knew all the particulars of Kamahasanyi's case, as well as the principal players in his life. All were heavily involved in his treatment, along with most of the rest of the local community. The treatment itself consisted of many long hours of intense drumming and singing by everyone, punctuated by periods of cupping the patient with antelope horns affixed to his body; after each cupping, the patient shook violently, as if in a convulsion. After a few hours of this, everyone wanted the patient to be well; the Ndembu doctor must skillfully manage the feelings of the crowd as well as those of the primary patient. Several of those involved in the formation of Kamahasanyi's disorder were made to participate in the ritual drama: his unfaithful wife, for example, had to publicly reaffirm her marital vows and obligations. Kamahasanyi himself spoke out against the kin and neighbors who had hurt him in various ways. Finally, after further cuppings, fits, and drama, the shaman drew a human tooth out of the patient with more than a little legerdemain: the tooth represented the spirit that was "eating" him and causing his pain.

Turner reports that the whole village fairly emanated goodwill and warmth at the end of this curing ritual, and that, even more remarkably, the cure was very much still in effect when he revisited the village over a year later. Kamahasanyi had become a man of some influence and prestige, and was apparently happily still married to his formerly unfaithful wife. Simply put, the whole community, including what in modern parlance is called the "family system," was treated, rather than an individual isolated from family and friends.

Even when no treatment is culturally prescribed, in spite of community recognition of disorder in an individual, the individual is often integrated into the community rather than isolated. For example, the British anthropologist Peter Wilson (1974) has written an eloquent case study of a behaviorally disordered individual, Oscar Bryan, on the small remote Caribbean island of Providencia. Even though he was by most measures what we in American society would call "a pain in the ass," Oscar was widely accepted by, and integrated into, his society, even performing important functions. He exposed hypocrisy, blew the covers off things hidden, said what others would sometimes like to but could not. The islanders in effect had decided that Oscar's role was "a dirty job, but somebody's gotta do it."

In addition to being communalistic, the treatment of disorder in simple non-Western preindustrial cultures is generally what we would characterize as religious. Both diagnosis and treatment usually contain elements of the spiritual or magical, as was evident in the treatment of Kamahasanyi. For example, the Tarahumara of

Chihuahua, Mexico, like many Native American groups, attribute most sickness, whether physical or emotional, to either soul-loss or sorcery: accordingly, treatment is an amalgam of religious and shamanistic ritual (Kennedy 1978). On the other side of the world, in the Highlands of Papua New Guinea in Melanesia, the Fore people, like their neighbors, attribute all illness to either sorcery or malicious nature-spirits, and treat it with countermagic (Lindenbaum 1979). Field (1960) has shown how Ashanti men and women in rural Ghana utilize the shrines of a new religious cult to treat a variety of psychiatric disorders, including depression, anxiety, paranoia, schizophrenia, and obsessive-compulsive disorder, all attributable to spirit possession. Often the ritual treatment is combined with ethnopharmacological treatment; Robert Edgerton (1971b) describes a Tanzanian Hehe ethnopsychiatrist who blends the supernatural with a variety of herbal and mineral preparations, many of which work quite well and are in fact chemically similar to many Western preparations.

While the great variety of non-Western approaches make generalization difficult and perhaps even ill-advised, they do exhibit two characteristics that should be taken seriously by Western psychiatrists and allied professionals. First, the community, particularly family and friends, should probably be more involved in the treatment of behavioral and emotional disorder in our own society than they currently are: family systems approaches are a step in the right direction. Second, although no one advocates a return to religious and magical treatment, this widespread approach does illustrate the importance of cultural consistency in treatment: if a treatment is to be maximally effective, it should be consistent with the patient's cultural belief system.

The role of culture is basic in the treatment of "mental illness" everywhere, in complex as well as simple societies. The Nigerian psychiatrist Thomas Lambo (1978) has argued that modern and traditional psychiatric methods must be blended for the best result. In Africa and much of the "non-West," therapy is not a private matter as it is for Americans, but a matter of community and religion, both of which must be involved. Africans and Americans, Asians and Europeans—all human beings—must find a place for disorder in their communities, rather than simply casting it out.

"Alcoholism":
Another Culture-bound Disorder in the United States

No discussion of behavioral and emotional disorder written in the United States of America in the 1990s for an American reading audience would be complete without some discussion of the pet "disease" of our times: drug or "substance" abuse, including "alcoholism." I will focus primarily on alcoholism, although much of the research on alcoholism and its treatment applies equally to the use and abuse of other drugs, since both behavioral patterns are perceived in the United States as manifestations of the "disease" of addiction; the particular drug does not really matter beyond the issue of legality.

Alcoholism and its treatment are a perfect example with which to close this chapter: it is psychocultural with regard to cause, manifestation, and treatment, and it illustrates how subjective cultural belief and morality are ultimately more important than objective science when it comes to setting public policy or capturing the popular imagination (Stein 1985). In fact, in the case of alcoholism research, cultural morality has directly shaped research. Finally, the most widely accepted and medically and governmentally recommended treatment is enrollment in a religious cult.

I have no interest in reviewing the tens of thousands of pages of research on alcoholism, a project well beyond the scope of this book and for the most part irrelevant to it; rather I target the relatively small body of research that bears on the *psychocultural* aspects of alcoholism and addiction in general. Some of my conclusions are based on my own thirty-month (1982–1985) study of Alcoholics Anonymous, alcohol counseling, Al-Anon, and Adult Children of Alcoholics, employing the "experiential research" strategy pioneered by the anthropologist David K. Reynolds (see Reynolds and Farberow 1976, 1977) along with traditional participant observation.

Let me explore briefly some of the terminology associated with alcoholism and related subjects before going any farther. As generally used in the United States, the term "alcoholism" refers to a medical disease believed to be biochemically based and incurable;

it is manifested chiefly in a loss of control over one's consumption of alcohol, with regard to quantity, or frequency, or appropriateness; abstinence and regular attendance at Alcoholics Anonymous meetings are the only widely recommended treatments. Some believers in the biomedical model of alcoholism consider it to be a *physical* disease, while others consider it to be a *mental* illness; for my purposes, this difference is not really very significant since, as I have already argued, the American biomedical model implies an ultimately physical basis for mental as well as physical illness. The term "alcohol abuse" implies "alcoholism," so these two terms are roughly equivalent. The term "addiction" as commonly used in the United States refers to a medical disease manifested by an inability to control a certain behavior, and the frequent repetition of that behavior; while "addiction" is most often used to refer to alcoholism or drug abuse, it is also applied to love and sex, work, shopping, gambling, and so forth, all of which are increasingly seen as diseases. Alcoholism and drug abuse, then, are subcategories of the larger disease of addiction.

Although alcohol is obviously a drug, for cultural reasons it is usually semantically separated from other drugs such as cocaine, heroin, LSD, and cannabis, largely because these latter drugs and others are illegal, whereas alcohol, along with the drugs caffeine and nicotine, is legal. Hence "drug abuse," and more cryptically, "substance abuse" (as in "controlled substance"), usually refer only to illegal drugs and exclude alcohol, caffeine, and nicotine. Prescription drugs also fall under the rubric of drug or substance abuse because while legal, they are also "controlled"—they can only be obtained legally by means of a physician's prescription for a specific condition, or illegally on the street.

I argued earlier in this chapter that the biomedical model is the culturally preferred—actually, culturally *mandated*—model for explaining deviance and behavioral and/or emotional disorder in the United States; unusual behavior is perceived as a symptom of a deeper biological sickness. I noted further that drug and alcohol abuse have been thoroughly medicalized in this country and that furthermore this biomedical model has become moral as well as scientific orthodoxy (Stein 1990). It is extremely difficult and problematic in the United States in 1990 to argue against this model of alcoholism. Nevertheless, it is important to do so, since there are quite simply *no* scientific data that uphold a purely biomedical model (that is, one that ignores other factors) of alcoholism or addiction in general, and psychological anthropology has much to contribute, at least potentially, to a more accurate understanding of addictive behaviors, especially in regard to their psychocultural dimensions.

That alcoholism is not accurately labeled a disease has been demonstrated over and over again in article after article, book after book, research study after research study, but all of these have been virtually ignored by the alcoholism establishment: they are heretical and do not fit into the dominant cultural norms of morality. For example, the philosopher and addiction consultant to the World Health Organization Herbert Fingarette (1988, 1990) has argued logically and persuasively in numerous articles and in his book *Heavy Drinking: The Myth of Alcoholism as a Disease,* that excessive use of alcohol is a sociocultural and psychological problem rather than a biological and medical one. By defining it and studying it incorrectly, we decrease our ability to offer real help to those who do suffer from this behavioral problem. Fingarette states that the disease model is based on four untrue assumptions: (1) there is a unitary pattern of steady deterioration for problem drinkers; (2) the condition is involuntary; (3) medical expertise is required to help the alcoholic; and (4) alcoholics are not responsible for either their drinking or its consequences, since they are victims of an involuntary disease. In reality, patterns of heavy drinking fluctuate from drinker to drinker, the causes of heavy drinking vary from drinker to drinker, and education and psychological counseling are more helpful than medical therapy (bear in mind that attendance at AA meetings is nonmedical, even though that group advocates a medical model). In addition, if alcoholics are treated as irresponsible, they are thus excused from self-destructive and/or antisocial behavior, in effect being rewarded for abusing alcohol; the Supreme Court has consistently ruled that alcoholics *are* responsible for their drinking and their behavior in general (Fingarette 1990:4–6).

Another major critic of the disease concept of alcoholism and addiction whom the reader would do well to consult is the social psychologist Stanton Peele (1981, 1987, 1989), who has spent a career uncovering the scientific falseness of the disease approach to addiction. In his most recent book, *Diseasing of America: Addiction Treatment Out of Control,* he notes that anything and everything can become an addiction; in the United States of 1990, that seems to be exactly what is happening. His thesis, consistent with psychocultural understandings of behavior, is that human beings are active agents, not passive victims, of their addictions (Peele 1989:3). Addiction "disease" is a new, third-generation disease: the first generation were physical; later the medical establishment expanded its purview to include emotional disorders, the second-generation "diseases" or mental illnesses; now addictions are the third generation of disease-category expansion, with alcoholism serving as the model for other newly medicalized deviant behaviors such as compulsive gambling (Peele 1989:21). Peele argues forcefully that alcoholism and other addictions represent ordinary human behaviors which are social, cultural, and psychological in nature. They reach problematic levels when people lose their sense of self-efficacy, when they feel hopeless and powerless against their environment and the future. Psychologist David McClelland also found that heavy drinking is associated with feelings of powerlessness (McClelland et al. 1972).

This analysis concurs with cultural and ethnological research. Is it just a coincidence, for example, that simple small-scale societies, many of whom have used indigenous alcoholic beverages for centuries, only begin to experience significant levels of problem drinking *after* loss of political sovereignty and economic self-sufficiency? What applies to individual problem drinkers in the United States, in other words, also seems to apply to entire cultures in other times and places. Among the Kpelle of Liberia, I noted an obvious relationship between degree of involvement in "modern" life—that is, level of urbanization of community, proximity to motor roads, effectiveness of secret societies, working for cash, and so forth—and incidence of problem drinking. The more rural, economically self-sufficient, and embedded in traditional, older customs was the community, then the lower was the level of what we would call alcoholism. In Micronesia, too, I found the feelings of impotence and frustration among young heavy drinkers to be almost palpable.

Many studies have documented the strong role that ethnicity and culture play in the incidence of alcoholism. For example, there are huge differences among Asians, Native Americans, Irish, Jews, and Italians, to name only five groups. Even those who argue that alcoholism is a disease, such as Harvard researcher George Vaillant (who, as an M.D., continues to advocate the disease model even though his own impressive longitudinal study in no way supports it), find impressive cultural differences among drinking populations (Vaillant 1983). Are there "racial" and genetic differences among cultural groups, even when those groups live side by side for generations, so powerful that they overwhelm learning, will, and responsibility? The proposition is absurd—and untrue. Not only are psychocultural factors an important cause of problem drinking, but cultural factors underlie the notion of alcoholism-disease itself: it is a culture-bound syndrome. Even a nonanthropologist, in this case the prominent sociological alcohol researcher Robin Room (1984:176), asserts that any "disease concept centering on loss of control . . . is at its heart a culture-bound syndrome, a concept which has meaning only in a culture in which individual self-control is the normative mode of social control." Culture thus underlies both Western theories of "alcoholism" and the use of alcohol everywhere.

Cultural and psychological anthropologists have contributed significantly to discussions of drinking, although as I have noted in other contexts earlier in the book, their "exotic" findings are often ignored. Space permits me only to mention a few of these findings. In an important cross-cultural study, anthropologist Robert Edgerton, working with Craig MacAndrew, found that culture patterns not only the actual consumption of alcohol but also the way people behave when inebriated; in other words, culture reaches way down into areas where we in the West keep insisting that control is lost (MacAndrew and Edgerton 1969). One of the foremost anthropological researchers on alcoholism is Mac Marshall (1979; Marshall and Marshall 1990), who has focused on problem drinking in the islands of Truk in central Micronesia. Like MacAndrew and Edgerton, Marshall (1979) shows conclusively that excessive drinking is shaped by the norms and beliefs of Trukese culture. It is a problem primarily among young men, who in the past would have been warriors; in a sense, excessive drinking, along with the brawling that often accompanies it, is a latter-day substitute for warfare, establishing the *pwara* (machismo) of the men. Even when extremely drunk, these young men adhere to strict norms concerning who is fair game for violence and abuse, use of language, location of alcohol consumption, reciprocity, and so on. These "drinking norms" are not everyday norms, of course, and in fact would violate community standards of behavior in a sober context: drinking norms exist in the permissive context of release from ordinary constraints; they are nonetheless cultural norms, albeit norms of a special sort. Marshall (1979) found that when these heavy drinkers reach middle age, most of them join the church and cease drinking; in other words, they "mature out" with the aid of religion.

In many societies, the consumption of alcoholic beverages is a central part of culture, filling many positive functions. East African cattle-herding men, for example, drink with those they were initiated with, their age-set, in important sociable contexts. Mary Douglas (1987) has edited a book, *Constructive Drinking*, full of anthropological examples from all over of the positive effects of drinking in society, to counterbalance the largely negative reputation of alcohol in the United States. John Kennedy (1978) shows how central the consumption of maize beer, or *tesguino*, is to the Tarahumara Indians of northern Mexico, a group that has gained minor notoriety among American athletes for their frequent long-distance mountain runs and races. Not only are beer parties the linchpins of an entire social and ritual complex vital to the culture's integration, but in spite of all the drinking, the Tarahumara live nonviolently and emphasize nonviolence as an important cultural value. It would seem very clear that alcohol use as well as abuse is an adaptational response to the cultural environment.

The most commonly recommended treatment for alcoholism in the United States, participation in Alcoholics Anonymous, is also a product of American culture; several studies of AA support a psychocultural rather than a biomedical model of problem drinking. In my own study, for example, I discovered numerous contradictions and inconsistencies, similar to those one would find if studying a religious group. The AA program and its members call it "the only treatment that works," yet there exist absolutely no statistics on its effectiveness. In my study, only a hard core of members attended regularly; most attendees at any given meeting dropped out for good or for a while, clearly *not* helped by the program. Some of the regulars drank heavily every few months or so: why wasn't the program working for them? Members insisted that they could never stop drinking on their own; yet on their own, they stopped drinking and went for help, they abstain on their own, and they attend meetings on their own; the founder of AA, Bill Wilson, quit drinking on his own. Many members of AA know people who had drinking problems who abstained or cut back on their own. In spite of these contrary data, however, official AA dogma—and the majority of members apparently agree—insists that no one can quit drinking on his or her own.

Members insist that they must abstain, not cut down, and do so forever, not temporarily, although the permanent abstinence is achieved "one day at a time." If they ever take a drink, the dogma goes, they will drink alcoholically in very short order. Again, although many members do indeed drink again (a "slip"), often without excess, and then return to the fold, and know many former problem drinkers who have changed to moderate drinking, persons in AA continue to believe that they can never drink again. In fact, this strong belief that they will never be able to control their consumption of alcohol often becomes a self-fulfilling prophecy. People who have been sober for years without AA are viewed skeptically: "Oh, he'll drink eventually. Just wait. You can't do it without the program." This view leads to absurdities: several of my informants said that they refused to eat any dish in a wine sauce. When I pointed out that all alcohol evaporates early in the cooking process, they remained adamant: "You can never be sure." Liqueur-based desserts, cough syrups, cold medicines were out. Most members, although not all, felt the same way about nonalcoholic beers and wines.

Members are, in other words, addicted to AA meetings, replacing one dependency with another. In my study sample, marriages frequently broke up, not because of drinking, but because of the all-consuming attention to, and dependency on, AA. The drug nicotine kills several times as many people as alcohol each year (346,000 versus 125,000 in 1988, according to the National Institute on Drug Abuse ["War on Drugs" 1990]), yet in the groups I studied most of the members were heavy smokers; some consumed as many as four or five packs of cigarettes a day. Three members died of lung, throat, or oral cancer during the thirty-month study period. In spite of this, everyone seemed to view nicotine, the "permitted vice" (as they called it), as rather benign compared with alcohol. Nonsmokers' meetings were unpopular, and AA literature subtly encourages smoking: in the official newsletter, *The Grapevine*, AA members are shown in cartoons often with cigarette in hand. (I must note that New York state law regarding smoking in public places has recently made all AA meetings, in effect, nonsmokers' meetings.) Alcoholics Anonymous members' addiction to caffeine is legendary.

Another contradiction centers on the notion of the "alcoholic personality": officially (according to AA), alcoholism is a disease that has absolutely nothing to do with the type of person one is, and nothing to do with life's problems. Yet in testimony after testimony, I listened while people proclaimed themselves "typical alcoholic personalities" and talked about how they had begun drinking during a "rough time" in their lives. Autobiographies are often unconsciously restructured so that rather than having drunk because of the hopelessness and powerlessness engendered by a set of serious problems, the problems themselves were caused by drinking.

The contradictory beliefs in the importance of individual psychological factors are so important that they underlie another article of faith, that abstaining by itself is not enough. If one simply does not drink, one is only "dry," not "sober." If people do not "work the program," that is, work through the requisite "Twelve Steps," they might even start behaving in as obnoxious a fashion as they did when they were drinking; this remarkable state of nonalcoholic drunkenness is officially designated a "dry drunk" (Solberg 1982, 1983)! Such semantic games are an important part of the AA belief system and are geared to foster dependency on, and attendance at, AA meetings. New members ("pigeons") are encouraged to attend "90 meetings in 90 days," especially if they have just come out of "rehab." I met several people who frequently attended more than one meeting a day.

Such bombardment is akin to recruitment into religious cults. Novices are free to leave, but warned of dire consequences to body and mind if they do leave. In the groups I attended, members were repetitively reminded that the *only* alternatives to attendance at AA meetings were "death or insanity." Not surprisingly, members of Alcoholics Anonymous are very fearful of leaving the program.

From a psychocultural viewpoint, AA *is*, in fact, a religious cult, having all the characteristics of a religious sect. Like Mac Marshall's Trukese, drinkers who join up stop drinking when they "get religion." The Alcoholics Anonymous literature, as well as the members of AA, insist that the program is not religious, but that it is rather a "spiritual" program. Yet I have never been able to ascertain the difference between the two; in fact there is no real difference, since spirituality, which pertains to an incorporeal soul, is a clearly religious concept.

Other aspects of the program bear out this religious dimension. The group has a creation myth complete with culture-heroes, Bill W. and Dr. Bob, laid out in its sacred scripture, the "Big Book" (Alcoholics Anonymous 1955). Stories of the lives of the early disciples follow the creation myth in the Big Book. The program insists on its members' following a strict moral code, like the Ten Commandments, laid down by the alcoholic ancestors—the "Twelve Steps" and the "Twelve Traditions" (Alcoholics Anonymous 1955). A belief in a Higher Power ("HP") is required; officially, this can be any power higher than oneself—the group itself, for example. Unofficially, it is the traditional Christian male God; members in my study sample were strongly pressured to make God their higher power. The use of "the group" or "nature" or the like as the higher power was only tolerated patronizingly as a temporary substitute for God. The word "God" is used explicitly four times in the Twelve Steps themselves. Some members spoke unselfconsciously of their "Savior Jesus Christ." The religious themes of redemption and salvation are evident in most meetings, as is the practice of "witnessing" and "testifying," also found in fundamentalist, evangelical Christian churches. The meetings I attended always closed with members all holding hands and praying directly to God, the official "Serenity Prayer." AA was founded on an explicitly religious basis. The conduct of meetings, the Twelve Steps, the uses of simple aphorisms, the anti-intellectualism, the attitude of unquestioning acceptance, and so on were lifted directly from an evangelical Christian movement known as the Oxford Group Movement or Moral Rearmament (Eister 1950). This movement was very active during the 1930s, when Bill Wilson was founding Alcoholics Anonymous.

Perhaps the most significant contradiction in AA philosophy for psychocultural purposes is its relationship to American biomedicine. Official AA literature promotes the idea that alcoholism is a disease or an allergy, a physical condition whose only treatment is complete abstinence. The members of my groups repeatedly said that alcoholism was "just like cancer" or "just like diabetes." Yet the treatment itself, with the possible exception of medically supervised detoxification of the heaviest drinkers, is wholly nonmedical; indeed the members of AA are very skeptical of both the medical and scientific establishments, in spite of the fact that the American Medical Association treats alcoholism as a disease. Only fellow alcoholics have credibility to those in AA; as a result, alcoholism counselors at rehabilitation facilities and at mental health centers are usually recovering alcoholics themselves. (It is as if only former cancer patients could become oncologists or only chronic depressives or schizophrenics could become psychiatrists.)

I want to stress that AA clearly helps a significant number of people to lead sober and productive lives. But that benefit does not in any way buttress the idea that alcoholism is a physiological disease. Observational studies of AA support the psychocultural nature of both alcoholism and its treatment, while in no way supporting the medical model. The sociologist David Rudy (1986), who also conducted a participant observation study of Alcoholics Anonymous, arrived at conclusions parallel to my own. He concluded that alcoholism was a product of social interaction, and that participation in Alcoholics Anonymous, rather than heavy drinking itself, leads to the acquisition of an "alcoholic identity," a transformation of the self. His study led him to define alcoholism as follows: "*Alcoholism is a characterization attached to drinkers by others when these others question the drinkers' behavior and when the drinkers lack the power or desire to negotiate another explanation*" (Rudy 1986:99; emphasis in original).

The AA program, along with the Twelve Steps, has been adapted for the treatment of a wide range of other addictions, addictions to drugs, food, gambling, and others. This spread means only that evangelism and conversion are successful in American culture; it does not mean that addiction is a disease. Addictions, including the repetitive and excessive drinking of alcohol or ingestion of drugs, are rather unremarkable panhuman behaviors, not diseases that separate their "victims" from the rest of the population, those who are "normal" and "healthy."

A psychocultural theory of addiction remains to be developed, but a few propositions emerge from the research available. Addictions are basically habits: in fact, the word "addiction" itself meant "habit" until about midtwentieth century; then the word began to connote bad habit, then finally out-of-control habit (Szasz 1974). In any case, alcohol and drugs do not produce involuntary addictions; rather, addictions to either substances or activities are, like other psychocultural behaviors, *learned.* "[The] addict must learn the culturally defined methods of response which vary from one subculture to another" (Coleman 1976:140). "The *experience itself* is what the person becomes addicted to . . . it is the *feeling* to which the person becomes addicted" (Peele 1989:151). Addictions do things for people, allowing them to deal "with feelings and situations with which addicts cannot otherwise cope" (Peele 1989:146).

Addiction is the product of a relationship, a relationship between an individual and an experience, not simply the product of a drug or of an emotionally disturbed individual. Its occasionally runaway character seems to be a type of feedback that the anthropologist Gregory Bateson (1958 [orig. 1936]:178–188) long ago labeled schismogenesis: an escalating attempt to recapture some originally satisfying experience, resulting in a distortion of self and behavior. Human beings seem to derive comfort and satisfaction from repetitive behaviors: perhaps this stems from the intellectual craving for order and predictability I emphasized earlier. Addictions in this sense appear to be related to ritualism, a panhuman trait defined by the psychological anthropologist Anthony Wallace (1966:236–242): "Ritual [is] stereotyped communication, solitary or interpersonal, which reduces anxiety," enlarges confidence, and restructures cognitive and affective states within the self, the subjects of the next chapter. Habits, rituals, addictions—all are subtypes of normal, necessary patterns of human behavior that help people get along and survive in their cultural environments.

SUGGESTED READINGS

By far the best and most thorough critique of the American biomedical model of deviance is *Deviance and Medicalization: From Badness to Sickness* by sociologists Peter Conrad and Joseph Schneider (1980). American biomedicine as a belief system is discussed by the medical anthropologists Atwood Gaines and Robert Hahn (1985) in their article "Among the Physicians: Encounter, Exchange and Transformation" included in their intriguing edited volume *Physicians of Western Medicine*. Anthropological psychiatrist Arthur Kleinman (1988b) offers a sociocultural critique of Western psychiatry from an insider's perspective in *Rethinking Psychiatry: From Cultural Category to Personal Experience.*

The culture-bound syndromes have for decades provided a major focus for dialogue between psychiatry and anthropology. A good, although technical, overview is Pow M. Yap's (1969) "The Culture-bound Reactive Syndromes," in *Mental Health Research in Asia and the Pacific,* edited by W. Caudill and T. Lin. Anthony Wallace's (1972) classic piece, "Mental Illness, Biology, and Culture," not only discusses the culture-bound syndrome *pibloktoq* but also treats the complex interaction of biological and cultural factors in the creation of behavioral and emotional disorders.

Turning to American society, Michael Kenny (1986), in *The Passion of Ansel Bourne,* shows how spirit possession and multiple personality disorder may be essentially the same disorder shaped differently by different cultural times and places. Elaine Abelson (1989), in "The Invention of Kleptomania," published in the feminist journal *Signs,* demonstrates that kleptomania stems from specific historical, social, and cultural circumstances.

Social psychologist D. L. Rosenhan's (1973) "On Being Sane in Insane Places," published in *Science,* remains the benchmark scientific critique of psychiatric diagnoses, mental hospitals, and related matters. It is a must for every student of psychology and culture.

The most trenchant and comprehensive critique of the categorization of addictions as illnesses is social psychologist's Stanton Peele's (1989) *Diseasing of America;* it will forever change your view of addiction. In an important ethnographic study of drinking among the young men of the Truk Islands, *Weekend Warriors,* Mac Marshall (1979) convincingly illustrates how culture patterns drinking patterns and inebriation itself. Finally, sociologist David Rudy (1986) carried out an ethnographic investigation of Alcoholics Anonymous utilizing the method of participant observation, and found that alcoholism and the identity of "alcoholic" were socially constructed rather than physiologically based. He reports his findings in *Becoming Alcoholic: Alcoholics Anonymous and the Reality of Alcoholism.*

6

Cogito Sentio Ergo Sum:
The Thinking, Feeling Self

Intellect and affect, thinking and feeling, knowing and sensing, reason and sentiment, cognition and emotion—no matter what words are used to describe it, this dualism pervades psychological studies. Unfortunately, these two faces of the self are often portrayed as sealed off from each other, or even as opposites, rather than as intertwined qualities that can only exist in tandem. The thinking faculty has long been associated with the mind, while feelings have been connected with the body: hence the paraphrase of Descartes's famous aphorism, "I think, therefore I am" in the chapter title. "I feel (*Sentio*), therefore I am" is just as correct, that is, just as wrong. The two equally and together define the human experience. *Star Trek*'s Mr. Spock—all cognition (logic) and no emotion—is not human.

While psychology and psychiatry have maintained this Cartesian split until fairly recently, cultural anthropology has sinned even more grievously, virtually ignoring both cognition and emotion until the 1960s. In the classic ethnographies of the thirties, forties, and fifties, cognition was rarely mentioned as such, but was in any case implicitly reduced to the slavish following of cultural rules; emotion was similarly subjugated to formal expression in ritual. In the sixties, however, a field labeled somewhat misleadingly as "cognitive anthropology" began to look at certain aspects of cognition, followed in the 1970s by educational anthropology; psychological and symbolic anthropology entered the fray with studies of emotion in the 1980s. Of course, the actual timeline was not so neat, and outlying early studies set the tone for work carried out much later, but I believe that the general temporal trend is accurate.

This chapter presents a brief look at recent and new directions in psychological anthropology; when it is taken together with the contemporary emphasis on the self and on gender and sexuality discussed earlier, a reasonably reliable picture of the future of the field comes into focus. I will first review recent work on cognition and culture, then the newer studies on the cultural construction of emotion.

Culture and Cognition

Until roughly 1960, cultural anthropologists paid very little attention to cognitive processes. Much of the work of Jean Piaget, a founding father of cognitive science so influential in Europe in the middle third of this century, was not even translated into English, and what was translated was ignored by anthropologists. Anthropological work before midcentury that did treat the relationship of culture with cognition was rare indeed.

One such exception is Franz Boas, the father of American cultural anthropology. In *The Mind of Primitive Man* (1938 [orig. 1911]), he argued forcefully that race had nothing to do with intelligence and that, while culture shapes the expression of cognition and intellect, the underlying cognitive processes are the same for all human beings everywhere, regardless of how "primitive" their cultures might appear to Western eyes. This very modern and liberal thesis was a counter argument to then-fashionable ideas of "primitive mentality," especially popular among French intellectuals: primitive people think primitive thoughts. He was especially interested in disproving the thesis of the French sociologist Lucien Levy-Bruhl, who in *How Natives Think* (1926 [orig. in French, 1910]) and other writings argued that primitive people thought like children, concretely and without abstraction. In *Growing Up in New Guinea*, Margaret Mead (1930) applied ethnographic research to the same problem, showing that Manus children believed less in spiritual entities than did their parents: their ideas of causation were more practical and empirical and less fanciful than adults'. In other words, much of the alleged evidence for childish thought among primitives was simply varying cultural beliefs and expression, ethnocentrically interpreted.

It was not until the sixties, however, that serious anthropological interest in cognition developed. At that time, a controversial movement swept through anthropology, a movement variously labeled "new ethnography," "ethnoscience," "ethnosemantics," "cognitive structuralism," and finally "cognitive anthropology." Much if not most of it was more methodological than psychological in orientation and so is not germane to the subject of this book; I will briefly review some of the more influential studies.

The study of kinship, including the analysis of the world's diverse systems of kinship terminology, has long been central to cultural anthropology. Ward Goodenough (1956), influenced by developments in the field of linguistics, introduced a new methodology for analyzing kinship terminology in the late fifties, a method he called "componential analysis," the breaking down of kin terms into their several "components" of meaning. For example, in American society a "sister" is (1) a female (2) in a given speaker's own generation, who is (3) in the speaker's own nuclear family. The numbered dimensions are the basic *components* of the kin-term "sister." The year before, Harold Conklin (1955) had published a similar analysis of categories of color among the Hanunóo of the Philippines.

The response was quite sensational: dozens of studies were published in the next few years on a dizzying variety of topics, generally taking apart linguistic categories (domains). The largest number consisted of formal analyses of kinship terminology (e.g.,

Lounsbury 1964; Hammel 1965; Goodenough 1967), but others included everything from disease categories (Frake 1961) to firewood (Metzger and Williams 1966); critics in fact commented on ethnoscientists' seeming preoccupation with ethnographic trivia. At first, these analyses remained at the level of semantics, that is, the researchers claimed only to be explaining the meanings of concepts and words within a linguistic taxonomy. Soon, however, "semantic" became "cognitive"; these analyses were said to accurately represent the cognitive world of the people under study (Frake 1962; Wallace 1962): at last, ethnographers wishfully stated, we are truly following Bronislaw Malinowski's dictum to reproduce "the native's point of view." A series of "how to" articles purported to guide the reader through the intricacies of foreign and even homegrown cognition: how to ask for a drink among the Subanun of the Philippines (Frake 1964), how to navigate in the Micronesian Pacific (Gladwin 1964), and how to drive to work in Philadelphia (Wallace 1965a). Ethnoscientific analyses, according to their practitioners, were "psychologically real" (Wallace and Atkins 1960; Wallace 1965b).

These studies do not argue that cognition was culturally constructed but rather that culture *is* cognition: the two are isomorphic (see, e.g., Tyler 1969:13). Culture in this view is an intricate structure of cognitive "rules, maps, and plans" for behavior (Spradley 1972). The ethnographer's task is to study native cognition and then to present it as accurately as possible. The majority of ethnographers, however, did not agree with this approach to fieldwork; nor did many anthropologists or psychologists agree that culture, semantics, and cognition were more or less the same thing. But cognitive anthropology, now more informed by cognitive psychology and shorn of its earlier preoccupation with trivia, did feed into the new and developing interdisciplinary field of cognitive science, where it continues to thrive.

Attention shifted away from semantic studies in the late sixties to more traditional cognitive concerns: cognitive development and the putative differences in thinking patterns between people in literate, industrial cultures and those in nonliterate, nonindustrial cultures—in many respects a return to the concerns of Boas, Levy-Bruhl, and Mead. An interdisciplinary convergence of scholars in

cultural anthropology, cognitive psychology, and education produced a series of remarkable studies of the cultural construction
of cognition, only a few of which can be discussed here.

One of our most persistent myths, exemplified by Levy-Bruhl
above, is that nonliterate people in less developed countries possess
a "primitive mentality" different from, and inferior to, our own. It
is like a child's mind, Levy-Bruhl argued. The "primitive mind" is
highly concrete, whereas the "Western mind" is highly abstract; the
"primitive mind" connects concrete ideas by rote association,
whereas the "Western mind" connects abstract ideas by general
principles of relationship; the "primitive mind" is illogical and contradictory, whereas the "Western mind" is logical and consistent.
The logical extension of this set of dichotomies is that the alleged
difference is genetically based: Third World peoples (and by further extension, nonwhites everywhere) are just not as intelligent as
Euro-American whites.

What is the other side of this racist myth? That there are no
differences? But there are, and they are well-documented. That
the differences are learned? Yes, but how? Exactly what are the
differences? Do they occur in all circumstances or only in certain
contexts? Why do they exist at all? As Boas (1938 [1911]) noted,
ethnographers must probe much more deeply than they were used
to doing in order to understand any people in other cultures: if
they do not, they might mistake their own lack of understanding
for stupidity on the part of the "natives."

The French anthropologist Claude Lévi Strauss (1966) has proposed a simplistic but catchy and much-cited update of the "primitive mentality" notion. "Primitive" thinking is akin to the activities
of a *bricoleur*, a jack-of-all-trades in rural France: he has a limited
tool kit which he must apply to any job he encounters. In other
words, he does not always have "the right tool for the job" but must
make do. Similarly, tribal peoples apply a limited set of magical and
mythical ideas to all problems, whether old or new. Western educated thought, on the other hand, is like engineering. The engi-
neer creates new tools, if necessary, to solve new problems.

Lévi-Strauss, of course, offers only a metaphor to elucidate cultural cognition. One researcher, not so easily dismissed, who does
not at all consider "mythical" the proposition that non-Western
nonliterate peoples might think in ways qualitatively different from

those of Western educated peoples, is the maverick British social anthropologist C. R. Hallpike. In his impressive compendium of ethnographic fieldwork and Piagetian psychological research, *The Foundations of Primitive Thought*, Hallpike (1979) argues that "primitive" (an aggressively provocative adjective, guaranteed to anger fellow anthropologists) thought is indeed childish, in fact preoperational and only occasionally concrete-operational. In effect, whole cultures can be stuck in a childlike egocentric preoperational world. He completely rejects any genetically based analysis, insisting that basic cognitive process is everywhere the same and that differing cognition is learned rather than innate. But he also argues that "primitive" cognition is not simply a matter of cultural difference: "primitive thought is based on an incomplete logic rather than on a different logic from that which we know" (Hallpike 1979:489). His theory is thus universalist rather than cultural-relativist.

More recently, Hamill (1990) challenged Hallpike's thesis as ethnocentric. His own thesis is radically cultural-relativist: no culture can be "higher" or "more complex" than another; "all cultures are equally complex and equally modern" (Hamill 1990:106). He investigated the use of logical syllogisms among the speakers of four different language groups, and found that all people are equally logical, but that logic cannot ever be separated from meaning. Reasoning, which Hamill calls "ethno-logic," is embedded in a cultural meaning-system: if it is separated from this meaning-system, and interpreted by researchers in other cultures with other meaning-systems—a description of much cross-cultural psychological research—the results will be ethnocentric or worse. Cognition cannot be fully understood divorced from symbolic meanings generated by particular cultures.

Perhaps the most influential body of work in culture and cognition to address these issues in recent years was carried out by the cross-cultural cognitive psychologist Michael Cole and his colleagues; they studied the Kpelle of Liberia, the subjects of some of my own research, as well as the Vai of Liberia and other groups elsewhere in the world. Although Hallpike draws liberally on Cole's and his colleagues' data, and although both are investigating similar questions concerning the relation of culture and cognition, they arrive at very different conclusions.

The findings of Cole and colleagues are experimental-psychological rather than participant-observational, but have nonetheless had a lasting influence on psychological anthropologists and their research; the results fill dozens of articles, but much of it is summarized in three books (Gay and Cole 1967; Cole, Gay, Glick, and Sharp 1971; Scribner and Cole 1981). Cognitive anthropologists had confined their work primarily to cultural (cognitive) *content*, whereas Cole, like most psychologists, was interested in cognitive *process*. To achieve an adequate understanding of pan-human cognition, a research strategy combining the most fruitful approaches of anthropology, linguistics, and psychology was needed: anthropology emphasizes the importance of naturalistic observation in context; linguistics emphasizes native categories and semantic codes; and psychology emphasizes controlled experimentation. In arguing for such a synthesis of disciplines, Cole echoes a scholar who deeply influenced him, the great Soviet psychologist, Lev S. Vygotsky (1962, 1978). Vygotsky argued in the twenties and thirties that cognition was profoundly social in origin and could not adequately be studied without employing the findings of the social sciences, linguistics, and philosophy, along with psychology. (I should note here that Hallpike also agrees with, and draws heavily upon, Vygotsky.)

The Cole research focuses on the relation between a person's culture and that same person's cognitive skills; the latter, as Vygotsky also argued, must not be isolated from ordinary life-activities. Further, the group wants to be able to characterize accurately the nature of any changes in habitual thinking and problem-solving brought about by cultural changes such as Western-style schooling or literacy (Cole, Gay, Glick, and Sharp 1971; Scribner and Cole 1981). Cole assumes "psychic unity," that is, that humans everywhere think by means of identical cognitive processes and utilize intelligent, adaptive behaviors daily. The trick is to use "experimental anthropology" and fine-grained ethnography to reveal these processes.

In their highly innovative initial fieldwork, Gay and Cole (1967) were trying to learn why Kpelle children had such a hard time with mathematics when they attended Western-style schools. After extensive investigation, they found that even relatively brief schooling did improve performance on some (but, importantly, not all) experimental tasks, but that an adequate understanding of Kpelle cognition requires going well beyond the simplistic concrete/abstract dichotomy so widely accepted. While not denying a tendency toward concreteness in Kpelle thinking, they found that habitual thinking varies according to context, with better performance on tasks typical of Kpelle culture. For example, Kpelle are better than Americans at the task of estimating the number of cups of rice in a larger container of rice (a skill useful at market) or the number of stones in a pile (used as markers). They also perform better than their American counterparts in logical problems where the Kpelle language makes finer distinctions that English, and even use verbal mediation (linguistic labeling of reasons for responses), a skill long associated only with literate subjects, as long as the mediation is within the conceptual capacities provided by their language and habitualized by their traditional and customary life.

Cole's later research built on these findings. He found that Western-style education led to the acquisition of new intellectual skills as well as to a change in the situations to which various cognitive skills are applied: educated subjects are more likely to treat individual stimulus presentations as subproblems of some larger problem, whereas noneducated subjects are more likely to see each presentation as a separate instance, without seeking some underlying principle (Cole, Gay, Glick, and Sharp 1971). Cole resists the temptation to conclude that nonliterate Africans are incapable of conceptual thinking or of combining subinstances to solve a more general problem, but rather concludes that people in differing cultures, and in differing contexts within a given culture, solve problems by means learned and used for particular situations. The tendency for American schoolchildren to learn things according to some general scheme is so strong that it can even interfere in the performance of tasks where any such general principle is lacking. Kpelle adults are perfectly capable of hypothetical reasoning but do not use it in experimental tasks because they fail to see its applicability (Cole, Gay, Glick, and Sharp 1971:187 ff.) In other words, cognitive skills and the behavior that results are functional and adaptational within cultures, reflecting the central thesis of this book. In Chapter 1, I discussed how Ogbu (1974, 1978) applied this thesis to his analysis of educational failure by minorities both in the United States and internationally. This important idea, "that cultural differences in cognition reside more in the situations to which cognitive processes are applied" than in the presence or absence of a process in a particular cultural group, is applicable to Western subcultures as well: we must learn to tap into cognitive "street skills" and apply them to the school setting (Cole, Gay, Glick, and Sharp 1971:233–234).

The latest investigations concerning how culture structures cognition reflect similar partnerships between cognitive psychology and cultural anthropology. Cole (1985) continues to propose a Vygotskian theoretical and methodological marriage between anthropology and psychology, since culture and cognition are inseparable and interactive. Such a union is indeed essential if there is to be a cross-culturally viable theory of human cognition. However, even quite sophisticated interdisciplinary studies of this sort often arrive at very different conclusions, typically at opposite ends of a relativist-universalist continuum, as we have seen in the case of the Cole versus Hallpike researches.

In the studies outlined above, Cole argues that while underlying cognitive processes are everywhere the same, their surface manifestations in characteristic thinking, problem-solving, and learning—what Scribner and Cole (1973) call "functional learning systems"—are shaped by local cultures and everyday situations. This Vygotskian perspective, with its universal depths and culturally relative surfaces, informs a good deal of recent research in culture and cognition.

Barbara Rogoff (1984) refers to the characteristic thinking shaped by recurring social contexts as "everyday cognition"; Sylvia Scribner (1984) refers to it as "working intelligence." They and their colleagues, very much influenced by Cole, appropriately focus on the cognitive consequences of everyday recurrent social experience, utilizing research on factory work, grocery-shopping, weaving, skiing, and a variety of other settings and activities (Rogoff and Lave 1984). They show that everyday thinking is practical and adaptive, in the service of action, and geared to contextual efficiency. With a particularly apt turn of phrase, Sheldon White and Alexander Siegel (1984:253) suggest that children are always and everywhere adaptationally "building selves to fit a set of social worlds."

Rogoff (1990) applies this seminal notion to the entire process of cognitive development, which she calls a process of "apprentice-ship in thinking." Drawing on Vygotsky and Piaget (e.g., 1967), her own field research in Guatemala and the United States, as well as parallel research by others, Rogoff builds a truly cultural and con-textual theory of cognitive development. Space limitations pre-clude my doing justice to her rich and detailed findings and speculations, but throughout her study, she emphasizes the *shared* nature of learning and thinking; earlier psychological research often emphasized the *independence* of the child as a developing organism. According to Rogoff (1990), cognitive development is always social-contextual, thinking is practical, learning is a collab-orative process of social sharing and guidance by peers and adults with greater skills, and children must be seen as interdependent with significant others in their cultures.

In an article in which he offers suggestions for integrating sym-bolic anthropology, with its concern for meaning-systems, and cog-nitive anthropology, with its emphasis on the cultural shaping of cognition, Bradd Shore (1991) also stresses shared cognition, which he refers to as "intersubjectivity." If social action is collec-tively meaningful, then cultural cognition, arising from shared ex-perience, must also be collectively meaningful, a proposition which might seem obvious to the reader but which is (incredibly) rejected by a few antiscience "postmodern" anthropologists (who in any case typically reject the notion of "culture" as a shared structure: see, e.g., Clifford 1988 and Rosaldo 1990). Cultures provide indi-viduals with conventional cognitive schemata—representations of reality—with which they cognitively construct experience and in the process of so doing, make it personally meaningful. Cognitive "meaning thus has a double birth, once through the social and his-torical evolution of such conventional schemata, and once through (personal) schematization" (Shore 1991:16). Cognition is at once psychological and individual, and cultural and collective.

The Cultural Construction of Emotion

We in the West seem to value intellect over affect. We endlessly ruminate over the nature of cognition but attend less seriously to emotional life, as if we were vaguely embarrassed by it. No weighty treatises deal with the differences between "us" and "them" in affect, but many discuss the mind and thought. Older works in anthropology sometimes implied that "primitives" are more subject to their emotions—wilder, less controlled—than are Westerners, but little systematic research was applied to the topic until quite recently. The early idea of the "wild man" of tribal society was little more than the ethnocentric expression of discomfort on the part of emotionally repressed male European intellectuals. Savages were seen as closer to beasts, while civilized people were closer to angels. In fact, recent research shows clearly that emotions are if anything *more* controlled in many non-Western preindustrial societies than in the West. Sociocentric selves would seem more likely to repress certain emotions in the service of society than would the more egocentric selves of the West.

Prior to 1980 or so, studies of emotional life within anthropology were linked to studies of personality and were often psychoanalytic in nature; in addition, they usually emphasized the universality of basic emotions, since the seat of emotions is in a primitive part of the brain, and emotions are therefore evolutionarily older than cognition, consciousness, or culture. Culture simply manages the expression or display of emotions. For example, Hildred Geertz (1974 [orig. 1959]:250) states that the socializing of emotions is a process of narrowing perceptions of self and feeling-states, and that this feature of learning "can be a key to the understanding of personality differences found between members of different cultures." In her study of the socialization of emotions among Javanese, she focused on "respect," a key component of Javanese character. Respect itself has to do with external behavior more than internal emotion, but is closely associated with feelings of shame, guilt, and fear. As children grow, they must become "Javanized" regarding respect. This means that Javanese culture, transmitted by the significant adults in the children's world, provides suggestions about not only how to show respect appropriately but also *"how to feel"* about it within particular situations (Geertz 1974:263).

Similarly, the transcultural psychologist Robert Levy (1969) focused on the cultural management of anger in the socialization process on Tahiti. Children are trained in such a way that they learn to be afraid of being hurt and of the possible social disruption a display of anger might cause. Levy suggests that not only anger but all strong, intense expressions of feeling are avoided by Tahitians: their character is one of mildness and control, their emotions inhibited. Levy seems surprised to report that Tahitians do not appear to suffer from frustrated anger or repressed hostility, concluding simply that other features of Tahitian culture and socialization reduce intrapsychic tension which might otherwise result from repressing anger. In a more detailed study of Tahitian character, Levy (1973) analyzes other aspects of Tahitian emotional life as well, emphasizing how Tahitians actually experience it personally and culturally. For example, Tahitian culture frequently translates the feelings of loneliness and sadness associated with the loss of a loved one into experienced "illness" of the body (Levy 1973:272).

In a landmark study in the anthropology of emotion, Jean Briggs (1970) presents a powerful portrayal of the emotional life of a Canadian Inuit family, although her study is essentially devoid of analysis. As in Tahiti, the repression of anger is a central concern (the book's title is *Never in Anger*); in fact, emotional volatility in general is despised. The ethnographer herself was ostracized by the community for a time for simply being volatile (in ways that would be viewed as absolutely unremarkable in the dominant Canadian or American cultures). An important feature of the book is the inclusion of a range of Inuit categories of and terms for emotion. "As a warm, protective, nurturant, even-tempered person represents the essence of goodness, so an unkind, bad-tempered person represents the opposite" (Briggs 1970:328). Displays of bad temper towards others are always wrong once one is past toddlerhood, although it is fine to express anger toward dogs. Like Levy, Briggs emphasizes the cultural management of universally felt emotions.

Recently, some anthropologists have begun to question the alleged universality of emotions, at least as they are linguistically labeled in the Western languages used in scientific research. Is Western thinking about feelings, focused as it is on those feeling-states labeled happiness, sadness, anger, fear, disgust, surprise, and so forth, simply ethnocentric? Is it, in other words, merely one ethnopsychology among many? These are questions addressed by some of the most recent ethnographic research on self and emotion.

Freud of course argued that the human psyche is a veritable cauldron of bubbling emotions stemming from universal conflicts; in fact, it is the repression of emotions that is largely responsible for the development of culture and civilization (see, e.g., Freud 1913, 1930). Since Freud, the universality of the conventionally described emotions has been assumed as an article of faith. As Briggs, Levy, and others have shown, the expression of feeling can be managed culturally through socialization, community pressure, and other means, but the basic underlying emotions are the same in all cultures. Some research seems to confirm this universality of affect. A much-cited study by psychologist Paul Ekman (1974 [orig. 1970]) on facial expressions of emotion, for example, argues for a universal biological or learned basis for such expressions. Several techniques were employed, but the method of greatest relevance to our concerns here involved the presentation of pictures of faces illustrating fear, disgust, anger, surprise, sadness, and happiness to subjects in five culturally varying industrial societies, along with the preindustrial Fore of Papua New Guinea. All subjects agreed on the emotions portrayed, although the Fore did tend to confuse surprise with fear. From this and other experiments, Ekman rather hyperbolically concludes that there is a universal basis for the facial expression of emotion, while culture governs what elicits particular emotional displays, the rules of display, and the behavioral consequences of display. Another psychologist, C. E. Izard (1983:310–311), argues more complexly that at the experiential level, wherein "emotion is a quality of consciousness or *feeling* . . . the emotion state is invariant across cultures" but that emotions are also cognized, and cognition is shaped by culture; these "affective-cognitive structures" thus vary cross-culturally.

Since about 1980, some symbolic anthropologists, moving away from the earlier psychodynamic approaches taken by culture-and-personality researchers, have rejected assumptions of universality in the study of emotion, and in so doing have opened up a new and energetic line of research. The late Michelle Rosaldo's (1980) *Knowledge and Passion: Ilongot Notions of Self and Social Life* is generally credited with bringing about this theoretical shift. In her studies of the emotional life of the Ilongot of the Philippines, Rosaldo (1980, 1983) argues forcefully that emotions at every level are cultural constructions. Culture shapes not only our beliefs but also how we feel about them. "Affects . . . are no less cultural and no more private than beliefs. They are instead, cognitions . . . always culturally informed, in which the actor finds that body, self, and identity are immediately involved" (Rosaldo 1984:141). Ilongot emotion is connected to a set of symbolic cognitions concerning "heaviness" as well as motion, and to culturally derived morals concerning social balance and equality. Unlike in the West, shame is a healthy stimulus to action for Ilongot, inhibited anger is forgotten, and violence (in headhunting) brings relief rather than guilt (Rosaldo 1983:148). Killing and taking heads removes Ilongot male anger, "lightening" the self and relieving tension (Rosaldo 1980).

Catherine Lutz (1983, 1985, 1988) is another radical cultural relativist in the field of "emotional anthropology" who takes her cue from Rosaldo. She studied the ethnopsychology of the people of Ifaluk, a tiny Micronesian atoll, including local theories of emotion and the role of emotion in the development and maintenance of the self. She reports that basic Ifaluk values such as nonviolence, cooperation, and obedience according to the local system of social ranking are intimately connected with and supported by the emotion of *metagu* (fear/anxiety) which, like all Ifaluk emotion words, is defined situationally (Lutz 1983). *Metagu* is felt when one has to visit a strange household or be in the midst of a large group of people; it is experienced when in danger of encountering ghosts or sharks or when one is alone in a canoe on the ocean; it is also felt when one is the object of another important emotional category, the emotion of moral outrage/justifiable anger (*song* in Ifaluk) (Lutz 1983:249–250). A third ethno-emotion is *fago*, a state that connotes at once compassion, love, and sadness, a feeling of morally good, mature adults that reflects caring and nurturance for others (Lutz 1988:140–144).

As interesting as Lutz's ethnographic work is, however, its real importance may lie in its theoretical uses since Lutz, like Rosaldo before her, uses her research discoveries as a springboard for theoretical polemics. Her ethnography of Ifaluk, *Unnatural Emotions* (1988), is unconventional: it is as much a critique of Western anthropological, psychological, and philosophical approaches to the study of emotion—witness its subtitle, *Everyday Sentiments on a*

Micronesian Atoll and Their Challenge to Western Theory—as it is an ethnography of Ifaluk emotional life. Lutz (1985:37–38) considers academic psychology and its approach to the emotions to be itself an ethnospychology, and a pernicious one at that because of its great influence. Some peculiar ideas about emotion in Western culture include its dichotomizing of the social and the individual, subjective and objective reality, thought and action, cognition and emotion, and public and private. Western cultural conceptualizations of emotion typically associate it with devalued qualities, according to Lutz (1988:76): they are "irrational, physical, unintentional, weak, biased, and female," although they can also be "an expression of personal (moral) values."

The critique offered by Rosaldo, Lutz, and other "interpretive" symbolic anthropologists is an important challenge which must be heeded, but in my view, they have gone overboard. If their polemics are taken literally, an ethnology (the comparative study of culture) of emotions is impossible, since there is, according to them, no universal emotional baseline, and the ethnopsychological categories and concepts are by definition culture-specific and noncomparable. I am not alone in my skepticism. Levy (1984:217), for example, refers to Rosaldo's position as "extreme" and simplistic in her argument that affect is purely cultural and therefore unique. Comparative scientific study becomes impossible, replaced by "endless local exegeses, ... atheoretical natural history" (Levy 1984:233). Comparison and explanation should be retained as goals, and field data and ethnographic analysis should lie somewhere "between the locally unique and the universal" (Levy 1983:133).

Psychological anthropologist Philip Bock (1988) also disputes Rosaldo's and Lutz's theoretical conclusions about cultural emotional uniqueness, finding more similarities than differences when comparing Rosaldo's Ilongot texts with Shakespeare's plays on dimensions of emotions. He suggests that she might be inadvertently supporting "the ethnocentric distinction between *them* ... and *us* ... implying not just a difference but a superiority of self-awareness and self control in 'ourselves'"(Bock 1988:201). Needless to say, this is the last thing Rosaldo (or Lutz) intend!

Few anthropologists would dispute the claim that emotions are culturally constructed—note the title of this section. But I must agree with Bock (1988:202) and disagree with Lutz and Rosaldo on the notion of universal psychobiological bases for emotional states. One cannot simply wish biology away. An anthropology of cognition and emotion that recognizes and accommodates human universals—whether biological, psychological, developmental, sociological, or existential—is a richer anthropology, and an anthropology consistent with its historical grounding in evolutionary theory, both biological and cultural. Deep interpretation can only be deepened further by such recognition and inclusion.

One recent treatise, Walter Goldschmidt's (1990) *The Human Career: The Self in the Symbolic World,* shows the way. He melds evolutionary, functionalist, developmental, psychocultural, and symbolic approaches in a seamless understanding of the human self progressing through the life course within culture—with cognition and emotion squarely at the center. Cognition makes possible the symbolic world of meaning which is the essence of language and culture. Emotion makes this world subjectively one's own. A hunger for positive affect from others in one's cultural community, satisfied by the attainment of culturally defined prestige, is the basis for self-esteem and the fuel that motivates actors in every society. The entire process of moving through the human career is, in Goldschmidt's (1990:243) words, "a deeply emotional activity." Culture is cognitively stimulating and emotionally satisfying to the self. I hope others follow his lead, moving upward toward synthesis rather than descending into theoretical sectarianism.

SUGGESTED READINGS

The reader who wishes to explore further the impact of culture on cognition would do well to start with Michael Cole and Sylvia Scribner's *Culture and Thought: A Psychological Introduction* (1974). Barbara Rogoff's *Apprenticeship in Thinking* (1990) is a recent theoretical synthesis focusing on cognitive development.

Catherine Lutz and Geoffrey White provide a thorough overview of studies of culture and emotion in "The Anthropology of

Emotions," published in the 1986 edition of *Annual Review of Anthropology* (vol. 15). Lutz's *Unnatural Emotions* (1988) and Michelle Rosaldo's *Knowledge and Passion: Ilongot Notions of Self and Social Life* (1980) are two excellent ethnographies that represent the newer interpretive symbolic approach to the study of emotional life. Robert Levy's *Tahitians: Mind and Experience in the Society Islands* (1973) is an excellent example of the older psychodynamic culture-and-personality approach to emotion (and cognition).

Walter Goldschmidt's *The Human Career: The Self in the Symbolic World* (1990) is a new synthesis of the self, emotion, and symbolic cognition.

Epilogue

Throughout this book I have tried to demonstrate that culture shapes the human self and its behavior, and that the self and behavior are in turn adapted to culture. In Chapter 1 I reviewed basic concepts, along with theories of psychocultural adaptation, as well as applications and criticisms of those theories. Chapter 2 dealt with the formation of the self within the culturally patterned process of socialization. In Chapter 3 I showed how gender and sexuality are culturally constructed and adaptive. The specific topics of initiation and homosexuality provided a focus to illustrate the psychocultural adaptational qualities of gender and sexuality. The cultural patterning of collective behavior was the subject of Chapter 4, especially the historical concepts of modal personality and national character. I argued that these concepts were actually statements about collective normality. Patterns of behavior away from the norm are therefore deviant; yet deviance is as essential as normality for the long-term survival of a culture. In Chapter 5, I explored the idea of deviance and disorder in greater detail. I especially challenged the American biomedical model of behavioral and emotional disorder, arguing instead for a psychocultural model wherein disorders are shown to be culturally constructed, as are their treatments. The phenomenon of culture-bound syndromes was reviewed; I provided examples from societies around the world, including American society. So-called mental illness was shown to be shaped by culture. To illustrate how culture shapes behavior, whether ordered or disordered, and to critique the biomedical model of deviant behavior, I explored in some depth an important American culture-bound syndrome, alcoholism, and its treatment, Alcoholics Anonymous. Finally, Chapter 6 treated newer areas and directions in psychological anthropology, the study of cognition and emotion. Most anthropological approaches to these two psychological areas emphasize their cultural construction.

Throughout this study, other examples could have been chosen, and other topics discussed, but the conclusion would have remained the same: that psychocultural adaptation is basic to human life, and that culture constructs our very selves. A psychocultural and anthropological understanding of the human self and human behavior shows the profound role culture plays in shaping human adaptation and survival, satisfaction and behavior, socialization and career, the self and personality, and cognition and emotion, revealing the integrated self in all its dimensions.

Bibliography

Abelson, Elaine S. 1989. "The Invention of Kleptomania." *Signs* 15(1):123–143.

————. 1990. *When Ladies Go A-Thieving: Middle-Class Shoplifters in the Victorian Department Store.* New York: Oxford University Press.

Alcoholics Anonymous. 1955. *Alcoholics Anonymous: The Story of How Many Thousands of Men and Women Have Recovered from Alcoholism.* Rev. ed. New York: Alcoholics Anonymous World Services.

American Psychiatric Association. 1987. *Diagnostic and Statistical Manual of Mental Disorder (DSM III-R).* Third ed., rev. Washington, D.C.: American Psychiatric Association.

Bandura, Albert. 1977. *Social Learning Theory.* Englewood Cliffs, N.J.: Prentice-Hall.

Barker-Benfield, G. J. 1976. *The Horrors of the Half-Known Life: Male Attitudes Toward Women and Sexuality in Nineteenth-Century America.* New York: Harper and Row.

Barnouw, Victor. 1985. *Culture and Personality*. Fourth ed. Homewood, Ill.: Dorsey Press.

Barry, Herbert, III; Bacon, Margaret K.; and Child, Irvin L. 1957. "A Cross-Cultural Survey of Some Sex Differences in Socialization." *Journal of Abnormal and Social Psychology* 55:327–332.

Barry, Herbert, III; Child, Irvin L.; and Bacon, Margaret K. 1959. "Relation of Child Training to Subsistence Economy." *American Anthropologist* 61:51–63.

Barzini, Luigi. 1964. *The Italians*. New York: Atheneum.

———. 1983. *The Europeans*. New York: Simon and Schuster.

Bateson, Gregory. 1958 (orig. 1936). *Naven*. Second ed. Stanford, Calif.: Stanford University Press.

Benedict, Ruth F. 1934a "Anthropology and the Abnormal." *Journal of General Psychology* 10:59–82.

———. 1934b. *Patterns of Culture*. Boston: Houghton Mifflin.

———. 1946. *The Chrysanthemum and the Sword*. Boston: Houghton Mifflin.

Berger, Peter, and Luckmann, Thomas. 1966. *The Social Construction of Reality*. Garden City, N.Y.: Doubleday.

Bernstein, Richard. 1990. *Fragile Glory: A Portrait of France and the French*. New York: Knopf.

Bettelheim, Bruno. 1955. *Symbolic Wounds: Puberty Rites and the Envious Male*. Glencoe, Ill.: Free Press.

Bharati, Agehananda. 1985. "The Self in Hindu Thought and Action." In *Culture and Self: Asian and Western Perspectives*, ed. Anthony J. Marsella, George DeVos, and Francis L. K. Hsu. New York: Tavistock.

Bledsoe, Caroline. 1980. *Women and Marriage in Kpelle Society*. Stanford, Calif.: Stanford University Press.

Boas, Franz. 1938 (orig. 1911). *The Mind of Primitive Man*. Rev. ed. New York: Macmillan.

Bock, Philip K. 1988. *Rethinking Psychological Anthropology: Continuity and Change in the Study of Human Action*. New York: W. H. Freeman.

Boehm, Christopher. 1982. "A Fresh Outlook on Cultural Selection." *American Anthropologist* 84(1):105–125.

Bolton, Ralph. 1973. "Aggression and Hypoglycemia among the Qolla: A Study in Psychobiological Anthropology." *Ethnology* 12:227–257.

———. 1978. *Aggression and Hypoglycemia in Qolla Society*. New York: Garland.

Bourguignon, Erika. 1989. "Multiple Personality, Possession Trance, and the Psychic Unity of Mankind." *Ethos* 17(3):371–384.

Briggs, Jean. 1970. *Never in Anger*. Cambridge, Mass.: Harvard University Press.

Bronfenbrenner, Urie. 1970. *Two Worlds of Childhood: U.S. and U.S.S.R.* New York: Russell Sage Foundation.

Broude, Gwen J. 1975. "Norms of Premarital Sexual Behavior: A Cross-Cultural Study." *Ethos* 3:381–402.

Brown, Judith K. 1963. "A Cross-Cultural Study of Female Initiation Rites." *American Anthropologist* 65:837–853.

Burton, Roger V., and Whiting, John W. M. 1961. "The Absent Father and Cross-Sex Identity." *Merrill-Palmer Quarterly of Behavior and Development* 7:85–95.

Carrier, James. 1983. "Masking the Social in Educational Knowledge: The Case of Learning Disability Theory." *American Journal of Sociology* 88:948–976.

Chagnon, Napoleon. 1983. *Yanamamo: The Fierce People.* Third ed. New York: Holt, Rinehart and Winston.

Chapple, Steve, and Talbot, David. 1989. *Burning Desires: Sex in America.* New York: Doubleday.

Chodorow, Nancy J. 1974. "Family Structure and Feminine Personality." In *Woman, Culture, and Society,* ed. Michelle Z. Rosaldo and Louise Lamphere. Stanford, Calif.: Stanford University Press.

———. 1978. *The Reproduction of Mothering: Psychoanalysis and the Sociology of Gender.* Berkeley: University of California Press.

———. 1990. *Feminism and Psychoanalytic Theory.* New Haven, Conn.: Yale University Press.

Chu, Godwin C. 1985. "The Changing Concept of Self in Contemporary China." In *Culture and Self: Asian and Western Perspectives,* ed. Anthony J. Marsella, George DeVos, and Francis L. K. Hsu. New York: Tavistock.

Clifford, James. 1988. *The Predicament of Culture.* Cambridge, Mass.: Harvard University Press.

Cohen, Yehudi A. 1964. *The Transition from Childhood to Adolescence.* Chicago: Aldine.

Cole, Michael. 1985. "The Zone of Proximal Development: Where Culture and Cognition Create Each Other." In *Culture, Communication, and Cognition: Vygotskian Perspectives,* ed. James V. Wertsch. Cambridge: Cambridge University Press.

Cole, Michael; Gay, John; Glick, Joseph A.; and Sharp, Donald W. 1971. *The Cultural Context of Learning and Thinking.* New York: Basic Books.

Cole, Michael, and Scribner, Sylvia. 1974. *Culture and Thought: A Psychological Introduction.* New York: Wiley.

Coleman, James William. 1976. "The Myth of Addiction." *Journal of Drug Issues* 6(2):135–141.

Coles, Gerald. 1987. *The Learning Mystique*. New York: Pantheon.

Conklin, Harold C. 1955. "Hanunóo Color Categories." *Southwestern Journal of Anthropology* 11:339–344.

Conrad, Peter, and Schneider, Joseph. 1980. *Deviance and Medicalization: From Badness to Sickness*. St. Louis: Mosby.

Danielsson, Bengt. 1956 (orig. 1954). *Love in the South Seas*. New York: Reynal.

Dentan, Robert K. 1979. *The Semai: A Nonviolent People of Malaya*. Fieldwork ed. New York: Holt, Rinehart and Winston.

DeVos, George. 1968. "Achievement and Innovation in Culture and Personality." In *The Study of Personality: An Interdisciplinary Appraisal*, ed. E. Norbeck, D. Price-Williams, and W. M. McCord. New York: Holt, Rinehart and Winston.

———. 1973. *Socialization for Achievement: Essays on the Cultural Psychology of the Japanese*. Berkeley: University of California Press.

———. 1978. "The Japanese Adapt to Change." In *The Making of Psychological Anthropology*, ed. George D. Spindler. Berkeley: University of California Press.

———. 1985. "Dimensions of the Self in Japanese Culture." In *Culture and Self: Asian and Western Perspectives*, ed. Anthony J. Marsella, George DeVos, and Francis L. K. Hsu. New York: Tavistock.

DeVos, George, and Suarez-Orozco, Marcelo. 1990. *Status Inequality: The Self in Culture*. Newbury Park, Calif.: Sage.

DiGiacomo, Susan M. 1987. "Biomedicine as a Cultural System: An Anthropologist in the Kingdom of the Sick." In *Encounters with Biomedicine: Case Studies in Medical Anthropology*, ed. Hans A. Baer. New York: Gordon and Breach.

Douglas, Mary, ed. 1987. *Constructive Drinking: Perspectives on Drink from Anthropology*. Cambridge: Cambridge University Press.

DuBois, Cora. 1961 (orig. 1944). *The People of Alor: A Social-Psychological Study of an East Indian Island*. New York: Harper and Brothers.

Edgerton, Robert B. 1971a. *The Individual in Cultural Adaptation: A Study of Four East African Peoples*. Berkeley: University of California Press.

———. 1971b. "A Traditional African Psychiatrist." *Southwestern Journal of Anthropology* 27:259–278.

———. 1976. *Deviance: A Cross-Cultural Perspective*. Menlo Park, Calif.: Cummings.

Eister, Allan W. 1950. *Drawing-Room Conversation: A Sociological Account of the Oxford Group Movement*. Durham, N.C.: Duke University Press.

Ekman, Paul. 1974 (orig. 1970). "Universal Facial Expressions of Emotion." In *Culture and Personality: Contemporary Readings*, ed. Robert A. LeVine. Chicago: Aldine.

Ember, Carol R. 1973. "Feminine Task Assignment and the Social Behavior of Boys." *Ethos* 1(4):424–439.

Erchak, Gerald M. 1974. "The Position of Women in Kpelle Society." *American Anthropologist* 76(2).

———. 1976. "The Nonsocial Behavior of Young Liberian Kpelle Children and the Acquisition of Sex Roles." *Journal of Cross-Cultural Psychology* 7(2):223–234.

———. 1977. *Full Respect: Kpelle Children in Adaptation.* New Haven, Conn.: HRAF Publications.

———. 1979a. "*Nyai Meni* and Kpelle Children." *Liberian Studies Journal* 8(2):159–161.

———. 1979b. "Socialization and Subsistence, Symbol and Surgery: Women in a West African Society." *Sociologus* 29(1):84–96.

———. 1980. "The Acquisition of Cultural Rules by Kpelle Children." *Ethos* 8(1):40–48.

———. Forthcoming. "Kpelle." In *Encyclopedia of World Cultures*, gen. ed. David Levinson, Africa ed. John Middleton. New York: G. K. Hall/ Macmillan.

Erchak, Gerald M., and Rosenfeld, Richard. 1989. "Learning Disabilities, Dyslexia, and the Medicalization of the Classroom." In *Images of Issues: Typifying Contemporary Social Problems*, ed. Joel Best. New York: Aldine de Gruyter.

Evans-Pritchard, Edward E. 1970. "Sexual Inversion among the Azande." *American Anthropologist* 72:1428–1434.

Field, M. J. 1960. *Search for Security: An Ethno-Psychiatric Study of Rural Ghana.* Evanston, Ill.: Northwestern University Press.

Fingarette, Herbert. 1988. *Heavy Drinking: The Myth of Alcoholism as a Disease.* Berkeley: University of California Press.

———. 1990. "We Should Reject the Disease Concept of Alcoholism." *Harvard Medical School Mental Health Newsletter* 6(8):4–6.

Fisher, Lawrence E. 1980. "Relationships and Sexuality in Contexts and Culture: The Anthropology of Eros." In *Handbook of Human Sexuality*, ed. Benjamin B. Wolman and John Money. Englewood Cliffs, N.J.: Prentice-Hall.

Fogelson, Raymond D. 1965. "Psychological Theories of Windigo 'Psychosis' and a Preliminary Application of a Models Approach." In *Context and Meaning in Cultural Anthropology*, ed. Melford E. Spiro. Glencoe, Ill.: Free Press.

Ford, Clellan S., and Beach, Frank A. 1951. *Patterns of Sexual Behavior.* New York: Harper and Row.

Fortes, Meyer, and Evans-Pritchard, Edward E., eds. 1940. *African Political Systems.* Oxford: Oxford University Press.

Foulks, Edward. 1972. *The Arctic Hysterias of the North Alaskan Eskimo*. Anthropological Studies 10. Washington, D.C.: American Anthropological Association.

Frake, Charles O. 1961. "The Diagnosis of Disease among the Subanun of Mindanao." *American Anthropologist* 63:113–132.

———. 1962. "The Ethnographic Study of Cognitive Systems." In *Anthropology and Human Behavior*, ed. Thomas Gladwin and William Sturtevant. Washington, D.C.: Anthropological Society of Washington.

———. 1964. "How to Ask for a Drink in Subanun." *American Anthropologist* 66(6):2:127–132.

Frayser, Suzanne G. 1985. *Varieties of Sexual Experience: An Anthropological Perspective on Human Sexuality*. New Haven, Conn.: HRAF Press.

Freilich, Morris; Raybeck, D.; and Savishinsky, Joel, eds. 1991. *Deviance: Cross-Cultural Perspectives*. Westport, Conn.: Bergin and Garvey/Greenwood.

Freud, Sigmund. 1913. *Totem and Taboo*. Standard ed., vol. 8. London: Hogarth.

———. 1916–17. *Introductory Lectures on Psychoanalysis*, part 3. Standard ed., vol. 16. London: Hogarth.

———. 1930. *Civilization and Its Discontents*. Standard ed., vol. 21. London: Hogarth.

Gaines, Atwood D., and Hahn, Robert A. 1985. "Among the Physicians: Encounter, Exchange and Transformation." In *Physicians of Western Medicine: Anthropological Approaches to Theory and Practice*, ed. Robert A. Hahn and Atwood D. Gaines. Boston: D. Reidel.

Gay, John, and Cole, Michael. 1967. *The New Mathematics and an Old Culture: A Study of Learning among the Kpelle of Liberia*. New York: Holt, Rinehart and Winston.

Geertz, Clifford. 1984. "'From the Native's Point of View': On the Nature of Anthropological Understanding." In *Culture Theory: Essays on Mind, Self, and Emotion*, ed. Richard A. Shweder and Robert A. LeVine. New York: Cambridge University Press.

Geertz, Hildred. 1974 (orig. 1959). "The Vocabulary of Emotion: A Study of Javanese Socialization Processes." In *Culture and Personality: Contemporary Readings*, ed. Robert A. LeVine. Chicago: Aldine.

Gibbs, James L., Jr. 1963. "Marital Instability among the Kpelle: Towards a Theory of Epainogamy." *American Anthropologist* 65(3):552–573.

———. 1965. "The Kpelle of Liberia." In *Peoples of Africa*, ed. James L. Gibbs, Jr. New York: Holt, Rinehart and Winston.

Gil, Eliana. 1983. *Outgrowing the Pain: A Book for and about Adults Abused as Children*. San Francisco: Launch Press.

Ginsburg, Herbert, and Opper, Sylvia. 1969. *Piaget's Theory of Intellectual Development: An Introduction.* Englewood Cliffs, N.J.: Prentice-Hall.

Gladwin, Thomas. 1964. "Culture and Logical Process." In *Explorations in Cultural Anthropology: Essays in Honor of George Peter Murdock,* ed. Ward H. Goodenough. New York: McGraw-Hill.

Goethals, George W. 1971. "Factors Affecting Rules Regarding Premarital Sex." In *Studies in the Sociology of Sex,* ed. James M. Hanslin. New York: Appleton-Century-Crofts.

Goffman, Ervin. 1959. *The Presentation of the Self in Everyday Life.* Garden City, N.Y.: Doubleday.

———. 1961. *Asylums.* Garden City, N.Y.: Doubleday.

———. 1963. *Behavior in Public Places.* New York: Free Press.

———. 1971. *Relations in Public.* New York: Basic Books.

Goldschmidt, Walter. 1971. "Introduction: The Theory of Cultural Adaptation." In *The Individual in Cultural Adaptation,* by Robert Edgerton. Berkeley: University of California Press.

———. 1986. *The Sebei: A Study in Adaptation.* New York: Holt, Rinehart and Winston.

———. 1990. *The Human Career: The Self in the Symbolic World.* Cambridge, Mass.: Basil Blackwell.

Goodenough, Ward H. 1956. "Componential Analysis and the Study of Meaning." *Language* 32:195–216.

———. 1967. "Componential Analysis." *Science* 156(3779):1203–1209.

Gorer, Geoffrey. 1948. *The American People.* New York: Norton.

———. 1955. *Exploring English Character.* New York: Criterion Books.

———. 1962 (orig. 1949). "The Psychology of Great Russians." In *The People of Great Russia: A Psychological Study,* by Geoffrey Gorer and John Rickman. New York: Norton.

Goslin, David, ed. 1969. *Handbook of Socialization Theory and Research.* Chicago: Rand McNally.

Granger, L., and Granger, B. 1986. *The Magic Feather: The Truth about "Special Education."* New York: Dutton.

Gregersen, Edgar. 1983. *Sexual Practices: The Story of Human Sexuality.* New York: Franklin Watts.

Gregor, Thomas. 1985. *Anxious Pleasures: The Sexual Lives of an Amazonian People.* Chicago: University of Chicago Press.

Guthrie, George M. 1973. "Culture and Mental Disorder." Addison-Wesley Module in Anthropology no. 39. Reading, Mass.: Addison-Wesley.

Hallowell, A. Irving. 1955. "The Self and Its Behavioral Environment." In *Culture and Experience,* by A. Irving Hallowell. Philadelphia: University of Pennsylvania Press.

Hallpike, C. R. 1979. *The Foundations of Primitive Thought.* Oxford: Clarendon Press of Oxford University Press.

————. 1986. *The Principles of Social Evolution.* Oxford: Oxford University Press.

Hamill, James F. 1990. *Ethno-Logic: The Anthropology of Human Reasoning.* Urbana, Ill.: University of Illinois Press.

Hammel, E. A., ed. 1965. *Formal Semantic Analysis.* Special publication. *American Anthropologist* 67(5), part 2.

Harris, Grace Gredys. 1989. "Concepts of Individual, Self, and Person in Description and Analysis." *American Anthropologist* 91(3):599–612.

Harris, Marvin. 1964. *The Nature of Cultural Things.* New York: Random House.

————. 1968. *The Rise of Anthropological Theory.* New York: Thomas Y. Crowell.

————. 1979. *Cultural Materialism: The Struggle for a Science of Culture.* New York: Random House.

————. 1981. *America Now: The Anthropology of a Changing Culture.* New York: Simon and Schuster.

————. 1987. *Cultural Anthropology.* Second ed. New York: Harper and Row.

Heider, Karl. 1976. "Dani Sexuality: A Low Energy System." *Man* 11:188–201.

Herdt, Gilbert. 1981. *Guardians of the Flutes.* New York: McGraw-Hill.

————. 1987. *The Sambia: Ritual and Gender in New Guinea.* New York: Holt, Rinehart, Winston.

————. 1989. "Father Presence and Ritual Homosexuality: Paternal Deprivation and Masculine Development in Melanesia Reconsidered." *Ethos* 17(3):326–370.

————, ed. 1982. *Rituals of Manhood: Male Initiation in Papua New Guinea.* Berkeley: University of California Press.

————, ed. 1984. *Ritualized Homosexuality in Melanesia.* Berkeley: University of California Press.

Herdt, Gilbert, and Stoller, Robert J. 1990. *Intimate Communications: Erotics and the Study of Culture.* New York: Columbia University Press.

Hezel, Francis X. 1985. "Trukese Suicide." In *Culture, Youth and Suicide in the Pacific: Papers from an East-West Center Conference,* ed. Francis X. Hezel, Donald H. Rubinstein, and Geoffrey M. White. Honolulu: Pacific Islands Studies Program, Center for Asian and Pacific Studies, University of Hawaii.

Hostetler, John A., and Huntington, Gertrude Enders. 1971. *Children in Amish Society: Socialization and Community Education.* New York: Holt, Rinehart and Winston.

Hsu, Francis L. K. 1975. *Iemoto: The Heart of Japan.* Cambridge, Mass.: Schenkman.

———. 1985. "The Self in Cross-Cultural Perspective." In *Culture and Self: Asian and Western Perspectives,* ed. Anthony J. Marsella, George DeVos, and Francis L. K. Hsu. New York: Tavistock.

Inkeles, Alex. 1968. *Social Change in Soviet Russia.* Cambridge, Mass.: Harvard University Press.

Ito, Karen I. 1985. "Affective Bonds: Hawaiian Interrelationships of Self." In *Person, Self, and Experience,* ed. Geoffrey M. White and John Kirkpatrick. Berkeley: University of California Press.

Izard, C. E. 1983. "Emotions in Personality and Culture." *Ethos* 11(4):305–312.

Johnson, Frank. 1985. "The Western Concept of Self." In *Culture and Self: Asian and Western Perspectives,* ed. Anthony J. Marsella, George DeVos, and Francis L. K. Hsu. New York: Tavistock.

Kaminer, Wendy. 1990. "Chances Are You're Codependent Too." *The New York Times Book Review* (Feb. 11).

Kardiner, Abram. 1939. *The Individual and His Society: The Psychodynamics of Primitive Social Organization.* New York: Columbia University Press.

———. 1945. "The Concept of Basic Personality Structure as an Operational Tool in the Social Sciences." In *The Science of Man in the World Crisis,* ed. Ralph Linton. New York: Columbia University Press.

Katz, Richard. 1982. *Boiling Energy: Community Healing among the Kalahari Kung.* Cambridge, Mass.: Harvard University Press.

Kennedy, John G. 1978. *Tarahumara of the Sierra Madre: Beer, Ecology, and Social Organization.* Arlington Heights, Ill.: AHM.

Kenny, Michael G. 1986. *The Passion of Ansel Bourne: Multiple Personality in American Culture.* Washington, D.C.: Smithsonian Institution Press.

Kernberg, Otto. 1975. *Borderline Conditions and Pathological Narcissism.* New York: Jason Aronson.

Kinsey, Alfred C.; Pomeroy, Wardell B.; and Martin, Clyde E. 1948. *Sexual Behavior in the Human Male.* Philadelphia: Saunders.

Kinsey, Alfred C.; Pomeroy, Wardell B.; Gebhard, Paul; and Martin, Clyde E. 1953. *Sexual Behavior in the Human Female.* Philadelphia: Saunders.

Kirkpatrick, John T. 1985. "Some Marquesan Understandings of Action and Identity." In *Person, Self, and Experience,* ed. Geoffrey M. White and John Kirkpatrick. Berkeley: University of California Press.

Kirkpatrick, John T., and White, Geoffrey M. 1985. "Exploring Ethnopsychologies." In *Person, Self, and Experience,* ed. Geoffrey M. White and John Kirkpatrick. Berkeley: University of California Press.

Kitahara, Michio. 1984. "Female Physiology and Female Puberty Rites." *Ethos* 12(2):132–150.

Kleinman, Arthur. 1980. *Patients and Healers in the Context of Culture.* Berkeley: University of California Press.

———. 1986. *Social Origins of Distress and Disease: Depression, Neurasthenia and Pain in Modern China.* New Haven: Yale University Press.

———. 1988a. *The Illness Narratives: Suffering, Healing and the Human Condition.* New York: Basic Books.

———. 1988b. *Rethinking Psychiatry: From Cultural Category to Personal Experience.* New York: Free Press.

Kleinman, Arthur, and Good, Byron, eds. 1985. *Culture and Depression.* Berkeley: University of California Press.

Kohn, Melvin. 1977. *Class and Conformity: A Study of Values.* Homewood, Ill.: Dorsey.

Kohut, Heinz. 1971. *The Analysis of the Self.* New York: International Universities Press.

———. 1977. *The Restoration of the Self.* New York: International Universities Press.

Laing, R. D. 1960. *The Divided Self.* London: Tavistock.

———. 1967. *The Politics of Experience.* New York: Pantheon.

———. 1969. *The Politics of the Family and Other Essays.* New York: Pantheon.

Laing, R. D., and Esterson, Aaron. 1964. *Sanity, Madness and the Family.* New York: Basic Books.

Lambo, Thomas Adeoye. 1978. "Psychotherapy in Africa." *Human Nature* (March).

Langness, Lewis L. 1974. "Ritual, Power, and Male Dominance." *Ethos* 2:189–212.

Lasch, Christopher. 1979. *The Culture of Narcissism.* New York: Norton.

———. 1984. *The Minimal Self.* New York: Norton.

Lebra, Takie Sugiyama. 1983. "Shame and Guilt: A Psychocultural View of the Japanese Self." *Ethos* 11(3):192–209.

Lee, Dorothy. 1986 (orig. 1976). *Valuing the Self.* Prospect Heights, Ill.: Waveland Press.

Lee, Richard B. 1979. *The !Kung San: Men, Women and Work in a Foraging Society.* Cambridge: Cambridge University Press.

Leiderman, P. H.; Tulkin, S. E.; and Rosenfeld, R., eds. 1977. *Culture and Infancy: Variations in Human Experience.* New York: Academic Press.

LeVine, Robert A. 1963. "Child Rearing in Sub-Saharan Africa: An Interim Report." *Bulletin of the Menninger Clinic* 27:245–256.

———. 1969. "Culture, Personality and Socialization: An Evolutionary View." In *Handbook of Socialization Theory and Research,* ed. David Goslin. Chicago: Rand McNally.

———. 1974. "Parental Goals: A Cross-Cultural View." *Teachers College Record* 76(2):52–65.

———. 1977. "Child Rearing as Cultural Adaptation." In *Culture and Infancy: Variations in Human Experience*, ed. P. H. Leiderman, S. E. Tulkin, and R. Rosenfeld. New York: Academic Press.

———. 1982. *Culture, Behavior, and Personality*. Second Ed. New York: Aldine.

LeVine, Robert A., and LeVine, Barbara. 1977 (orig. 1966). *Nyansongo: A Gusii Community in Kenya*. Malabar, Fla.: Robert E. Krieger.

Lévi-Strauss, Claude. 1966. *The Savage Mind*. Chicago: University of Chicago Press.

Levy, Robert I. 1969. "On Getting Angry in the Society Islands." In *Mental Health Research in Asia and the Pacific*, ed. William Caudill and Tsung-Yi Lin. Honolulu: East-West Center Press.

———. 1973. *Tahitians: Mind and Experience in the Society Islands*. Chicago: University of Chicago Press.

———. 1983. "Introduction: Self and Emotion." *Ethos* 11(3):128–134.

———. 1984. "Emotion, Knowing, and Culture." In *Culture Theory: Essays on Mind, Self, and Emotion*, ed. Richard A. Shweder and Robert A. LeVine. New York: Cambridge University Press.

Levy-Bruhl, Lucien. 1926 (orig. in French, 1910). *How Natives Think*. London: Allen and Unwin.

Lindenbaum, Shirley. 1979. *Kuru Sorcery: Disease and Danger in the New Guinea Highlands*. Palo Alto, Calif.: Mayfield.

Lounsbury, Floyd G. 1964. "The Formal Analysis of Crow- and Omaha-Type Kinship Terminologies." In *Explorations in Cultural Anthropology: Essays in Honor of George Peter Murdock*, ed. Ward H. Goodenough. New York: McGraw-Hill.

Lutz, Catherine A. 1983. "Parental Goals, Ethnopsychology, and the Development of Emotional Meaning." *Ethos* 11(4):246–262.

———. 1985. "Ethnopsychology Compared to What? Explaining Behavior and Consciousness among the Ifaluk." In *Person, Self, and Experience: Exploring Pacific Ethnopsychologies*, ed. Geoffrey M. White and John Kirkpatrick. Berkeley, Calif.: University of California Press.

———. 1988. *Unnatural Emotions: Everyday Sentiments on a Micronesian Atoll and Their Challenge to Western Theory*. Chicago: University of Chicago Press.

Lutz, Catherine A., and White, Geoffrey M. 1986. "The Anthropology of Emotions." In *Annual Review of Anthropology*, vol. 15, ed. Bernard J. Siegel, Alan R. Beals, and Stephen A. Tyler. Palo Alto, Calif.: Annual Reviews.

MacAndrew, Craig, and Edgerton, Robert B. 1969. *Drunken Comportment: A Social Explanation*. Chicago: Aldine.

Malinowski, Bronislaw. 1929. *The Sexual Life of Savages in North-Western Melanesia*. New York: Harcourt, Brace and World.

Manson, William C. 1988. *The Psychodynamics of Culture: Abram Kardiner and Neo-Freudian Anthropology.* Westport, Conn.: Greenwood.

Marshall, Donald S., and Suggs, Robert C., eds. 1971. *Human Sexual Behavior: Variations in the Ethnographic Spectrum.* New York: Basic Books.

Marshall, Mac. 1979. *Weekend Warriors: Alcohol in a Micronesian Culture.* Palo Alto, Calif.: Mayfield.

Marshall, Mac, and Marshall, Leslie B. 1990. *Silent Voices Speak: Women and Prohibition in Truk.* Belmont, Calif.: Wadsworth.

Masters, William H., and Johnson, Virginia E. 1966. *Human Sexual Response.* Boston: Little, Brown.

———. 1970. *Human Sexual Inadequacy.* Boston: Little, Brown.

———. 1979. *Homosexuality in Perspective.* Boston: Little, Brown.

Mazur, Tom, and Money, John. 1980. "Prenatal Influences and Subsequent Sexuality." In *Handbook of Human Sexuality*, ed. Benjamin B. Wolman and John Money. Englewood Cliffs, N.J.: Prentice-Hall.

McClelland, David C. 1961. *The Achieving Society.* Princeton, N.J.: Van Nostrand.

McClelland, David C., et al. 1972. *The Drinking Man.* New York: Free Press.

McGuiness, Diane. 1985. *When Children Don't Learn: Understanding the Biology and Psychology of Learning Disabilities.* New York: Basic Books.

Mead, George Herbert. 1964 (orig. 1934). *On Social Psychology*, ed. Anselm Strauss. Chicago: University of Chicago Press.

Mead, Margaret. 1928. *Coming of Age in Samoa.* New York: William Morrow.

———. 1930. *Growing Up in New Guinea.* New York: William Morrow.

———. 1942. *And Keep Your Powder Dry.* New York: William Morrow.

———. 1955. (orig. 1951). *Soviet Attitudes Toward Authority.* New York: William Morrow.

Mead, Margaret, and Metraux, Rhoda, eds. 1953. *The Study of Culture at a Distance.* Chicago: University of Chicago Press.

Metzger, Duane, and Williams, Gerald. 1966. "Some Procedures and Results in the Study of Native Categories: Tzeltal 'Firewood.'" *American Anthropologist* 68:389–407.

Middleton, John, and Tait, David, eds. 1958. *Tribes Without Rulers.* London: Routledge and Kegan Paul.

Minturn, Leigh, and Lambert, William W. 1964. *Mothers of Six Cultures: Antecedents of Child Rearing.* New York: Wiley.

Moffatt, Michael. 1989. *Coming of Age in New Jersey.* New Brunswick, N.J.: Rutgers University Press.

Money, John, and Wiedeking, Claus. 1980. "Gender Identity Role: Normal Differentiation and Its Transpositions." In *Handbook of Human Sexuality*, ed. Benjamin B. Wolman and John Money. Englewood Cliffs, N.J.: Prentice-Hall.

Murdock, George Peter. 1964. "Cultural Correlates of the Regulation of Premarital Sex Behavior." In *Process and Pattern in Culture: Essays in Honor of Julian H. Steward*, ed. Robert A. Manners. Chicago: Aldine.

Murphy, H. B. M. 1976. "Notes for a Theory on *Latah*." In *Culture-Bound Syndromes, Ethnopsychiatry, and Alternative Therapies: Mental Health Research in Asia and the Pacific*, ed. William P. Lebra. Honolulu: University Press of Hawaii.

Murphy, Jane. 1976. "Psychiatric Labeling in Cross-Cultural Perspectives (Yoruba and Eskimo)." *Science* 191:1019–1028.

Murphy, Yolanda, and Murphy, Robert F. 1974. *Women of the Forest*. New York: Columbia University Press.

Myers, Fred R. 1979. "Emotions and the Self: A Theory of Personhood and Political Order among Pintupi Aborigines." *Ethos* 7(4):343–370.

Nanda, Serena. 1990. *Neither Man nor Woman: The Hijras of India*. Belmont, Calif.: Wadsworth.

Ogbu, John U. 1974. *The Next Generation: An Ethnography of Education in an Urban Neighborhood*. New York: Academic Press.

———. 1978. *Minority Education and Caste: The American System in Cross-Cultural Perspective*. New York: Academic Press.

O'Nell, Carl W., and Selby, Henry A. 1968. "Sex Differences in the Incidence of Susto in Two Zapotec Pueblos: An Analysis of the Relationships Between Sex Role Expectations and a Folk Illness." *Ethnology* 7:95–105.

Ortner, Sherry B. 1974. "Is Female to Male as Nature Is to Culture?" In *Woman, Culture, and Society*, ed. Michelle Z. Rosaldo and Louise Lamphere. Stanford, Calif.: Stanford University Press.

Parker, Seymour. 1960. "The Wiitiko Psychosis in the Context of Ojibwa Personality and Culture." *American Anthropologist* 62(4).

Parsons, Talcott. 1949. *The Social System*. Glencoe, Ill.: Free Press.

Peele, Stanton. 1981. *How Much Is Too Much: Healthy Habits or Destructive Addictions*. Englewood Cliffs, N.J.: Prentice-Hall.

———. 1987. *The Meaning of Addiction*. Lexington, Mass.: Lexington Books/D. C. Heath.

———. 1989. *Diseasing of America: Addiction Treatment Out of Control*. Lexington, Mass.: Lexington Books/D. C. Heath.

Peele, Stanton, with Brodsky, Archie. 1975. *Love and Addiction*. New York: Signet.

Piaget, Jean. 1967. *Six Psychological Studies*. New York: Random House.

Piaget, Jean, and Inhelder, Barbel. 1969. *The Psychology of the Child*. New York: Basic Books.

Pontius, A. 1977. "Dani Sexuality." *Man* 12:166–167.

Read, Kenneth E. 1965. *The High Valley*. London: Allen Unwin.

Reynolds, David K., and Farberow, Norman L. 1976. *Suicide: Inside and Out.* Berkeley: University of California Press.

————. 1977. *Endangered Hope: Experiences in Psychiatric Aftercare Facilities.* Berkeley: University of California Press.

Riesman, David. 1950. *The Lonely Crowd: A Study of the Changing American Character.* New Haven, Conn.: Yale University Press.

Robarchek, Clayton A. 1977. "Semai Nonviolence: A Systems Approach to Understanding." Ph. D. dissertation, Department of Anthropology, University of California, Riverside.

————. 1989. "Primitive Warfare and the Ratomorphic Image of Mankind." *American Anthropologist* 91(4):903–920.

Rogoff, Barbara. 1984. "Introduction: Thinking and Learning in Social Context." In *Everyday Cognition: Its Development in Social Context*, ed. Barbara Rogoff and Jean Lave. Cambridge, Mass.: Harvard University Press.

————. 1990. *Apprenticeship in Thinking: Cognitive Development in Social Context.* New York: Oxford University Press.

Rogoff, Barbara, and Lave, Jean, eds. 1984. *Everyday Cognition: Its Development in Social Context.* Cambridge, Mass.: Harvard University Press.

Room, Robin. 1984. "Alcohol and Ethnography: A Case of Problem Deflation?" *Current Anthropology* 25(2):169–191.

Rosaldo, Michelle Z. 1980. *Knowledge and Passion: Ilongot Notions of Self and Social Life.* Cambridge: Cambridge University Press.

————. 1983. "The Shame of Headhunters and the Autonomy of Self." *Ethos* 11(3):135–151.

————. 1984. "Toward an Anthropology of Self and Feeling." In *Culture Theory: Essays on Mind, Self, and Emotion*, ed. Richard A. Shweder and Robert A. LeVine. New York: Cambridge University Press.

Rosaldo, Renato. 1990. *Culture and Truth.* Boston: Beacon Press.

Rosenhan, D. L. 1973. "On Being Sane in Insane Places." *Science* 179:250–258.

Rubel, A. J. 1964. "The Epidemiology of a Folk Illness: Susto in Hispanic America." *Ethnology* 3:268–283.

Rubinstein, Donald H. 1983. "Epidemic Suicide among Micronesian Adolescents." *Social Science and Medicine* 17:657–665.

————. 1985. "Suicide in Micronesia." In *Culture, Youth and Suicide in the Pacific: Papers from an East-West Center Conference*, ed. Francis X. Hezel, Donald H. Rubenstein, and Geoffrey M. White. Honolulu: Pacific Islands Studies Program, Center for Asian and Pacific Studies, University of Hawaii.

Rudy, David R. 1986. *Becoming Alcoholic: Alcoholics Anonymous and the Reality of Alcoholism.* Carbondale, Ill.: Southern Illinois University Press.

Schafer, Roy. 1989. "Narratives of the Self." In *Psychoanalysis: Toward the Second Century*, ed. Arnold Cooper, Otto Kernberg, and Ethel Person. New Haven, Conn.: Yale University Press.

Schlegel, Alice, and Barry, Herbert, III. 1979. "Adolescent Initiation Ceremonies: A Cross-Cultural Code." *Ethnology* 18(2):199–210.

———. 1980. "The Evolutionary Significance of Adolescent Initiation Ceremonies." *American Ethnologist* 7(4):696–715.

Scribner, Sylvia. 1984. "Studying Working Intelligence." In *Everyday Cognition: Its Development in Social Context*, ed. Barbara Rogoff and Jean Lave. Cambridge, Mass.: Harvard University Press.

Scribner, Sylvia, and Cole, Michael. 1973. "Cognitive Consequences of Formal and Informal Education." *Science* 182(4112):553–59.

———. 1981. *The Psychology of Literacy.* Cambridge, Mass.: Harvard University Press.

Shore, Bradd. 1991. "Twice-Born, Once Conceived: Meaning Construction and Cultural Cognition." *American Anthropologist* 93(1):9–27.

Shweder, Richard A., and Bourne, Edmund J. 1984. "Does the Concept of the Person Vary Cross-Culturally?" In *Culture Theory: Essays on Mind, Self and Emotion*, ed. Richard Shweder and Robert LeVine. Cambridge: Cambridge University Press.

Slater, Philip. 1970. *The Pursuit of Loneliness.* Boston: Beacon Press.

Solberg, R. J. 1982. *The Dry-Drunk Syndrome.* Center City, Minn.: Hazelden.

———. 1983. *The Dry Drunk Syndrome.* Rev. ed. Center City, Minn.: Hazelden.

Spindler, George. 1968. "Psychocultural Adaptation." In *The Study of Personality: An Interdisciplinary Appraisal*, ed. E. Norbeck, D. Price-Williams, and W. M. McCord. New York: Holt, Rinehart and Winston.

Spindler, George, ed. 1978. *The Making of Psychological Anthropology.* New York: Holt, Rinehart and Winston.

Spindler, George, and Spindler, Louise. 1971. *Dreamers without Power: The Menomini Indians.* New York: Holt, Rinehart and Winston.

Spradley, James P. 1972. "Foundations of Cultural Knowledge." In *Culture and Cognition: Rules, Maps, and Plans*, ed. James P. Spradley. San Francisco: Chandler.

Starr, Paul. 1982. *The Social Transformation of American Medicine.* New York: Basic Books.

Stein, Howard F. 1985. "Alcoholism as Metaphor in American Culture: Ritual Desecration as Social Integration." *Ethos* 13(3):195–235.

———. 1990. *American Medicine as Culture.* Boulder, Colo.: Westview.

Stent, Gunther S. 1975. "Limits to the Scientific Understanding of Man."
Science 187:1052–1058.

Stephens, William N. 1962. *The Oedipus Complex: Cross Cultural Evidence.*
Glencoe, Ill.: Free Press.

Szasz, Thomas S. 1963. *Law, Liberty and Psychiatry.* New York: Macmillan.

———. 1965. *Psychiatric Justice.* New York: Macmillan.

———. 1970. *The Manufacture of Madness.* New York: Harper and Row.

———. 1974. *The Myth of Mental Illness.* Rev. ed. New York: Harper and
Row.

———. 1976. *Schizophrenia: The Sacred Symbol of Psychiatry.* New York: Basic
Books.

———. 1978. *The Myth of Psychotherapy.* Garden City, N.Y.: Doubleday.

Torrey, E. Fuller. 1972. *The Mind Game: Witchdoctors and Psychiatrists.* New
York: Emerson.

———. 1974. *The Death of Psychiatry.* Radnor, Penn.: Chilton.

———. 1980. *Schizophrenia and Civilization.* New York: Jason Aronson.

———. 1986. *Witchdoctors and Psychiatrists: The Common Roots of Psychotherapy and Its Future.* New York: Harper and Row.

Turnbull, Colin M. 1972. *The Mountain People.* New York: Simon and
Schuster.

———. 1983. *The Human Cycle.* New York: Simon and Schuster.

Turner, Victor W. 1967. *The Forest of Symbols.* Ithaca, N.Y.: Cornell University Press.

Turner, Victor W., and Bruner, Edward M., eds. 1986. *The Anthropology of
Experience.* Urbana, Ill.: University of Illinois Press.

Tyler, Stephen A., ed. 1969. *Cognitive Anthropology.* New York: Holt, Rinehart and Winston.

Vaillant, George E. 1983. *The Natural History of Alcoholism: Causes, Patterns,
and Paths to Recovery.* Cambridge, Mass.: Harvard University Press.

Valentine, Charles A. 1968. *Culture and Poverty: Critique and Counter Propos-
als.* Chicago: University of Chicago Press.

Van Gennep, Arnold. 1960 (orig. 1908). *The Rites of Passage.* Chicago: University of Chicago Press.

Varenne, Hervé. 1977. *Americans Together: Structured Diversity in a Midwestern Town.* New York: Teachers College Press.

Vygotsky, Lev S. 1962. *Thought and Language.* Cambridge, Mass.: M.I.T.
Press.

———. 1978. *Mind in Society: The Development of Higher Psychological Processes.* Cambridge, Mass.: Harvard University Press.

Wallace, Anthony F. C. 1952. *The Modal Personality Structure of the Tuscarora
Indians, as Revealed by the Rorschach Test.* Bulletin 150, Bureau of
American Ethnology. Washington, D.C.: Smithsonian Institution.

———. 1962. "Culture and Cognition." *Science* 135(3501):351–357.

———. 1965a. "Driving to Work." In *Context and Meaning in Cultural Anthroplogy*, ed. Melford E. Spiro. New York: Macmillan.

———. 1965b. "The Problem of the Psychological Validity of Componential Analyses." In *Formal Semantic Analysis*, ed. E. A. Hammel. Special publication, *American Anthropologist* 67(5):2 229–248.

———. 1966. *Religion: An Anthropological View.* New York: Random House.

———. 1972a. *The Death and Rebirth of the Seneca.* New York: Random House.

———. 1972b. "Mental Illness, Biology, and Culture." In *Psychological Anthropology*, rev. ed., ed. Francis L. K. Hsu. Cambridge, Mass.: Schenkman.

Wallace, Anthony F. C., and Atkins, John. 1960. "The Meaning of Kinship Terms." *American Anthropologist* 62:58–80.

"War on Drugs: Now Who Is the Enemy?" 1990. *Utne Reader* (Jan.–Feb).

Wegscheider, Sharon. 1981. *Another Chance: Hope and Health for the Alcoholic family.* Palo Alto, Calif.: Science and Behavior Books.

White, Geoffrey M. 1985. "Premises and Purpose in a Solomon Islands Ethnopsychology." In *Person, Self, and Experience*, ed. Geoffrey M. White and John Kirkpatrick. Berkeley: University of California Press.

White, Sheldon H., and Siegel, Alexander W. 1984. "Cognitive Development in Time and Space." In *Everyday Cognition: Its Development in Social Context*, ed. Barbara Rogoff and Jean Lave. Cambridge, Mass.: Harvard University Press.

Whiting, Beatrice B. n. d. "General Introduction to the Observation of Social Behavior." Unpublished mimeo. Department of Anthropology, Harvard University.

———. ed. 1963. *Six Cultures: Studies of Child Rearing.* New York: Wiley.

Whiting, Beatrice B., and Edwards, Carolyn P. 1973. "A Cross-Cultural Analysis of Sex Differences in the Behavior of Children Aged Three through Eleven." *Journal of Social Psychology* 91:171–188.

———. 1988. *Children of Different Worlds: The Formation of Social Behavior.* Cambridge, Mass.: Harvard University Press.

Whiting, Beatrice B., and Whiting, John W. M. 1973. "Methods for Observing and Recording Behavior." In *Handbook of Methods in Cultural Anthropology*, ed. Y. Cohen and R. Naroll. New York: Columbia University Press.

———. 1975. *Children of Six Cultures: A Psycho-Cultural Analysis.* Cambridge, Mass.: Harvard University Press.

Whiting, John W. M., and Child, Irvin. 1953. *Child Training and Personality.* New Haven, Conn.: Yale University Press.

Whiting, John W. M.; Kluckhohn, Richard; and Anthony, Albert. 1958. "The Function of Male Initiation Ceremonies at Puberty." In *Readings in Social Psychology*, third ed, ed. Eleanor E. Maccoby, Theodore M. Newcomb, and Eugene L. Hartley. New York: Holt.

Wilson, Peter J. 1974. *Oscar: An Inquiry into the Nature of Sanity.* New York: Random House.

Woititz, Janet G. 1983. *Adult Children of Alcoholics.* Hollywood, Fla.: Health Communications.

Yap, Pow Meng. 1952. "The Latah Reaction." *Journal of Medical Science* 98:515–564.

———. 1969. "The Culture-bound Reactive Syndromes." In *Mental Health Research in Asia and the Pacific*, ed. William Caudill and Tsung-Yi Lin. Honolulu: East-West Center Press.

Young, Frank W. 1965. *Initiation Ceremonies: A Cross-Cultural Study of Status Dramatization.* Indianapolis: Bobbs-Merrill.

Index